AF622042

FAITHS AND BELIEFS IN THE KATHĀSARITSĀGARA

FAITHS AND BELIEFS IN THE KATHĀSARITSĀGARA

DR. NIRMAL TRIKHA, Ph.D.
Department of Sanskrit,
Daulat Ram College,
University of Delhi.
Ex. Teacher Fellow,
Department of Sanskrit,
University of Delhi.

with a Foreword by

DR. SATYA VRAT SHASTRI
Professor, Department of Sanskrit,
University of Delhi.
Ex. Vice-Chancellor,
Shri Jagannath Sanskrit University,
Puri, Orissa.

Eastern Book Linkers
DELHI (INDIA)

Published by :
EASTERN BOOK LINKERS,
5825, New Chandrawal, Jawahar Nagar,
DELHI - 110007.

© AUTHOR

Ist. Edition : 1991

ISBN: 81- 85133 - 50 - 6

EASTERN BOOK LINKERS EBL RS. 500-

Printed by :
Orient Offset,
Delhi-110032.

Laser typeset by :
Compu-Media-The D.T.P. People
43, Bungalow Road, Delhi-110007. ☎ 2911869.

DEDICATED
TO

The sacred memory of my father Rāja-Jyotishi Pt. Devi Lal Sharma, a votary of the Goddess Durgā and a constant source of inspiration to me.

FOREWORD

I have great pleasure in introducing to the world of scholars Dr. Nirmal Trikha's work : Faiths and Beliefs in the *Kathāsaritsāgara*.

Literature is generally the mirror to the age in which it is produced. Whatever its motivation, the urges and aspirations of the people, the mould of their thinking, as a matter of fact, their entire way of life gets reflected in it. It, therefore, is the surest medium and a fairly reliable at that in gauging the make-up of a society of a given age. It is bound to contain within it bits of information on its varied aspects which when pieced together can yield a fairly clear picture of the contemporary society.

The bigger the work, the greater the scope for this excersize. It is in this context that the importance of the present study can be realized. Herein is dealt with a voluminous work, the *Kathāsaritsāgara* which, as the title itself makes out, is an ocean of stories. With an enormous variety of plots woven in them, they are a veritable 'ocean' of information to a sociologist, an anthropologist and a historian.

Dr. Nirmal Trikha has dived deep into the ocean in search of the faiths and beliefs of the people of the age. It is extremely gratifying that she has come out with very valuable material in that connection. She has been quite systematic and thorough in her approach. Nothing of value has escaped her searching eye. With proper documentation she has tried to focus the spotlight on the religious persuations of the people, Hinduism and Buddhism. Even in Hinduism she has turned the torch on its different sects. And even among sects, the division among sub-sects. The Śaivas she divides into the Kāpālikavratas, the Kāpālikas, the Mahāvratins and the Pāśupatas. She then goes into their special characteristics which distinguish them from others. She then gives the different names of the Lord as they occur in the work under study followed by the three-fold functions that the Lord performs. She proceeds next to mention the places sacred to the Śaivas. The same system she follows in her treatment of the Gāṇapatyas and the Vaiṣṇavas with the result that a reader forms a fairly accurate idea of the religious side of the society of the period of the *Kathāsaritsāgara*. Through it he comes to know that it consisted of people following different faiths and sects with their fixed codes of conduct. In their devotion to their particular deity they would touch the extreme of downgrading other deities while glorifying theirs. This is the religious plane.

On the social plane the *Kathāsaritsāgara* depicts a society having deep faith in omens and dreams, good or bad, a superstitious kind of society where the outcome of the coming events is foreseen through certain good or bad signs manifesting themselves at the start of any venture, the signs which could indicate the impending trouble or happy event. Interestingly, the signs fit almost into a pattern and are fairly traditional. The throbbing of the right limbs of a man and those of a woman are taken to represent something good or bad respectively. The sound of a female jackal is taken to portend evil. The red sky and the rough weather are taken to be indicative of impending disaster. The sight of owl is considered inauspicious. These omens and others are taken to represent the same good or bad effects throughout the ancient literature, from the Brāhmaṇas to the epics and the Purāṇas, from the Purāṇas to later classical works and so on with little deviation. Nowhere is owl considered auspicious as in the West. No where is the cat crossing the path is taken to be good as in China. The beliefs got infixed in the Indian psyche. Nobody has ever bothered to verify them, accepted as they have been as gospel truth, for, they have been taken to represent the experiences of the earlier generations. And in this India is not alone. Wherever the beliefs have grown, they have come to stay, meeting with unquestioned approval of the populace. Barring some which may be common, every region of the world has its own set of such beliefs. One fine morning the writer of these lines saw a beehive sprung up on a branch of a plant on the terrace of his house in Bangkok. Taking bees hovering around as a potential threat, he talked to the house owner to have the beehive removed, to which he did not agree pointing out that as per the Thai belief the bees bring good luck and it would be inadvisable to drive away the good luck from the house. The bees did bring good luck to the house for it was in that house the writer of these lines could complete the biggest of his Sanskrit Mahākāvyas in record time. Just as it happened with the present writer, it must have happened with many others. And that is how the beliefs would have grown. Just as with this belief, it must have been so with other beliefs. And so starts the chain.

Just as with omens, so is it with dreams. As a matter of fact, the interpretation of dreams is now a regular science. A full corpus of literature is available on it. Which of the dreams indicate what is a fascinating study. There is a whole lot of material on it in India's ancient literature which needs to be subjected to a searching scrutiny. Viewed in this light the present study deserves warm welcome.

Dr. Nirmal Trikha through her work has presented a conspectus of the social ethos of the period of the *Kathāsaritsāgara*. To wade through the mass of work was itself quite a task which she has accomplished with singular success. And to draw a complete picture of the society of the time in the faiths and beliefs it followed shows the greater depths to which she was taken that task for which she deserves full approbation of the scholarly community.

Satya Vrat Shastri
Professor of Sanskrit,
University of Delhi.
Ex-Vice-Chancellor,
Shri Jagannath Sanskrit
University, Puri, Orissa.

Delhi.
26.6.1991

PREFACE

श्रद्धयाग्निः समिध्यते श्रद्धया हूयते हविः ।
श्रद्धां भगस्य मूर्धनि वचसा वेदयामसि ॥
श्रद्धां प्रातर्हवामहे श्रद्धां मध्यन्दिनं परि ।
श्रद्धां सूर्यस्य निम्रुचि श्रद्धे श्रद्धापयेह नः ॥

ऋग्वेद – 10.151.1,5.

Faiths and beliefs are the important aspects of the multi-traditional incomprehensible Indian Culture as these have substantially contributed to the making of Indian Thought. The importance of the study of faiths and beliefs is proved by the fact that faiths and beliefs have entered the wrap and woof of Indian Life and give a meaning and a purpose to it. The study helps us in understanding the psychic make-up of the people.

The Kathāsaritsāgara (1063-1081 A.D) of Somadeva is a Sanskrit version of the lost Bṛhatkathā of Guṇāḍhya. As the work contains floating stories spread over from the Pre-Vedic Age to the eleventh centuary A.D., it is indispensable for having an insight into the faiths and beliefs of the Indian Society. The existing works based on the study of the Kathāsaritsāgara do not fully explore the aspects of faiths and beliefs from it. The present work is an attempt to give an exhaustive and comprehensive survey of faiths and beliefs in the Kathāsaritsāgara. Moreover, about two thousand foot-notes have been added to give the relevant information on the subject.

It is my solemn duty to offer my sincere thanks to all those scholars and organizations who have helped me in carrying the work to completion. I am thankful to all those scholars whose published works have been gratefully acknowledged by me in the foot-notes and in the Bibliography.

I offer my regards to Dr. Rāmāshraya Sharma, Senior Lecturer in Sanskrit, Zakir Husain College, University of Delhi, and a recipient of a prestigious award in 1991 from the Sanskrit Academy for his zeal to promote the cause of Sanskrit. But for his deep interest, worthy guidance, perennial encouragement and constant inspiration, I would never have been able to complete the work.

I express my deepest gratitude to Prof. Satya Vrat Shastri, Department of Sanskrit, University of Delhi, who has always inspired me by his thorough wisdom and enriched the present work with his critical and constructive Foreword.

I am highly thankful to the University Grants Commission for awarding me Long Term Teacher-Fellowship for my research work.

I am grateful to the University of Delhi for granting me the permission to publish my Ph.D. thesis.

I express my sincere thanks to the authorities of the Delhi University Library, Archaeological Survey of India, Delhi, and National Museum Library, Delhi, for their kindness in allowing me access to all the relevant books and journals available with them.

I express my deep sense of admiration, gratitude and regards to all my teachers, friends and well-wishers who have taken keen interest in my work and have always encouraged me.

I owe the highest sense of regards, appreciation and gratefulness to Shri Karan Singh Gautam, a Senior and a learned teacher in Govt.S.S.School, Netaji Nagar, Delhi, who initiated me into the world of knowledge at Jangpura Ext., New Delhi in 1953 and whose all-round personality has always been the greatest source of inspiration and guidance throughout my life.

The work could not have seen the light of the day without the moral support of my mother and the co-operation of my family members. My special thanks are due to my husband Dr.R.K. Trikha, Reader, Department of Chemistry, Hansraj College, for his constant help and constructive suggestions. Our children Smriti, Stuti and Sakshi too have rendered great help to me for this work.

I express my sincere thanks to Shri Sham Lal, Proprietor Eastern Book Linkers, 5825, New Chandrawal Road, Delhi, for expidiating the arduous task of publishing the book so efficiently.

Department of Sanskrit, Nirmal Trikha
Daulat Ram College,
University of Delhi.
Delhi - 110007.
2.9.1991

Scheme of Transliteration

अ	a	ठ्	ṭh
आ	ā	ड्	ḍ
इ	i	ढ्	ḍh
ई	ī	ण्	ṇ
उ	u	त्	t
ऊ	ū	थ्	th
ऋ	ṛ	द्	d
ॠ	ṝ	ध्	dh
लृ	lṛ	न्	n
ए	e	प्	p
ऐ	ai	फ्	ph
ओ	o	ब्	b
औ	au	भ्	bh
ं	ṁ	म्	m
ः	ḥ	य्	y
क्	k	र्	r
ख्	kh	ल्	l
ग्	g	व्	v
घ्	gh	श्	ś
ङ्	ṅ	ष्	ṣ
च्	ch	स्	s
छ्	chh	ह्	h
ज्	j	क्ष्	kṣ
झ्	jh	त्र्	tr
ञ्	n̂	ज्ञ्	jn̂
ट्	ṭ		

Mode of Citation from the Kathāsaritsāgara

In case of the Kathāsaritsāgara, citations are given by reference to Lambakas, Taraṅgas and Verses. To take an example in 1.1.12, the first figure refers to the Lambaka (i.e. first Lambaka), the second to the Taraṅga (i.e. first Taraṅga), and the last to the Verse (i.e. twelfth Verse).

Abbreviations

Ab.	Abridged
A.D.	anno Domini (in the year of our Lord)
Cf.	Compare
comm.	Commentary
comp.	Compiled by
Ed.	Edited
Eng.	English
ff.	Following
f.n.	Foot Note
H.	Hindi
ibid.	ibidem = in the same place
i.e.	id est = that is
KSS.	Kathāsaritsāgara
Mss.	Manuscripts
No.	Number
Nos.	Numbers
Ocean.	The Ocean of Story Ed. by N.M. Penzer
p.	page
pp.	pages
Speyer-review	Studies of the Kathāsaritsāgara by J.S. Speyer. A book-review by C.H. Tawney, Journal of the Royal Asiatic Society of Great Britain and Ireland, 1908.
Trans.	Translated
viz.	videlicet, namely
Vol.	Volume

CONTENTS

PART II : BELIEFS

INTRODUCTION

Faith and belief are often regarded as synonyms and used interchangeably in common speech. However, there is a subtle difference in the meaning of these words. Belief was the earlier word for what is now commonly called faith. The word faith, derived through old French *fei, feith*, the etymological representative of Latin *fides,* began in the 14th century to be employed in sense of belief, and in the course of time almost superseded the latter especially in theological language.[1] Now, faith has become a religious word for an inner attitude, conviction or trust. It applies to any system of religious belief and worship that is clearly formulated and definitely accepted.[2]

The Sanskrit word Śraddhā conveys the meaning of faith. Śraddhā is a religious belief.[3] Śrīmaddayānanda Sarasvatī too explains Śraddhā as strong conviction in Īśvara and ethical virtues.[4]

Faith implies full assent of the mind, and therefore certitude, but it adds to this a strong implication of complete trust or confidence.[5] It represents the mind's act or state only when something is assented to on grounds other than merely those of the evidence of one's senses or of conclusions entirely supported by reason.[6] One holds it with will and emotion.[7] None can doubt it because it is beholded as if supernaturally sanctioned.[8]

Belief is less restricted in its application than faith. It includes every degree of conviction from the feeblest to the strongest. Whereas religious beliefs come under faiths, all other forms of conviction pertaining to secular sphere are known as beliefs.[9] The Sanskrit word Viśvāsa is commonly used in the sense of belief. It implies one's particular manner of breathing or figuratively thinking (Chittavṛttibhede).

An ordinary secular belief is different from a religious belief. Unlike a religious belief, it may or may not imply certitude or certainty in the one who assents. It may even suggest nothing more then one's mere mental acceptance.[10]

Again, any secular belief, rooted in and supported by an association and widely held, may be refused and contradicted by a few who have thought more about the facts in question.[11] Thus, a belief can be strengthened, weakened or even annulled by logical reasoning and excludes the moral element of trust or confidence contained in faith.

The present work considers faith and belief in their proper connotations. Here, these words denote religious and secular beliefs respectively. Thus, the present work is an attempt to know all the religious as well as secular beliefs depicted in the Kathāsaritsāgara.

Faiths and beliefs occupy a unique position in the life of every individual. It is natural for the mind to believe. There is an emotional necessity of holding faiths and beliefs. It can be well perceived that in this world, it is difficult to survive without beliefs of one form or the other. Every human being whether religious or non-religious holds innumerable beliefs. There are needs of various kinds-physical, logical, aesthetic and religious and that in experience of finding satisfaction for them we find belief.[12] Faiths and beliefs are indispensable for a person because without them, one will become to oneself a wilderness, a chaos. Infact, a man is a product of his beliefs.[13] One's environment, conduct and life-style can be measured in term of one's beliefs which enter into the warp and woof of every life to which they give a meaning and a purpose.

There is an immense scope for the depiction of faiths and beliefs in stories which are indispensable for their depiction of the various aspects of society. One can gather from them, a pretty exact image of the vicissitudes of people in every walk of life. Stories introduce us to a world of infinite originality, in which characters are real under the garb of imagination. Characters of stories are not only heroic warriors, virtuous kings and beautiful princesses, but also people of the most varied kind-- peasants, merchants, artisans, vagabonds, selfish Brāhmaṇas, hypocritical monks, courtesans and procuresses. Thus, stories through their variety of characters can give fuller and finer expressions to the faiths and beliefs of people.

The Kathāsaritsāgara, the treasure of these stories, is the most notable of the Sanskrit story books. It is unquestionably the largest single collection of stories in the world. It is as big as Illiad and Odyssey put together. It is almost three times bigger than the Bṛhatkathāmañjarī of Kṣemendra. It excels the Pañchatantra, the Hitopadeśa, the Vetālapañchaviṁśati, the Siṁhāsanadvātriṁśati and the Śukasaptati in bulk.

The Kathāsaritsāgara is a huge compilation comprising stories from heterogeneous sources. Somadeva himself admits that the attempt to write the Kathāsaritsāgara is in order to facilitate the collection of a multitude of various stories.[14] His work is adapted from the Paiśāchī Bṛhatkathā of Guṇāḍhya who in his own turn must have collected his material from the floating stories. The poet affirms in the Kathāpīṭha that he has followed his original with utmost fidelity.[15] A stupendous mass of remotely connected floating stories is accumulated in the text. The work contains many legends of the Ṛgvedic period, stories of the Rāmāyaṇa, the Mahābhārata, the Purāṇas and the Jātakas. It contains the recast of the first three books of the Pañchatantra and abstracts or versions of several of the well known books of Sanskrit stories such as the Hitopadeśa, the Vetālapañchaviṁśati, the Siṁhāsanadvātriṁśati and the Śukasaptati. Thus, the stories of the text cover a very long period.

The Kathāsaritsāgara contains astonishing profusion of the stories of every conceivable type. The title Kathāsaritsāgara means ocean formed by the rivers of stories. The work absorbs all stories as the ocean does all rivers. All the rivers of stories which having sprung out from all possible sources flow into this one ocean. Every stream of myth and mystery flowing down from the snowy heights of sacred Himālaya would sooner or later reach the ocean, other streams from other mountains would do likewise till at last fancy would create an ocean full of stories of every conceivable description.[16]

The comparison is apt from another point of view also. Rivers begin as tiny streams. As they move farther from their source, they swell more and more. Likewise stories that have been told and retold for centuries no longer remain episodic. They grow, their course becomes wide, they become powerful forces of cultural transmission. They irrigate vast tracts of the human consciousness. In Somadeva's classic it is not the tiny streams but these mighty currents that have been gathered together.[17] The work has become the most interesting collection of shrewd and well told stories in Sanskrit.

The stories of the Kathāsaritsāgara are diversified and well conceived. There is an infinite variety of theme in the text which contains myth, mystery, fact, fancy, fable, legend, tradition, romance and what not. Some of the stories are saturated with the spirit of piety and religious devotion while others reveal a refreshing secular and objective attitude of life. Statecraft and intrigue, magic and spells, treachery, trickery, murder and war, all provide matter for these stories. There is hardly any class of stories that is not found in the Kathāsaritsāgara.

Variety of atmosphere is another characteristic feature of the stories of the Kathāsaritsāgara. The text contains many stories of wonderful adventures on sea and land and stories of battle between divine and human beings. Many stories deal with the magical word where creatures and objects grow small and large, fly through the air, change form or become invisible.

There is an endless diversity of situation in the stories of the Kathāsaritsāgara. The text appears as a vast picture-gallery in which men and women are depicted filling a variety of roles in the drama of life.[18] Some of the characters live out their lives swayed by longings, passions, hopes and disappointments that are the common lot of all men. Other face unusual situations and cross into the magic realm of the supernatural. Still other characters adventure through normal situations.

The text contains a gallery of sketches from life, romantic as well as real. The poet has true knowledge of human nature. The work depicts a large variety of characters such as wondrous maidens, fearless lovers, virtuous kings, brave warriors, sweet princesses, venerable priests, hardworking farmers, manual workers, expert salesmen, skilled artisans, clever jugglers, cunning swindlers and rascals, selfish Brāhmaṇas, hypocrite monks, clever harlots, cunning procuresses, poor beggars, fools, selfless ascetics, drunkards, clever gamblers, blood sucking vampires, devils, goblins, ghouls, fairies and animals. Such characters are not just stereotyped figures but are often delineated with sharp individual traits.

The Kathāsaritsāgara with its variety of theme, atmosphere, situation and character provides a wide scope for the depiction of the faiths and beliefs of its society. Quite close to the masses by its subject matter, it keeps a taste for living reality. It introduces us to the mixed world where characters speak of men of their time.

The present work is divided into two parts containing eleven chapters. The first part is based on the faiths in the Kathāsaritsāgara. It comprises nine chapters. Chapters I to VII are devoted to the Hindu[19] Faith. The first part starts with the principal sectarian Faiths of the Hindus.

Chapters I and II attempt to present the Śaiva, Gāṇapatya, Vaiṣṇava, Brāhma, Śākta and the Saura Faiths.

Chapter III analyses the divine family which constitutes of various gods, goddesses, associates of gods, divine seers, divine races and enemies of gods. Lower mythology is also included into this chapter as it throws light on the religious beliefs of the people of those times.

All religious practices are the expressions of religious beliefs.[20] Therefore, religious practices such as fire-worship, sacrifices, temple-worship, sacred prostitution as also other religious practices including Devajāgaraṇa, Japa, vows, Bali and austerities are discussed in the fourth chapter. Pilgrimage to sacred places is an act of faith and religious festivals too are celebrated to express one's devotion towards different gods. Both these are included in this chapter.

Chapter V deals with such religious concepts as afterworld, heaven and hell, sin, curse and boon. Beliefs founded on Astrology and Astronomy are also taken into account.

Ethics is an inseparable element of all religions[21] as no spiritual development is possible without cultivating ethical virtues. Therefore, Ethics too comes into the purview of the Hindu Faith. Chapter V concludes with Hindu Ethics.

Religion and Philosophy are closely inter-related in the Hindu Faith. In fact, Philosophy forms it's basis. Therefore, beliefs about God, the soul, the world and salvation are considered in this work and chapter VI is devoted to them. The spiritual systems like Sāṁkhya and Yoga are also referred to in this chapter. The chapter ends with the belief in the doctrine of grace.

The Tāntrika practices too form a part of the religious beliefs. Chapter VII deals with these practices.

Chapter VIII analyses the Bauddha faith and throws light on its Ethics.

The second part, consisting of the last three chapters of the work, deals with beliefs in the Kathāsaritsāgara.

Chapter IX is based on omens. It refers to both good and evil omens. Omens from bodily signs are taken into account. Birth marks (Lakṣaṇas) and moles (Tilakas) on one's body too portend good or evil fortune to a superstitious mind. Therefore, these are also included in this chapter.

Chapter X points out belief in the significance of various types of dreams and gives superstitious interpretations of many dreams.

The last chapter deals with the belief in the existence of various evil spirits viz., the Rākṣasas, Piśāchas, Bhūtas and Pretas, Vetālas, water-spirits and witches. Belief in the evil effect of the fatal look is also considered in this chapter.

A consolidated picture of the faiths and beliefs, based on the study of the Kathāsaritsāgara, is presented in the conclusion.

Footnotes Of Introduction

1. The Oxford English Dictionary, Vol. IV, p.782.

2. Webster's Dictionary of Synonyms, p.692.

For faith as a religious belief vide Webster's Third New International Dictionary (unabridged), p.816; The New Century Dictionary of the English Language, Vol.I, p. 545; Harrap's Standard French and English Dictionary, Part II, p.97; The Random House Dictionary of the English Language (unabriged), p.511; The Reader's Digest Great Encyclopaedic Dictionary, Vol.I, p.312; Funk and Wagnalls New Practical Standard Dictionary of the English Language, Vol.I, pp.475-76; The New Funk and Wagnalls Encyclopaedia, Vol.13, pp.4691-92.

3. Cf. प्रत्ययो धर्म्मकार्येषु यथा श्रद्धेत्युदाहृता ।
धर्म्माः श्रद्धैव कीर्त्तिताः ॥

Both these lines are quoted by Rājā Rādhākāntadevabahādura. Vide- Śabdakalpadruma, Vol.V, p. 154.

4. ईश्वारसत्यधर्मादिगुणानामुपर्यत्यन्तं विश्वासः श्रद्धा

Ṛgvedādibhāṣyabhūmikā, p.108

5. Webster's Dictionary of Synonyms, p.113.

6. Ibid. p.113.

7. Solomen, E., Scepticism or Faith and Mysticism, Journal of the Oriental Institute, Baroda, Vol.VIII (1958-59), p.225.

8. Cf.

"Having such faith is thought to be a mark of divine grace. Men may exercise their own will to believe about other matters, but belief in the articles of religious faith is a gift that God himself bestows upon them." Great Treasury of Western Thought, pp.443-44.

9. Hamilton, E.J., Human Mind, p.101.

10. Webster's Dictionary of Synonyms, p.113.

11. Encyclopaedia of Religion and Ethics, Vol.II, p.461.

12. Encyclopaedia of Religion and Ethics, Vol.II, p.462.

13. Cf.
यो यच्छ्रद्धः स एव सः ।

Śrīmadbhagavadgītā 17/3-1.

14. वैदध्यख्यातिलोभाय मम नैवायमुद्यमः ।
किन्तुनानाकथाजाल स्मृति सौकर्य सिध्दये ॥

KSS. 1.1.12

15. बृहत्कथायाः सारस्य संग्रहं रच्याम्यहम् ॥
यथा मूलं तथैवैतन्न मनागप्यतिक्रमः ।
ग्रन्थविस्तरसंक्षेपमात्रं भाषा च भिद्यते ॥
औचित्यान्वयरक्षा च यथाशक्ति विधीयते ।
कथारसाविघातेन काव्याशंस्य च योजना ॥

KSS. 1.1.3, 10-11

16. Krishnamachariar, M., History of Classical Sanskrit Literature, pp. 420-21.

17. Naravane, V.S., Stories from the Indian Classics, p. 238.

18. Ibid, p. 238.

19. The word Hindu is generally used to distinguish the inhabitants of Hindustān from the Muslims and the Christians. But, in the present work, it is used in the restricted sense. Here the word Hindu stands for one who is the follower of Hindu religion.

20. Cf.

"Faith is the force that allows the performance of the rites." Renou, Louis., Vedic India, p.73.

21. According to Manu Smṛti (6.91-92) also religion comprises ethical virtues.

PART I

FAITHS

The Kathāsaritsāgara presents both the Hindu and the Bauddha Faiths. The Hindu Faith includes higher Hindu Faiths and lower Hindu Faiths. The higher Hindu Faiths consist of the body of beliefs regarding the divine or supernatural powers and the sense of dependence on those powers which is expressed by word in the form of prayer and praise or by act in the form of ritual and sacrifice. The lower Hindu Faiths contain the Tāntrika practices which are combined with the tenets of the Hindu Faith.

The Hindu writer Somadeva gives place to the Bauddha Faith along with his own Hindu Faith. He himself adores Jina (Buddha) along with the gods of the Hindu pantheon.[1]

The picture of both the Faiths from the Kathāsaritsāgara will be presented in this part.

Chapter I

HIGHER HINDU FAITHS

Writing on Hinduism, Monier Williams observes that Hindus are profoundly religious people. A religion of some kind they must have, a religion which will stir to depths of the heart, and give room for the exercise of faith and love.[2] This remark appears to be correct when we study the Kathāsaritsāgara which throws tremendous light on the faiths of its characters. The following are the principal sectarian Faiths in the Kathāsaritsāgara:

The Śaiva Faith

Śiva is the most prominent god in the Kathāsaritsāgara. The poet Somadeva himself is a Śaiva Brāhmaṇa of Kaśmīra. The invocation[3] of Śiva in the text shows his unbounded devotion to the god.[4] The origin of the 'the story of the Bṛhatkathā' is traced to Śiva.[5] The great Sanskrit grammarian Pāṇini is fabled to have seen rather than composed his grammar by the grace of Śiva.[6] Vararuchi is conquered by Pāṇini in the learning of grammar only due to the preference of Śiva for the latter grammarian.[7] The chief god of the Bṛhatkathāślokasaṁgraha is Kuvera and not Śiva. The prominence of Śiva in the Kāśmīrian version of Somadeva confirms that the poet is probably influenced by that form of the Śaiva Faith which was introduced into Kaśmīra by Vasugupta about two hundred and fifty years before the poet's time and which was subsequently made widely popular by his pupil Kallaṭa Bhaṭṭa. About one hundred years before Somadeva, this form of the Hindu Faith was further spread by Bhāskara, and then in Somadeva's own time made popular by Abhinavagupta and his pupils Kṣemarāja and Yogarāja.

The Śaivas form a powerful sect in the Kathāsaritsāgara. There are references to the Śaivas[8], Kāpālikavratas[9], Kāpālikas[10], Mahāvratins[11] and Pāśupatas[12]. The Kāpālikavratas or the Kāpālikas are the skull-bearing Śaiva ascetics who are seen white with ashes and with matted locks.[13] The bodies of the Mahāvratins or the Pāśupata Śaiva ascetics, who hold trident in their hands, are smeared with matted hair.[14] There is a description of a Pāśupata ascetic who is covered all over with hair white with ashes. His matted locks are yellow with lightning, and he looks like another Śiva. His body is emaciated with age and excessive asceticism.[15]

The Śaivas try to indicate the superiority of Śiva over all other gods by calling him Devadeva.[16] Both the gods and Asuras are said to bow down before Śiva.[17] The Śaivas show Śiva as superior to Brahmā and Nārāyaṇa by holding that both these gods propitiate Śiva with austerities and obtain boons from him.[18] They describe Brahmā as carrying out Śiva's command[19] and Indra is also made inferior to Śiva. They declare that even Indra seeks Śiva's favour in the destruction of Asuras.[20] The 'story of Vararuchi' also shows the supremacy of Śiva over Indra. Aindra grammar is exploded in the world by the terrible menancing sound of Śiva.[21] The thunderbolt of Indra is destroyed by the angry roar of Śiva.[22] All the weapons of other gods are also annihilated by the angry sound of Śiva.[23] The Śaivas show the superiority of Śiva over Viṣṇu, Brahmā and Indra by making them the devotees of Śiva. It is said that these gods perform severe penance in order to please Śiva.[24] Kuvera and Agni are shown inferior to Śiva. The former worships him[25] and the latter is afraid of his curse.[26] The Śaivas establish the supremacy of Śiva over other gods by arguing that of what importance are the hosts of other gods when Śiva is in arms.[27] The Pāśupatāstra or the weapon of Śiva is held as the most powerful of all the weapons of gods.[28] Thus, the tendency of the Śaivas to show other deities as inferior to Śiva is powerfully depicted in the Kathāsaritsāgara.

The Śaivas hold Śiva as the Supreme Reality. Śiva is called the all-pervading (Vibhu)[29] lord of the world (Viśveśa).[30] He is self-existent (Svayambhū)[31] and supremely chaste.[32] He, though his beloved takes up half his body is an ascetic, free from qualities (Nirguṇa). He assumes eight forms.[33] He is holy (Sthāṇu).[34] He sleeps on the ever-expanded lotus of the heart. He is the swan dwelling in the pure Mānasa lake[35] (pure mind) of his devotees. He is pure and of watery substance. He is to be seen by those whose sins are washed away.[36] His body is held as the bestower of emancipation.[37]

Śiva is represented as the ultimate cause of the universe. He creats the world by his mere will[38] and pervades the universe. He is called the source of the things, animate as well as inanimate.[39] He is the creator, preserver and destroyer of the world.[40] He is always producing new and wonderful creations. He does not feel the urge of love in order to have offspring.[41] Though free from Rāga (passion), his creation abounds in colours.

The conception of the world-egg is very common in Indian cosmology. It can be traced back to the Vedic period.[42] It is found at several places in the post Vedic period also.[43] The Kathāsaritsāgara connects the Cosmic Egg Theory with Śiva Śiva is held as the creator of the world egg. A myth in the text traces the origin of creation from Śiva. It is believed that long ago, when all things had been destroyed at the end of Kalpa, the universe was transformed into water. Śiva then cleft his thigh and let fall a drop of blood. The very drop of blood converted into an egg. From the egg sprang the Supreme Soul. From that Supreme Soul proceeded Nature, created by Śiva for the purpose of further creation. The Supreme Soul (Pumān) and Nature (Prakṛti) then together created other lords of the created beings (Prajāpatis). Those Prajāpatis, in turn, created all the beings. The Supreme Soul (Pumān) is called in the world the Pitāmaha. The world resembling a skull, rests in Śiva's hand. The two skull-shaped halves of the egg are called heaven and earth.[44] As destruction is considered a necessary prelude to creation, the Śaivas hold that the god of destruction is also the god of creation.[45]

The epithets of Śiva are directly connected with his twofold nature–the malevolent and the benevolent. Many names or epithets of

Śiva are found in the Kathāsaritsāgara. He is called Īśvara,[46] Īśāna,[47] Bhagavān,[48] Bharga,[49] Maheśvara,[50] Hara,[51] Śiva,[52] Śaṁkara,[53] Śambhu,[54] Śarva[55] and Rudra.[56] Out of all these names, Rudra and Śarva are indicative of his destructive energy and the rest refer to his benignant counterpart. Human-beings do not believe in a purely malignant power reigning the universe. The dreadful phenomena are attributed to the wrath of a god, which, however, can be appeased by prayer, praise and offerings. The god becomes Śiva or the benignant. This appears to be the natural process by which a belief in such a god as Rudra Śiva became established in India in ancient times.[57]

Being a moon-diademed god, Śiva is known as Induśekhara,[58] Chandramauli,[59] Niśākarakalāmauli and Śaśi-Śekhara. The crescent moon depicted on Śiva's head has a special significance. It points to that sovereignty which was assigned to him when the moon was recovered from the depths of the ocean. The crescent moon also symbolizes the power of Śiva over the measurement of time.[60]

Śiva is also called Dhūrjaṭa[61] (a god of matted locks). He is Trinetra[62] or Tryakṣa.[63] This perhaps is an allusion to either the three Vedas or time-past, present and future.[64]

As Kapālamālī[65], Śiva wears a garland of skulls. He takes delight in skulls and burning places.[66] It is held that having created the world, animate and inanimate, the spirit (Puruṣa) became arrogant. Then Śiva cut off his head. Through regret for what he had done, he undertook a difficult vow. Therefore, he carries skulls in his hands and loves cremation grounds.[67] The garland of skulls which Śiva wears, the corpse on which he is seated, the terrific shape in which he is adored as Mahākāla-the destructive god of time or death–all these items are so many indications that Śiva was regarded first as the ruler and then as the representative of the vast various classes of demonic beings who were created in the imagination of the superstitious by the fear and awe inspired by everything relating to death and the dead.[68] Association of Śiva with dead bodies has led some scholars to believe in the non-Aryan origin of Śiva.[69]

The 'story of the former birth of Pārvatī', narrated in the Kathāsaritsāgara, shows that once, the Prajāpati Dakṣa performs a sacrifice in which Śiva is not invited. On being asked by Pārvatī, he tells that Śiva is inauspicious because he wears garlands of skulls.[70] Then Pārvatī commits suicide and Śiva in his wrath destroys the sacrifice of Dakṣa. The story shows that originally there was no provision for giving Śiva, any portion of the sacrificial oblation. Śiva's antagonistic attitude towards Dakṣa has been explained as the struggle of a non-Aryan deity for participation in the sacrifices of the Aryans and his forcible entry in the Vedic pantheon.

Muir has refuted the view of the non-Aryan origin of Śiva.[71] It can be concluded that the cult of Rudra-Śiva, and of his consort, originally, perhaps, chiefly the property of tribes loosely or not at all connected with Brāhmaṇical society has in course of time been fully Brāhmaṇized.[72]

Pinākin,[73] Pinākabhṛt,[74] Śūlin[75] or Triśūlin are other epithets of Śiva in the Kathāsaritsāgara. The trident borne by Śiva is a symbol of government and authority.[76] The three-pronged symbols may denote creation, destruction and regeneration.[77]

The great god Śiva is also called Ambikāsakhā,[78] Ambikāpati,[79] Umāpati,[80] Girijāpati[81] and Gaurīpati.[82] All these refer to the belief that he is the consort of Pāravatī. He receives the name Tryambaka[83] which is common epithet in post-Vedic literature and which has been applied to Rudra in Vedic texts.[84] The epithet Giriśa[85] points at the association of Śiva with mountains. Another epithet of Śiva is Vṛṣadhvaja[86] or Vṛṣalakṣmaṇa.[87] As in the case of other gods of fertility, the bull is the appropriate emblem of Śiva.[88]

Being the enemy or destroyer of Tripura,[89] Śiva is variously known as Tripurāri,[90] Purārāti[91] and Purāri[92].

It is held that Śiva possesses a highly colourful appearance. He has a dark neck.[93] At the churning of the ocean poison comes to the surface and it is swallowed by Śiva[94] to save the universe from destruction. It is held by him in his throat and this accounts for the dark colour of the neck.

Śiva is describes as three eyed, bearing trident in hand, wearing yellow matted locks and putting on a lovely half moon crest. His eyes gleam with a lustre like that of the sun and the moon.[95] He bears Gaṅgā on his head. He is red on one side with saffron paint and white on the other with ashes.[96] He is also described as white with ashes and red with matted locks. His body is adorned with snakes.[97] His partiality for the serpents and his being the lord of spirits or Bhūtas, are probably due to the influence of serpent worship and the devilry of the savage tribe.[98]

Half of the body of Śiva is occupied by Pārvatī.[99] This symbolizes the union of Puruṣa and Prakṛti. Śiva's representation as half male and half female is emblematic of the indissoluble unity of the creative principle.

Śiva rides on a bull.[100] He is attended upon by Gaṇas, Vidyādharas and Siddhas.[101] Pāśupata or the Mahāpāśupatāstra is the great weapon of Śiva.[102] It is considered to be of irresistible might, of huge size, with a flame of fire streaming up from it, with three eyes, with four faces, with one leg and eight arms.[103] It is held that this weapon does not harm children, old men and fugitives.[104]

The terrible aspect of Śiva as Rudra[105] is also conceived in the Kathāsaritsāgara. The angry Rudra is believed to be formidable.[106]

Kailāsa is a mountain in the Himālayas, north of the Mānasa lake.[107] It is called the dwelling place of Śiva.[108] The pleasure-harbours of the slopes of this mountain, in which Śiva dwells with his wife, are believed to be made of the branches of Kalpa tree.[109] The abode of Śiva excels Svarga.[110] There blow winds of heavenly fragrance, the trees ever bear fruits and flowers, and Gandharvas begin their concert with the dancing of Apsarasas.[111] It is believed that one should not advance towards this mountain of Śiva because all the Vidhyās are destroyed by crossing this dwelling place of Śiva. One must pass to the other side of the mountain by the cave of Triśīrṣa.[112]

The peaks of the mountain Mandara are described as the pleasure groves of Śiva.[113]

There are many sacred earthly abodes of Śiva. The holy city of Vārāṇasī[114] is one of them. The city of Ujjayinī is also considered to be the dwelling place of Śiva.[115] Śiva, under the name of Mahākāla, dwells there.[116] It is held that this city, inferior only to Bhogavatī and Amarāvatī, was selected by Śiva himself as his habitation.[117] Vetālas and such other beings cannot enter this city which is guarded by the grace of Śiva.[118]

Vilāsapura[119] and Dhāreśvara are also considered as the dwelling places of Śiva. Kaśmīra is another sacred place of Śiva. It is believed that, here, Śiva, as self-existent deity, inhabits hundred shrines, forgetting his happy home in Kailāsa.[120] There is a famous holy place, dear to Śiva, called Vijayā in it.[121] Nandikṣetra, Mahādevagiri, Amaraparvata, the mountain of Sureśvarī and Kapaṭeśvara are the various holy places of Śiva in Kaśmīra. Śiva inhabits the lower regions in the form of Hāṭakeśvara.[122] Gokarṇa is also a sacred place associated with Śiva.[123]

In the Kathāsaritsāgara, worship of Śiva is considered to be the best form of worship. It is held that when Śiva, the god of gods is worshiped, all gods are worshipped.[124]

Śiva has a large number of devotees and notable among them are the King Hemaprabha and his queen,[125] Naravāhanadatta,[126] Sūryaprabha,[127] the King Udayana,[128] Chamaravāla,[129] Vīravara,[130] Somadatta,[131] Niśchayadatta,[132] Devadatta,[133] Hemaprabha[134] and many others.

Devotees of Śiva feel that god is kind to his votaries[135] and grants boons to them.[136] They think that god protects his devotees through his Gaṇas.[137] Even the sweat of god Śiva is believed to be the protector of his devotees.[138]

So strong is the faith of the devotees in Śiva that the King Chandraketu says that without pleasing Śiva, one cannot attain the fulfilment of one's desires.[139] A sage asks the King Merudhvaja to worship in order to obtain the desired object soon.[140] The King Hemaprabha has full faith that Śiva when adored will bless him with a son.[141] Many stories express the belief that Śiva can bless his devotee with a son. The King Kanakākṣa,[142] Jyotiṣprabha,[143] Ratnavarman,[144] Kusumasāra,[145] Pratāpasena,[146] Vīradeva,[147] Ratnākara[148] and Hemaprabha[149] obtain sons through the grace of Śiva. The worship of Śiva is also believed to give strength[150] and knowledge.[151]

Śiva is worshipped by his devotees for fulfilment of various desires such as knowledge,[152] suitable husband,[153] son,[154] success and so on.

The worship of Śiva is a revealing study. Devotees like Puṣkarākṣa worship Śiva everyday.[155] Some devotees worship Śiva thrice a day. The fourteenth and the eighth days of the both fortnights are considered to be sacred for his worship.[156] The King Pratāpamukha worships the god on the fourteenth day of a month.[157] The eight day of a month is considered to be sacred for going to the temple of Puṣpadanteśvara. The daughter of the King Suśarman, Śrī by name, goes to the temple of Puṣpadanteśvara on this day.[158] Śiva, in the form of Hāṭakeśvara, is worshipped on the fourteenth day of a month. On this day, the King Merudhvaja with his sons and his wife, worships him.[159]

The Kathāsaritsāgara refers to the temples of Śiva.[160] Śrīdatta beholds a splendid temple of Śiva[161] from which Naravāhanadatta hears music.[162] There is a reference to a temple of Śiva that stands on the bank of a river.[163] The temple at Gokarṇa is situated on the shore of a sea.[164] There is another temple of Śiva outside a city.[165] Temple of Śiva contains a sacred vessel.[166]

Devotees of Śiva go to such temples for worship. A female ascetic goes everyday to worship the lord in the temple of Amareśa.[167] In a temple of Svayambhū, the King Mahāsena with his attendants, remains totally absorbed in asceticism.

Image of Śiva is worshipped. There is a reference to a temple of Śiva with the image of Śiva having Pārvatī on his left and Ganeśa on his right.[168] There is an image of Śiva about which it is believed that if visited and worshipped, it gives enjoyment and even salvation.[169] There is a reference to an image of Śiva visible within a Liṅga.[170] There is an image of mighty Bhairava in the cemetery of Mahākāla which is worshipped by heroes.[171]

Śiva is pleased with circumambulation. Muktāphaladhvaja walks devoutly round the temple of Śiva three times keeping his right hand towards it.[172]

Water is the source of purity. Therefore, the devotees of Śiva take bath before worshipping him. The King Hemaprabha and his queen,[173] the King Chamaravāla,[174] Śarvavarman,[175] and a physician[176] take bath before worshipping the god

Nāmasaṁkīrtana which consists in enumerating as many names and epithets as possible pertaining to a certain god in order to please him, has been regarded as an effective and meritorious work of devotion. This mode of worship first appears in the Śatarudrīya which enumerated hundred names of god Rudra.[177] In the Kathāsaritsāgara also, uttering of Śiva's different names is considered to be auspicious. Chamaravāla worships Śiva by repeating his names referring to sixty-eight excellent parts of the body. These names are held auspicious, destroyer of sins and bestower of all desires.[178] Suvāsakumāra tells Sūryaprabha and others that they should extol Śiva with his eight thousand names as this will make the Gaṇas favourably disposed to them.[179]

Dance, songs and instrumental performances are regarded as vital means of pleasing gods. Devotees of Śiva make full use of them to win his grace. From a Svayambhū temple of Śiva. Naravāhanadatta hears the sound of singing, mixed with the notes of a heavenly lyre.[180] Anaṅgaprabhā sings devoutly in praise of Śiva.[181]

Flowers and garlands are offered to gods in order to please them. Śiva is also worshipped in this way. Naravāhanadatta pleases Śiva with the offering of lotuses.[182] Somadatta adores Śiva with many garlands.[183]

Devotees also kneel on the ground in humble devotion to Śiva.[184]

Among almost all people, fasting is considered as an important means of establishing direct communication with the supernatural. It is regarded as a form of personal sacrifice which propitiates gods. It leads to mystical experience and revelations. In the Kathāsaritsāgara, the worshippers of Śiva believe that the god is highly pleased with those devotees who undertake fast. Udayana and Vāsavadattā fast for three nights to please Śiva.[185] The King Hemaprabha also fasts for three nights to please him.[186] Guhasena observes a rigid fast thinking that god will show him some way of getting out of his difficulty.[187] Sometimes, the fast for pleasing Śiva is undertaken at some sacred place of pilgrimage. For instance, the King Chandraprabha goes to Vārāṇasī and fasts there for three days to worship Śiva.[188]

Various other vows are also undertaken to please Śiva.

The King Mahendrāditya observes many vows in order to please the god.[189]

Rudrayajña is considered to be superior to many other sacrifices including Aśvamedha. The Śaivas hold that the sacrifice of Rudra has no comparison. There is no need of performing other sacrifices.[190]

It is held that Śiva can be pleased by performing austerities. Dharmaśīla declares that object of his life is to please Śiva by practicing austerities.[191] Among other characters of the Kathāsaritsāgara, Devadatta,[192] Naravāhanadatta,[193] Sāgaravarman,[194] Somadatta[195] and Vararuchi[196] propitiate Śiva by undertaking austerities. Muktāphaladhvaja says to his father that he will perform a course of austerities to please Śiva.[197]

Devotees of Śiva perform penance to please him for obtaining various desired objects. The King Vīradeva pleases Śiva with penance for securing a son.[198] The King Hemaprabha fasts and goes through ascetic practices in front of the image of Śiva in order to obtain a son.[199] Like-wise, the King Karpūraka performs penance for pleasing Śiva in order to obtain offspring.[200]

Some places are considered to be especially sacred for undergoing penance to please Śiva. The temple of Mahākāla is one of them.[201] The mountain Himālaya is also regarded as suitable for such a penance. Vararuchi, by performing a severe penance on this mountain, pleases Śiva.[202] Many other devotees are seen observing penance in some holy temples of god. The King Mahāsena and the King Haṁsadvīpa practise penance in a temple of Svayambhū.[203]

The use of symbols in worship is quite common in many religions. The symbol is believed to be a necessary and helpful intermediary between the inadequate capacity of the mind of the worshipper and the incommunicable nature and fullness of the unknown whom he adores. Śiva-Liṅga is a prominent symbol used in the worship of this deity. Its connection with Śiva may probably be traced to his manifestation as a god of reproduction.[204] The prevalence of this ancient symbol of fertility and life in the cult of Śiva shows that in the more naive religion of the older age there was not yet that divorce between the physical and moral world which the spiritual law of modern religion has formulated.

The origin of the belief in Liṅga-worship is quite obscure and controversial. Many scholars have tried to show that the belief has been adopted from the Dravidian tribes of the South. To A.A. Macdonell, it seems to be a non-Aryan cult.[205] A.B. Keith observes that is as probable as anything can be that the phallus - worshippers were aborigines.[206] Stephenson also connects phallic worship with the non-Aryan tribes.[207] P. Thomas holds that there is every reason to believe that the worship of Liṅga is not of Aryan origin.[208] Lassen also traces this belief from the Dravidian races.[209] R.G. Bhandarkar remarks that just as the Rudra Śiva cult borrowed several elements from the dwellers in forests and stragglers in places out of the way, so it may have borrowed the element of phallic worship from the barbarian tribes with whom the Aryas came in contact.[210]

The view of the non-Aryan or Dravidian origin of the Liṅga-worship has, now been generally rejected. Competent authorities like E.W. Hopkins and A. Barth have completely refuted it.[211] Early traditions also associate the establishment of Liṅgam in North India with Aryan saints and worthies.[212] The facts, seem to indicate that, though the cult may have prevailed among some of the indigenous tribes, it was not confined to them, and that in the form in which it now appears, its extension was largely due to the Aryans.[213]

The Kathāsaritsāgara frequently refers to the Liṅga form of Śiva.[214] The text alludes to temples containing Liṅgas of Śiva.[215] Flame Liṅga (Jvālā-Liṅga) is a favourite emblem of Śiva.[216] It is believed that Śiva is ever manifest in the form of a Flame-Liṅga at Siddhiśvara on the Tridaśa mountain.[217]

Many devotees worship the Liṅga of Śiva.[218] Disrespect to the Liṅga is considered to be a great sin and an expiatory penance is prescribed for it's atonement. Vālmikī tells an expiatory penance for Lava and Kuśa because they play with the Liṅga which the former worships.[219]

The story of adventures of Puṣkarākṣa and Vinayavatī in a former life shows the belief that one gets a good birth by worshipping the Liṅga of Śiva.[220]

The Tāntrikas perform magic rites to please Śiva.[221]

Family of Śiva

Pārvatī

Pārvatī alias Umā,[222] is the consort of Śiva. The Kathāsaritsāgara describes her as the mother of the three worlds[223] and as Śakti of god Śiva.[224] According to one reference, she is believed to be an incarnation of Nārayāṇa.[225] It is said that, once, the god Nārāyaṇa wants a boon from Śiva and prays to become his devotee. Śiva grants the boon in pursuance of which Nārāyaṇa is born as Pārvatī.[226]

Many names and epithets of Pārvatī[227] occur in the Kathāsaritsāgara. She is called Girijā,[228] Girisutā,[229] Śailatanayā,[230] Gaurī,[231] Śarvāṇī,[232] Mṛḍānī,[233] Umā[234] and Ambikā.[235] She is described as the half of the body of Śiva.[236] Though enjoying the supreme love and regard of her lord, she is jealous of her co-wives Sandhyā and Gaṅgā.[237]

The 'Story of the present birth of Pārvatī' is narrated in the text. It is said that Śiva comes to the Himālayas to perform penance. The Himavat asks Pārvatī to look after the venerable guest. Then comes Kāma, sent by gods in order that they may obtain a son from Śiva to kill Tāraka. But, Kāma is consumed by the angry eye of Śiva. Later on, Pārvatī wins Śiva by her severe austerities.[238]

Like Śiva, Pārvatī is also highly adored by the characters of the Kathāsaritsāgara. Mṛgāṅkadatta[239] and the King Parityāgasena[240] worship her. Pārvatī is particularly worshipped by maidens for getting suitable husbands. Uṣā propitiates her for obtaining a husband.[241]

Devotees believe that the goddess Pārvatī is kind to her votaries[242] and grieves at their miseries.[243] There are many references in the text which point at the belief that the goddess fulfils the desires of her devotees. For instance, it is said that the King Mahāvarāha gets the daughter Anaṅgarati by pleasing the goddess.[244] Śaktiyaśas obtains all the magic sciences from Pārvatī.[245]

The Kathāsaritsāgara alludes to the temples of Pārvatī[246] with images of Pārvatī installed therein.[247]

The goddess is pleased by reciting hymns. Sundarasena praises her with mind humbled by devotion and recites prayers.[248] Śaktiyaśas also praises her by reciting hymns.[249] Jīmūtavāhana happens to see a beautiful maiden playing on the lyre, intent on pleasing Pārvatī in a temple.[250]

Flowers are frequently offered to the goddess. Muktāphalaketu worships the goddess with flowers.[251]

Fast is observed in reverence of the goddess. Śaktiyaśas propitiates her with fast.[252]

Devotees of Pārvatī feel that she can be pleased by practising penance. Many devotees are seen pleasing her by taking recourse to it. Vijayavatī propitiates her with it.[253] Padmāvatī goes to her temple with the intention of performing penance.[254]

A festival is held in her honour. Every year, during a feast on the fourteenth day of the bright fortnight of the month of Āṣāḍha, a large crowd comes to the Gaurītīrtha, south of the temple of Gaurī in the city of Śobhāvatī for a holy dip from every nook and corner of the world.[255]

Kārttikeya[256]

He is the son of Śiva. In the Kathāsaritsāgara, he is variously called Kumāra,[257] Swāmi-Kumāra,[258] Guha,[259] Skanda,[260] Ṣaḍānana[261] and Ṣaṇmukha[262] (six faced god). He holds spear in his hand[263] and rides on a peacock.[264] His having the peacock as his vehicle is consistent with his connection with Śiva, aspeacocksare found in forests of which Rudra and his attendants were gods.[265]

Kārttikeya has the brightness of the burning fire. He has five sons. He is described encircled by inauspicious planets and infant planets that submit to him as soon as he is born.[266]

The account of the birth of Kārttikeya is quite obscure. The Rāmāyaṇa represents him as the son of god of fire and Gaṅgā.[267] The Mahābhārata calls him the son of Agni and Svāhā.[268] The Kathāsaritsāgara refers to all the beliefs regarding the origin of this god. Thus, his origin is traced from Śiva, from the fire-cavity, from fire, from the thicket of reeds and from the Kṛttikas.[269] A detailed story of his birth[270] is given in Kathāsaritsāgara.

Kārttikeya is depicted as a mighty god. It is held that as soon as he is born, he makes the world bend by his irresistible might and kills the Asura Tāraka.[271] He is consecrated as general of his forces by Indra.[272]

Kārttikeya is worshipped for attaining desired objects. The wife of Śarvavarman tells him that in difficulty there is no refuge except Kārttikeya.[273] The god is particularly worshipped for attaining knowledge. For instance, Indradatta and Vyāḍi desiring to attain learning go to the southern region to propitiate the god.[274] Varṣa also worships him with the desire to attain knowledge.[275]

The eighth day of a month is held sacred for the worship of Kārttikeya.[276]

There are temples of the god.[277] There is a reference to the holy shrine of Kārttikeya in the Deccan. Śarvavarman sets out fasting for this shrine.[278] Many devotees worship Kārttikeya by performing austerities.[279]

The Gāṇapatya Faith

Closely associated with Śiva is Gaṇeśa[280] who is the chief of his Gaṇas. The Kathāsaritsāgara depicts Gaṇeśa not only as the son of Śiva and Pārvatī but also as an independent sectarian god. The Gāṇapatya Faith has emerged as a popular Faith in the text. Gaṇeśa is described as the god of gods.[281] All the three worlds with gods, Asuras and men are described as the worshippers of Gaṇeśa.[282] Even the chief of the gods are held as uttering his sixty-eight sin destroying names.[283]

Gāṇapatyas establish their supremacy over Brāhmas by declaring that even Brahmā needs the help of Gaṇeśa in order to accomplish the act of creation without any hindrance.[284] They hold that Gaṇeśa terrifies Brahmā by shaking the lotus, which is his throne.[285] They describe him as more powerful than Śiva, Viṣṇu and Indra. They call him the premature day of doom to the race of Daityas whom Śiva, Viṣṇu and Indra find hard to conquer.[286]

The Gāṇapatyas believe that even gods, Asuras and great ascetics do not attain success unless Gaṇeśa is pleased by them.[287] The 'Story of Gaṇapati' and the 'Story of the birth of Kārttikeya'[288] show that Pārvatī and Indra have to encounter obstructions (Vighna) for not worshipping Gaṇeśa. In' the story of the birth of Kārttikeya', when Pārvatī asks Śiva why a son has not been born to them, Śiva replies that obstruction in this matter has been caused by her not worshipping Gaṇeśa.[289] Śiva pleads with Pārvatī to worship Gaṇeśa.[290] Following his advice, Pārvatī worships him and a son is born to them.[291] She also worships him, in order that her husband might successfully accomplish conquest of Tripura.[292] The story also shows that Indra too cannot be successful in his undertakings if he neglects the worship of Gaṇeśa. The arm of Indra becomes stiff when he himself lifts the pitcher for consecrating Kārttikeya. On this, Śiva reveals the truth that the obstruction has appeared because Indra has not worshipped Gaṇeśa when he desired a general. He tells Indra that the latter should worship Gaṇeśa.[293] The arms of Indra becomes free only when he worships him.[294] The story is clearly an attempt of the Gāṇapatyas to show the competence of Gaṇeśa in the matter of creating obstructions in the actions of those who ignore him and in averting obstructions of those who worship him. The fact that even Śiva recommends the worship of Gaṇeśa to Pārvatī and Indra is a clear attempt of Gāṇapatyas to establish the supremacy of their Faith over the Śaivas.

Several references in the text testify to the supreme importance of Gaṇeśa. Gaṇeśa is conceived as the only refuge of the world,[295] the giver of boons,[296] and destroyer of one's ignorance.[297] His devotees believe that without propitiating him, no one can obtain any success in this world.[298] When one remembers him and praises him, fear produced by the battle field, by the king's court, by gambling, by thieves, by fire, by evil beings departs.[299]

In the Kathāsaritsāgara, the chief characteristic of Gaṇeśa is his power of averting all hindrances as is obvious from his many names such as, Vighnajit,[300] Vighneśvara,[301] Vighneśa,[302] Vighnarāja[303] and Vighnāntaka.[304] He is always described as the remover of obstacles and the main source of every kind of success.[305] Of his other names, Vināyaka[306] may be mentioned. He is called Vināyaka for his being associated with the Vināyakas who are reckoned among gods. These

Vināyakas are the observers of all the actions of men and removers of all evils.[307]

Gaṇeśa is held as pitcher bellied, the basked eared one, and the noose-handed god.[308] He has an elephant's head.[309] Rudra Śiva and the gods allied with him were connected closely with forests and wild places in which elephants also were found. The hide worn by Rudra and by his consort also in one of her forms was the hide of an elephant, and it perhaps suited the fancy of some men to place the head of that animal over the body of the god Gaṇeśa.[310]

Gaṇeśa is intimately associated with dance.[311]

Sometimes, Gaṇeśa is held as a tree spirit. There is a reference to a tree inhabited by him.[312]

As the remover of obstacles, Gaṇeśa is invoked at the beginning of every undertaking. He is worshipped before setting out on a journey. Maidens worship him for obtaining suitable husbands. Anaṅgamañjarī worships him inorder to obtain a universal monarch as her husband. A friend tells Kuvalayāvalī to worship Gaṇeśa so that she may obtain a suitable husband.[313]

The Kathāsaritsāgara refers to the temples of Gaṇeśa.[314] There is a reference to an image of Gaṇeśa carved in a tree.[315] Another passage refers to the image of Gaṇeśa carved out of a jewel.[316]

Gaṇeśa is worshipped with dance, songs and instrumental performances.[317] Some of the devotees observe fast and worship him. Mṛgāṅkadatta leaves food and worships him.[318] Austerities are also undertaken in honour of Gaṇeśa. Naravāhanadatta pleases him with austerities.[319]

The study of the Śaiva and the Gāṇapatya Faiths shows that the Śaiva is the most prominent of all the Faiths depicted in the Kathāsaritsāgara. Sectarian tendencies are clearly discernible in the text. Śiva is called superior to the other gods and his worship is considered to be the best form of worship. He is held as the Highest Reality and the ultimate cause of the universe. The Cosmic Egg Theory which explains the creation of the universe from the Cosmic Egg, is associated with him. Even his family members such as Pārvatī, Kārttikeya and Gaṇeśa are worshipped with great devotion. Phallic worship is performed by the Śaivas. The Śaiva Faith is influenced by Tāntricism. The Gāṇapatya is also a popular Faith. The tendency of the Gāṇapatyas to show the superiority of Gaṇeśa over other gods is celebrated in the text.

Footnotes Of Part I, Chapter I

1. धन्याः सरस्वतीस्कन्दो जिनश्च जगति त्रयः ।

K.S.S. 9.1.205.

2. Hinduism, p.184.

3. इदं गुरुगिरीन्द्रजाप्रणयमन्दरान्दोलना
त्पुरा किल कथामृतं हरमुखाम्बुधेरुद्गतम् ।
प्रसह्य रसयन्ति ये विगतविघ्नलब्धर्द्धयो
धुरं दधाति वैबुधीं भुवि भवप्रसादेन ते ॥

K.S.S. Benedictory Stanza.

4. Cf. "The Kathāsaritsāgara was written, very probably to be a part of a collection of pious Śaivaite Stories, a kind of Māhātmya."
Lacôte, Felix, Essai Sur Gunadhya Et La Brhatkatha, Trans. by Rev. Father A.M.Tabard, The Quarterly Journal of the Mystic Society, Vol.IV, pp.101 ff.

5. KSS. 2.1.2-3.

6. KSS. 1.4.20-22.

7. KSS. 1.4.24-25.

8. KSS. 17.1.17,19.

9. KSS. 3.5.74.

10. KSS. 5.3.250.

11. KSS. 7.9.172; 12.2.53.

12. KSS. 6.8.69.; 14.4.35.

13. KSS. 5.2.81.

14. KSS. 12.25.31.

15. KSS. 12.30.21-23.

16. KSS. 8.2.168.

17. चूडामणिषु यत्पादनखाग्रप्रतिमाङ्किताः ।
प्रसादप्राप्तचन्द्रार्धा इव भान्ति सुरासुराः ॥

KSS. 1.1.20.

18. KSS. 1.1.29.

19. KSS. 6.8.45.

20. KSS. 18.1.17.

21. KSS. 1.4.24-25.

22. ततः क्रुद्धः स कुलिशं जग्राह स सुराधिपः ।
    हुङ्कारं चाकरोदुद्रः कुलिशं च ननाश तत् ॥
    KSS. 8.7.84.

23. पर्यन्ते परमास्त्रं च यो यो यद्यत्सुरोऽक्षिपत् ।
    तस्य तस्य हरस्तत्तद्हुङ्कारेण व्यनाशयत् ॥
    KSS. 8.7.80.

24. तत्परास्ते हरिर्ब्रह्मा देवेन्द्रो दिविषद्गुरुः ।
    तेपिरे हरमुद्दिश्य चत्वारो दुश्चरं तपः ।
    KSS. 17.2.116.

25. KSS. 12.5.39.

26. KSS. 3.6.80.

27. किं तत्र देवनिवहैरन्यैर्यत्रोद्यतो हरः ।
    KSS. 8.2.29.

28. KSS. 8.7.67-69; 17.5.84.

29. KSS. 1.3.21; 2.1.1.

30. KSS. 2.3.32.

31. KSS. 9.2.15.

32. KSS. 7.1.102.

33. गौरीश तत्तद्व्योमादिभेदभिन्नाष्टमूर्त्तये ॥
    KSS. 7.1.99.
    Vide also KSS. 17.1.1.

34. KSS. 18.2.103.

35. KSS. 7.1.100.

36. KSS. 7.1.101.

37. मूर्तिः शांभवीवापवर्गदा ॥
    KSS. 17.1.17.

38. इच्छानिर्मितविश्वाय ।
    KSS. 7.1.102.

39. चराचरगुरुः ।

KSS. 1.1.17.

40. जगत्सर्गस्थितिसंहारहेतवे ।

KSS. 7.1.99.

41. KSS. 3.6.67.

42. Cf. Ṛg Veda, X.121; Śatapatha Brāhmaṇa, 11.1.6.1-11; Chhāndogya Upaniṣad, 3.19.1-2; 3.15.1; Nṛsiṁhatapanīya Upaniṣad, 1.1; Taittirīya Saṁhitā, v.6,4,2; vii. 1.5.1; Chhāndogya Brāhmaṇa, 5,19.

43. Cf. Manu Smṛti, I-14; Matsya Purāṇa, 2.27-29; Vāyu Purāṇa, 4.74-76; Viṣṇu Purāṇa, I.2.33-61.

44. पुरा कल्पक्षये वृत्ते जातं जलमयं जगत् ।
मया ततो विभिद्योरुं रक्तबिन्दुर्निपातितः ॥
जलान्तस्तदभूदण्डं तस्माद्द्वैधा कृतात्पुमान् ।
निरगच्छत्ततः सृष्टा सर्गाय प्रकृतिर्मया ॥
तौ च प्रजापतीनन्यान् सृष्टवन्तौ प्रजाश्च ते ।
अतः पितामहः प्रोक्तः स पुमान्जगति प्रिये ।
किं चैतन्मे कपालात्म जगद्देवि करे स्थितम् ।
पूर्वोक्ताण्डकपाले द्वे रोदसी परिकीर्त्तिते ॥

KSS. 1.2.10-12, 15.

This myth combines the Cosmic Egg Theory with the Sāṁkhya thought and traces the task of creation to Śiva. The Egyptian sun god 'Ra'similarly arose from the primordial waters as the sun-egg.

Mackenzie, Donald A., Indian Myth and Legend, p.101.

45. Thomas, p., Epics, Myths and Legends of India, p.38.

46. KSS. 1.1.54.

47. KSS. 2.2.32.

48. KSS. 1.2.9.

49. KSS. 1.2.34.

50. KSS. 1.2.17.

51. KSS. 1.1.45.

52. KSS. 3.6.69.

53. KSS. 1.1.33.

54. KSS. 1.1.43. 55. KSS. 1.2.8.

56. KSS. 8.2.28.

57. Bhandarkar, R.G., Vaiṣṇavism, Śaivism and Minor Religious Systems, p.102. Cf. also - "The deprecations of the wrath of Rudra gave rise to the euphemistic epithet 'auspicious' (Śiva) which became the regular name of Rudra's historical successor in the post-Vedic mythology." Macdonell,A.A., Vedic Mythology,p.77

58. KSS. 1.4.22. 59. KSS. 1.1.64.

60. Monier-Williams, M., Indian Wisdom, pp.325-26,f.n.1.

61. KSS. 1.7.112. 62. KSS. 3.6.65.

63. KSS. 4.2.167.

64. Monier-Williams,M., Indian Wisdom, pp.325-26,f.n.3.

65. KSS. 1.1.37. 66. KSS. 1.2.14.

67. एवं चराचरं सृष्ट्वा विश्वं दर्पमगादसौ ।
पुरुषस्तेन मूर्धानमथैतस्याहमच्छिदम् ॥
ततोऽनुतापेन मया महाव्रतमगृह्यत ।
अतः कपालपाणित्वं श्मशानप्रियता च मे ॥

KSS. 1.2.13-14.

68. Encyclopaedia of Religion and Ethics, Vol.II, p.812.

69. Cf. "Śiva was, in all probability a non-Aryan god adopted by Indo-Aryans." Thomas,P., Epics Myths and Legends of India, p.38. Cf. also "Śiva was originally a god of the Vrātyas or the non-Vedic nomadic people." Shastri,H.P., Journal of the Asiatic Society of Bengal, 1921, pp. xxi-xxiv.

70. KSS. 1.1.34. ff.

71. Cf. "There seems, no good reason to assign the origin of Śiva, the special Brāhmaṇa god,to the non-Aryan races, though his cultus may have been contaminated by their influence." Muir,IV,p349.

72. Encyclopaedia of Religion and Ethics, Vol.II, p.813.

73. KSS. 1.1.51. 74. KSS. 15.1.66.

75. KSS. 8.1.28; 8.7.144.

76. Encyclopaedia of Religion and Ethics, Vol.12, p.143.

77. Monier-Williams,M., Indian Wisdom, p.325, f.n.3.

78. KSS. 1.1.17. 79. KSS. 6.4.12.

80. KSS. 1.1.55. 81. KSS. 1.7.111.

82. KSS. 4.2.16. 83. KSS. 3.6.61.

84. Cf. Vājasaneyī Saṁhitā, 3.58; Śatapatha Brāhmaṇa, 2, 6,2.9. It appears to be referred to Śiva even in the Ṛg Veda, 7,59.12; Atharva Veda, xiv.1,17 and Taittirīya Saṁhitā, 1.8, 6.2.

85. KSS. 7.1.99. 86. KSS. 2.2.31.

87. KSS. 3.6.68.

88. Cf. Frazer, James, Adonis, pp.96,130, Golden Bough, ii,312,277 ff. Cults of Greek States, iii.11, v.97.

89. KSS. 17.2.108. 90. KSS. 2.1.7.

91. KSS. 8.1.22. 92. KSS. 3.6.60.

93. शम्भोः श्यामः कण्ठः । KSS. 1.1.1

94. KSS. 12.33.15.

95. त्रिलोचनं शूलपाणिं स्वच्छस्फटिकसंनिभम् ।
बद्धपिङ्गजटाजूटं चारुचन्द्रार्धशेखरम् ॥

KSS. 8.7.190-91.

Vide also- चन्द्राननार्धदेहाय चंन्द्रांशुसितभूतये ।
चन्द्रार्कानिलनेत्राय चन्द्रार्धशिरसे ---- ॥

KSS. 18.1.1.

and- भस्माङ्गरागसितया शेखरीकृतचन्द्रया ।
पिशङ्गजटयामूर्त्या शोभितं शूलहस्तया ॥
KSS. 4.3.4.

96. शोणैकपार्श्वः कैलासः शूरशोणितकुङ्कुमैः ।
भूतिश्वेतान्यपार्श्वश्च तथा गौरीशमन्वगात् ॥
KSS. 15.1.120.

97. शैवी तनुरिवोद्दामभोगिभूतिविभूषिता ।
KSS. 12.16.5.

98. Bhandarkar, R.C., Vaiṣṇavism, Śaivism and Minor Religious Systems, p.115.

99. KSS. 7.1.102.

100. KSS. 12.2.37.

101. गणैर्विद्याधरैः सिद्धैः सेव्यमाणो महेश्वरः ।
KSS. 1.1.17.

102. KSS. 17.5.23.

103. ददर्शालङ्घ्यतेजस्कमस्त्रं पाशुपतं महत् ॥
अतिप्रमाणमुद्वह्निज्वालं त्र्यक्षं चतुर्मुखम् ।
एकाङ्घ्रिमष्टबाहु च कल्पान्तानलसंनिभम् ॥
KSS. 17.5.75-76.

104.न हिनस्ति तदस्त्रं हि बालं वृद्धं पराङ्मुखम् ।
KSS. 17.2.35.

105. KSS. 12.8.44.

106. Śiva as Mahākāla sits naked with his head resting on his knee; his moon, his bull and elephant skin having been won at play by Devī:
देव्या द्यूतजितेष्विन्दुवृषकुञ्जरचर्मसु ।
जानुन्यस्तकपोलं ते नौमि नग्नाङ्गमासितम् ॥
KSS. 18.2.99.

107. Dowson, John , Classical Dictionary of Hindu Mythology and Religion, p.139.

108. अस्ति त्रिजगति ख्यातो नगेन्द्रो हिमवानिति ।
भूरिशृङ्गस्य तस्यैकं शृङ्गं गौरीपतेर्गिरि ॥

KSS.7.1.17.

109. KSS. 1.1.66.

110. शम्भोः स्वर्गाधिकं पदम् ।

KSS. 8.7.188.

111. दिव्यगन्धवहद्वातं सदापुष्पफलद्रुमम् ।
गन्धर्वारब्धसङ्गीतमप्सरोनृत्तसोत्सवम् ॥

KSS. 8.7.189.

112. न युक्तमिममुल्लङ्घ्य कैलासं गन्तुमग्रतः ।
हरास्पदस्य ह्येतस्य विद्या नश्यन्ति लङ्घनात्
त्रिशीर्षगुहया तस्य गन्तव्यं पार्श्वमुत्तरम् ।

KSS. 15.1.44-45.

Śiva is supposed to have been a trans-Himālayan god.He has many Himālayan characteristics. He is depicted as living in Kailāsa, attended by the Himālayan Gaṇas, Yakṣas, Gandharvas, etc. He marries the daughter of the Himālayas and carries the Ganges on his head.

113. अस्ति मन्दर इत्यद्रिराजो जगति विश्रुतः ।
कैलासाधिककान्तस्य यस्य शृङ्गाग्रभूमयः ।
नानासद्रत्नरचिता लीलोद्यानानि धूर्जटेः ।

KSS. 17.1.53,55.

114. अस्ति वाराणसी नाम पुरारिवसतिः पुरी ।

KSS. 12.8.59.

115. उज्जयिनी नाम पुरारिवसतिः पुरी ॥

KSS. 18.1.9.

116. यस्यां वसति विश्वेशो महाकालवपुः स्वयम् ।
शिथिलीकृतकैलासव्यसनो हरः ॥

KSS. 2.3.32.

Vide also-KSS. 6.1.136.

117. अस्ति गौरीतपःक्लेशवृतेन त्रिपुरारिणा।
असामान्यगुणोत्कर्षलुब्धेनैव स्वयं वृता ॥
भोगवत्यमरावत्योस्तृतीयोज्जयिनी पुरी ।

KSS. 12.25.9-10.

118. KSS. 12.35.20.

119. KSS. 7.6.42.

120. हिमवद्दक्षिणो देशः कश्मीराख्योऽस्ति ।
यत्र विस्मृत्य कैलासश्वेतद्वीपसुखस्थितिम् ।
स्वयम्भुवो स्थानशतान्यध्यासाते हराच्युतौ ॥

KSS. 10.7.53-54.

121. विजयाख्यं महाक्षेत्रं काश्मीरेष्वस्ति शाम्भवम् ।

KSS. 10.10.5.

122. अयं स देवः पातालनिलयो हाटकेश्वरः ।

KSS. 12.6.124.

123. KSS. 12.23.144. Gokarṇa is situated on the Malabar coast. Barth,A., The Religions of India, p.283.

124. अर्चिते देवदेवे च शम्भो देवो न कोऽर्चितः ।

KSS. 8.2.28.

125. KSS. 7.1.96.

126. KSS. 9.2.20.

127. KSS. 8.3.204.

128. KSS. 16.1.82.

129. KSS. 9.4.214.

130. KSS. 9.3.96.

131. KSS. 1.7.109.

132. KSS. 7.3.237.

133. KSS. 1.7.105.

134. KSS. 10.10.142.

135. भक्तवत्सलः

KSS.8.7.196;

भक्तकृपालुः

KSS. 10.3.171.

136. देवो वरदः

KSS. 1.3.18.

137. KSS. 5.1.7; 6.8.226.

138. KSS. 2.1.1.

139. तमनाराध्य न सन्तीप्सितसिद्धयः ।

KSS. 17.2.89.

140. KSS. 17.5.29.

141. मेने च तनयप्राप्तिं गौरीशाराधनाद् ध्रुवम् ।

KSS. 7.1.95.

142. KSS. 10.9.216.

143. KSS. 10.3.60.

144. KSS. 10.1.55.

145. KSS. 11.1.37.

146. KSS. 10.10.170-73.

147. KSS. 12.16.8-12.

148. KSS. 10.3.60.

149. KSS. 7.1.97,104,111.

150. KSS. 7.3.128.

151. KSS. 7.3.134.

152. KSS. 14.3.73-74.

153. KSS. 12.6.423.

154. KSS. 4.2.117.

155. KSS. 12.2.84.

156. KSS. 12.19.132; 17.6.85.

157. KSS. 5.2.128.

158. KSS. 1.7.71.

159. KSS. 17.5.154-56.

160. KSS. 10.9.226; 12.6.122; 12.25.26; 12.34.212; 17.6.90.

161. KSS. 2.2.30.

162. KSS. 9.1.23.

163. KSS. 7.6.89.

164. KSS. 12.23.144.

165. KSS. 12.36.119.

166. KSS. 1.8.33.

167. KSS. 10.9.226.

168. KSS. 7.5.138-39.

169. KSS. 9.2.15-16.

170. लिङ्गान्तर्दृश्यगौरीशमूर्तिरत्नमयम् ।

KSS. 17.6.99.

171. KSS. 12.35.7-9.

172. KSS. 17.6.106.

173. KSS. 7.1.96.

174. KSS. 9.4.214.

175. KSS. 1.7.8.

176. KSS. 7.6.91.

177. Cf. Vājasaneyī Saṁhitā, Section XVI; Taittirīya Saṁhitā, IV.5. Cf. also-Mahābhārata, VII.202. Mahābhārata, XII.284,16 ff, is a Śivasahasranāma stotra which praises Śiva in thousand names.

178. अष्टषष्टयुत्तमस्थाननियतैर्नामभिः शुभैः ।
यथावत्तं च तुष्टाव पापध्नैः सर्वकामदैः ॥

KSS. 9.4.215.

179. तन्नामाष्टसहस्रेण तमेव वरदं स्तुमः ॥
तेनेव ते प्रसीदन्ति तद्गणा इत्यवोचत ॥

KSS. 8.3.202-3.

180. KSS. 9.1.6.

181. KSS. 9.2.195.

182. KSS. 1.9.62.

183. KSS. 1.7.109.

184. KSS. 10.5.208.

185. KSS. 3.5.6-7; 4.1.143.

186. KSS. 7.1.103.

187. KSS. 2.5.77.

188. KSS. 12.26.82,84.

189. KSS. 18.1.15.

190. रुद्रयज्ञे हि विहितेऽन्यैः किमध्वरैः ।

KSS. 8.2.27.

191. ममैतज्जीवितफलं यच्छिवाराधनं तपः ॥

KSS. 9.1.35.

192. KSS. 1.7.53.

193. KSS. 14.3.81.

194. KSS. 9.2.388.

195. KSS. 1.7.109-10.

196. KSS. 1.4.27.

197. KSS. 17.5.123.

198. KSS. 12.16.8.

199. KSS, 7.1.97.

200. KSS. 7.9.144.

201. KSS. 16.2.180.

202. KSS. 1.4.87.

203. KSS. 12.34.212.

204. Macdonell, A.A, Vedic Mythology, p.75.

205. Ibid., p.155.

206. Keith, A.B., Religion and Philosophy of the Veda, p.10.

207. Stevenson, On the Anti-Brahmanical Religions of the Hindus, Journal of the Royal Asiatic Society, viii(1942), p.330.

208. Thomas, P., Epics, Myths and Legends of India, p. 106.

209. Lassen, Ind. Alterthumsk; t.i.p.924; t.iv.p.265. referred to by A.Barth in The Religions of India,p.261.

210. Bhandarkar,R.G., Vaiṣṇavism, Śaivism and Minor Religious Systems, p.106.

211. Vide-Barth. A., The Religions of India, p.261.

212. Muir, ii.202, iv.189 ff. 405 ff.

213. Encyclopaedia of Religion and Ethics, Vol.6, p.700.

The origin of the belief in the Liṅga form of worship is even traced to western nations, and even among the Greeks (Kittel, F-Veber den Ursprung des Lingakultus in India, p.46 referred to by A.Barth in the Religions of India, p.261). To James Frazer, it seems to be an aberrant form of the cult of stones and pillars that was widely distributed in the Greece, and among the semites (Frazer, Pausan, London, 1898 ii 539, iv.110, 115, 318 ff; v.314 ff; Cults of the Greek states iv.149, 307; Hastings Dictionary of the Bible iii.819 ff. v.110 ff). Fergusson believes that Liṅgam is in origin a miniature Buddhist 'dagoba' or relic-shrine (History of Indian Architecture, p.304 ff). There is divergence of opinion about the origin and antiquity of the Liṅga-worship (vide for details,

Karmarkar,A.P., The Religions of India, Vol.I,pp.79 ff; Banerjea,J.N., Pauranic and Tantric Religion, pp.78 ff; Bhandarkar,R.G., Vaiṣṇavism, Śaivism and Minor Religious Systems, pp.160-64). T.A.Gopinatha Rao concludes that Liṅga-worship is as old as the 2nd century B.C. (Rao,T.A.Gopinatha, Elements of Hindu Iconography, Vol.I, Part I, Introduction, p.6). Wilson believes that this worship of Śiva in this form probably spread throughout India at least as early as the 5th or 6th century A.D. (Wilson, Essays 77(i) 224). A.Barth observes it contemporaneously with Śaivism (The Religions of India, p.261).

214. KSS. 7.9.158; 12.2.153; 17.6.178; 18.1.119.

215. KSS. 12.34.224.

216. The other forms are ether, air, water, Earth, Sun, Moon and the sacrificing priest.

217. KSS. 17.2.110-11.

218. KSS. 9.1.95; 10.3.81; 11.1.65-66.

219. KSS. 9.1.95,98.

220. KSS. 12.2.155.

221. Vide pp. 177 ff. infra.

222. The name Umā is found first of all in the Kena Upaniṣad (III.12; 4.1). But she is not mentioned there as the wife of Śiva. The earliest reference to Umā as the wife of Rudra or Śiva occurs in the Taittirīya Āraṇayaka –

नमो हिरण्यबाहवे हिरण्यपतये अम्बिकापतये उमापतये नमो नमः ।

X.18.

223. त्रिजगज्जननी

KSS. 1.1.14.

224. KSS. 1.1.32.

225. यो हि नारायणः स त्वं शक्तिः शक्तिमतो मम ॥

KSS. 1.1.32.

226. KSS. 1.1.31-32. 227. KSS. 1.1.33.

228. KSS. 1.1.23. 229. KSS. 1.1.53.

230. KSS. 1.1.62. 231. KSS. 1.1.39.

232. KSS. 1.1.63. 233. KSS. 1.1.58.

234. KSS. 3.6.72. 235. KSS. 4.2.16.

236. KSS. 9.6.285. 237. KSS. 1.1.44.

238. KSS. 1.1.39-42. Cf. Kālidāsa, Kumārasambhavam, V.86.

239. KSS. 12.36.72. 240. KSS. 7.8.60.

241. KSS. 6.5.11.

242. भवानी भक्तवत्सला

KSS. 7.8.57.

भक्तानुकम्पिनी ।

KSS. 6.8.253.

243. सततानुवृत्तभृत्यावमाननविभावनासानुतापाम् ।

KSS. 1.1.66.

244. KSS. 9.2.93. 245. KSS. 10.3.13.

246. KSS. 12.13.23. 247. KSS. 7.3.9.

248. KSS. 12.34.302-4. 249. KSS. 10.3.12.

250. KSS. 12.23.41. 251. KSS. 17.3.14.

252. KSS. 10.3.12. 253. KSS. 12.5.35.

254. KSS. 17.3.17. 255. KSS. 12.13.5-6.

256. The origin of this god is assigned to the post Vedic period.

257. KSS. 3.6.95. Kārttikeya is considered a misogynist and bachelor (Kumāra) in Mahārāṣṭra. Here, women are not allowed to worship him at his shrines.

258. KSS. 1.2.44.

259. KSS. 9.5.158.

260. KSS. 1.7.9

261. KSS. 3.6.86

262. KSS. 9.5.180.

263. शक्तिहस्तः

KSS. 1.7.6.

264. बर्हिवाहनः

KSS. 9.5.173.

265. Bhandarkar, Vaiṣṇavism, Śaivism and Minor Religious Systems, p.150.

266. KSS. 8.7.183-84.

267. Cf.Rāmāyaṇa,1.37.7 ff.

268. Cf. Mahābhārata, iii.225 ff; ix.44 ff;xiii.84 ff.

269. महेश्वरादग्निकुण्डादग्नेः शरवणादपि ।
कृत्तिकाभ्यश्च शंसन्ति विचित्रं यस्य सम्भवम् ।

KSS. 8.6.239.

270. KSS. 3.6.60-100.

271. जातेनैव जगत्कृत्स्नं दुष्प्रधर्षेण तेजसा ।
आनन्द्य येन निहतो दुर्जयस्तारकासुरः ।

KSS. 8.6.240.

272. KSS. 3.6.95.

273. KSS. 1.6.152

274. KSS. 1.2.44.

Even in modern times, the worship of Kārttikeya is common in south India where the god is known generally by the name of Subrāhmaṇya. Vide-Rao,T.A. Gopinath, Elements of

Hindu Iconography, Vol.I, part I,Introduction, p.40; Barth,A., The Religions of India, p.183.

275. KSS. 1.2.60.

276. KSS. 17.1.115.

277. KSS. 9.5.174.

278. KSS. 1.6.152 ff. Vide also KSS.1.3.6.

279. KSS. 1.2.44.

280. Gaṇeśa is the latest of the Brāhmaṇical god. His worship starts from the Paurāṇic period. R.G.Bhandarkar holds that the Vināyakas had come to be objects of faith before the Christian era. But the one Gaṇapati Vināyaka, the son of Ambikā, was introduced into the Hindu pantheon much later. He concludes that between the end of the fifth and the end of the eighth century the Gaṇapati cult must have come into practice.

Vaiṣṇavism, Śaivism and Minor Religious Systems, p.148.

281. देवदेवः

KSS. 3.6.55.

282. जयससुरासुरमानुषभुवनत्रयपूजिताङ्घ्रिकमलयुग।

KSS. 12.33.45.

283. घटोदरः शूर्पकर्णो गणाध्यक्षो मदोत्कटः।
पाशहस्तोऽम्बरीषश्च जम्बकस्त्रिशिखायुधः।
एवमाद्यैः स्तुवन्ति स्म पापघ्नैरष्टषष्टिभिः।
तत्संख्यस्थाननियतैर्नामभिस्त्वां सुरोत्तमाः।

KSS. 9.5.165-66.

284. निर्विघ्नविश्वनिर्माणसिद्धये यदनुग्रहम्।
मन्ये स वव्रे धातापि तस्मै विघ्नजिते नमः।

KSS. 3.1.1.

285. लीलोत्क्षिप्तकराघातविद्युतासनपङ्कजम्।
ब्रह्माणमपि सोत्कम्पं कुर्वञ्जय गजानन।

KSS. 9.5.163.

286. हरहरिसुरपतिदुर्जयदितिजकुलाकालकल्पान्त।
KSS. 12.33.46.

287. सुरासुरमुनीन्द्राणामपि सन्ति न सिद्धयः।
अतुष्टे त्वयि - - - - - - - - - - - - - - ।
KSS. 9.5.164.

Cf. also -
- - - - - - - - देवानामपि सन्ति न सिद्धयः।
हेरम्बेऽनर्चिते - - - - - - - - ।
KSS. 3.6.100.

288. KSS. 3.6.60-100.
289. KSS. 3.8.83.

290. KSS. 3.6.100.
291. KSS. 3.6.84.

292. अभिमतसिद्ध्यैभर्तुस्त्रिपुरविजये गणेश गौर्याऽपि।
यः पूजितः - - - - - - - - ।
KSS. 12.33.48.

293. KSS. 3.6.97.
294. KSS. 3.6.98.

295. लोकैकशरण्ये KSS. 9.5.164.

296. वरदः KSS. 3.6.55.
297. KSS. 15.1.1.

298. तस्मिन्नपूजिते नास्ति सिद्धि कापिह कस्यचित्।
KSS. 3.6.58.

299. स्मरतः स्तुवतश्च त्वां विनश्यन्ति भयं प्रभो।
रणराजकुलद्यूतचोराग्निश्वापदादिजम्।
KSS. 9.5.167.

300. KSS. 4.1.1.
301. KSS. 3.6.62.

302. KSS. 9.5.162.
303. KSS. 3.6.101.

304. KSS. 17.1.2. Cf. Yājñavalkya Smṛti, I.270.

305. कारणं सर्वसिद्धीनां दुरितार्णवतारणम्।
KSS. 11.1.1.

निधानं सर्वसिद्धीनाम् ।

KSS. 12.6.378.

Cf. also - KSS. 4.1.1; 5.1.1; 6.1.1; 7.1.2; 12.1.1.; 17.1. 2; 18.1.2.

306. KSS. 12.6.116.

307. Pai, D.A.,India Among Hindus, p.86. According to Bhaviṣya-Purāṇa since Gaṇeśa leads the good in the path of righteousness, he is called Vināyaka. Another explanation of the name Vināyaka is given in the Vāmana Purāṇa to the effect that as he was born without a nāyaka or sire, he came to be named Vināyaka. Rao,T.A.Gopinath, Elements of Hindu Iconography, Vol.I, part I, p.47.

308. KSS. 9.5.165. 309. KSS. 9.5.163.

310.Bhandarkar,R.G.,Vaiṣṇavism, Śaivism and Minor Religious Systems, p.149. The images of Gaṇeśa at Ellora have the elephant's head.Cf. Bhavabhūti, Mālatīmādhava, Benedictory Stanza.

311. KSS. 1.1.2; 8.1.1; 9.1.1.; 12.6.377; 12.8.1.; 12.33. 1; 13.1.1.; 14.1.2; 15.1.1.; 16.1.526.

312. अस्मिन्गणपतिदेवः स्वयं वसति पादपे ।

KSS. 12.33.37.

313. तमुपागत्य भक्त्या त्वं पूजय प्रार्थितपदम् ।
येन निर्विघ्नमेवाशु स्वोचितं पतिमाप्स्यसि ।

KSS. 3.6.56.

314. KSS. 12.6.375.

315. तस्मिन्निखातरूपां च गणेशप्रतिमाम् ।

KSS. 12.4.60.

316. रत्नविनायकम् ।

KSS. 12.6.325.

317. KSS. 12.6.328.

318. KSS. 12.33.43.

319. KSS. 14.3.124.

Chapter II

HIGHER HINDU FAITHS - contd.

The Vaisanava Faith[1]

In the Kathāsaritsāgara, the Vaiṣṇavas call Viṣṇu as superior to all the other gods as they have attained various stages of prosperity by his favour.[2] Viṣṇu is called as the helper of gods in their fight against the Asuras.[3] Brahmā stays on the lotus of his naval.[4] Nārada and the other Gandharvas are described as chanting hymns in praise of Viṣṇu. Devas, Siddhas and the Vidyādharas bow before him.[5]

The Vaiṣṇavas believe that Viṣṇu is the Highest Reality. He is called omniscient.[6] He is the divine swan dwelling in the Mānasa lake in the form of the minds of the good and moving in the sky.[7] He transcends all, and dwells within all.[8] The idea of the all pervasiveness of Viṣṇu seems to have been developed out of the concept of Vedic Puruṣa who not only covers this world but also goes beyond it.[9] The etymology of the word Viṣṇu also points at his all pervasiveness. He is called Viṣṇu because He pervades all the creatures of the whole world by His unmanifested form.[10]

The idea of the Virāṭa form of Divinity goes back to the Ṛgvedic period. The Ṛg Veda describes universe as the form of the Puruṣa.[11] It narrates God as having eyes everywhere, arms everywhere and feet everywhere.[12] The Kathāsaritsāgara also describes Viṣṇu in his Virāṭa form. Sky is his head, directions his ears, the sun and the moon his eyes and the whole universe as his belly.[13]

Viṣṇu is held as the creator of the universe. From him, spring all creatures, as the host of sparks from the blazing fire, and when the time of destruction comes, they again enter his essence, as at the end of the day a flock of birds enters the great tree in which it dwells. He creates the lords of the worlds who are parts of him, as the ocean, disturbed with a continual flow creates the waves.[14]

Like Puruṣa of Sāṁkhya, Viṣṇu is untouched by the qualities of Sattva, Rajas and Tamas.[15] Though Viṣṇu is the creator, he is without activity. Though he is the support of the world, he is himself without support. None can understand his real nature.[16]

Many names and epithets of Viṣṇu occur in the text. He is called Achyuta,[17] Murāri,[18] Śauri[19] and Kṛṣṇa.[20] Viṣṇu is held as staying in the Kṣīrāmbudhi[21] and as reclining upon the snake Śeṣa.[22] He mounts on Garuḍa[23] and his chest is marked with a lotus.[24] In his hands, he bears Chakra,[25] Śaṁkha, Gadā and Padma.[26] He is known for his bravery. He cuts off the head of the wicked Rāhu.[27]

Viṣṇu manifests himself in all ages for the protection of the pious, for the destruction of the wicked and for the establishment of righteousness.[28] This is called Avatāra of God.[29] The ten incarnations of Viṣṇu are generally recognized.[30] The Kathāsaritsāgara refers to his four incarnations viz. Varāha, Vāmana, Rāma and Narasiṁha.

The earliest reference to boar (Varāha) in a cosmogonic character appears in the Śatapatha Brāhmaṇa.[31] But, it associates Varāha and Vāmana with Prajāpati and not with Viṣṇu. The Taittirīya Saṁhitā,[32] the Rāmāyaṇa,[33] the Viṣṇu Purāṇa,[34] the Garuḍa Purāṇa[35] and the Padma Purāṇa[36] also associate Varāha and Vāmana incarnations to Brahmā. But, the Kathāsaritsāgara, like the Nārāyaṇa section of the Mahābhārata[37] associates the two incarnations with Viṣṇu.

Viṣṇu in the form of a great boar enters the great ocean.[38] He delivers the earth and bears it for a long time on his arms, gladdening all men by his incarnation.[39]

In his Vāmana incarnation,[40] Viṣṇu strides across the earth and makes it tremble.[41] He grows bigger and bigger and steps into heaven.[42]

Rāma is considered to be an incarnation of Viṣṇu.[43]

Viṣṇu in the form of Narasiṁha destroys Hiraṇyakaśipu. The nails of Narasiṁha are curved and red with the blood, when he kills his enemy.[44]

Mathurā[45] and Kaśmīra[46] are held as the sacred earthly abodes of Viṣṇu.

In the Kathāsaritsāgara, there are many worshippers of Viṣṇu.[47] Haṁsāvalī is devoted to him even in her childhood.[48] She thinks that her sins can be washed away by worshipping the god.[49] Vibhīṣaṇa has unshakable faith in him.[50] The King Bhūnandana is exclusively devoted to him.[51] Viṣṇudatta calls to mind the god before starting out on a journey.[52]

Devotees of Viṣṇu feel that god is compassionate to his votaries.[53] He is their wish-yielding tree.[54] He is mainly worried about their safety[55] and grants them their desires.[56] He exonerates them from their sins, delivers them in this world and the next,[57] and confers boons upon them.[58]

The twelfth day of the bright fortnight is held sacred for the worship of Viṣṇu.[59]

There are many temples of Viṣṇu.[60] A lofty stone pillar is constructed in front of his temple, with a discus on its summit.[61]

A lotus, a club, a shell and a discus are offered to Viṣṇu.[62] Vibhīṣaṇa, out of his devotion to the god, entrusts to the care of Lohajaṅgha a lotus, a club, a shell and a discus all of gold to be offered to the god. Flowers are also offered to please Viṣṇu. Hamsāvalī worships Viṣṇu with flowers.[63]

Devotees please Visnu with songs also.[64] Some of them take fruits only,[65] while others resort to penance to please him.[66]

A festival is celebrated every year in honour of Viṣṇu in the Ratnakūṭa island on the Śuklā Dvādaśī of the month of Āṣāḍa. People from all over the country come to participate in it. Festive procession (Yātrā) is also arranged in course of this festival.[67]

Kaśmīra is a Vaiṣṇava place of pilgrimage. The Vaiṣṇavas hold that one's sins are washed away by a pilgrimage to the holy places of Vajayakṣetra, Nandikṣetra, Varāhakṣetra, Maṇḍapakṣetra and Uttaramānasa of Kaśmīra.[68]

Pañchatīrthī is also referred to as the sacred place of Vaiṣṇavas. It is held that the blessed water of Pañchatīrthī possesses the power of enabling those men who bathe in it and fast for five nights, to become devotees of Nārāyaṇa.[69]

It is held that the holy bathing place named Kramasaras arose from the foot fall of Viṣṇu in his dwarf incarnation. It is attended by the three gods Brahmā, Viṣṇu and Śiva, who have settled on the top of the neighbouring mountain in the form of peaks. And the foot of Viṣṇu created in Kaśmīra another Ganges, named Iṣuvatī, as if in emulation of the Vitastā.[70]

Ratnakūṭa is another Vaiṣṇava place of pilgrimage.[71] Śvetadvīpa[72] is an island where people assemble to worship Viṣṇu.

Consort of Viṣṇu (Lakṣmī)

Consort of Viṣṇu is Lakṣmī.[73] Lotus is her symbol. She has a lotus in her hand[74] and she plays with lotuses.[75] As goddess of beauty, she is intimately connected with the beautiful flower lotus.

Her origin is traced back to the ocean.[76] She lived in the ocean before it was churned.[77] Later on, she was carried away by gods.[78]

Like Viṣṇu, Lakṣmī is also worshipped in the Kathāsaritsāgara. The King Bhadrākṣa, desiring a son, worships her every day with one hundred and eight white lotuses.[79] Kālanemi pleases the goddess with Homa.[80]

The Brāhma Faith[81]

Devotees of Brahmā consider him as superior to Indra who with Bṛhaspati approaches him for help.[82] The weapon of Brahmā is considered to be very powerful. It cannot be repelled by any weapon except the weapon of Paśupati.[83] It is capable of destroying the whole world.

In the Kathāsaritsāgara, the ideas of creation and fate are personified in the concept of Brahmā.[84] The idea of creation is associated with Brahmā from the Vedic times.[85] In the Kathāsaritsāgara too, Brahmā is held as the creator of the world.[86] It is believed that every creature is what he is made by him.[87]

Being the creator of the world, Brahmā is conceived as the god who gives progeny. Sattvaśīla reflects that the creator has not given him a son.[88]

Many names or epithets of Brahmā occur in the Kathāsaritsāgara. Besides Brahmā,[89] he is called Viriñchi,[90] Pitāmaha,[91] Prajāpati,[92] Chaturmukha,[93] Vedhas,[94] Ambujāsana,[95] Kamalāsana,[96] Kamalasambhava,[97] Padmaja[98] and Padmayoni.[99] All the epithets of Brahmā relating to lotus show his origin from the naval of Viṣṇu.[100]

The 'story of Sūryaprabha' in the text points out that the conduct of Brahmā is not considered free from suspicion.[101]

The Kathāsaritsāgara discusses the cause that led to the lose of interest in the worship of Brahmā. It tells us that Brahmā has ceased to be very popular because once he wanted Śiva to become his son.[102] This argument is apparently a fancy of the Śaivas who consider their favourite god Śiva as far superior to Brahmā.

The Śākta Faith[103]

The Śākta Faith is the worship of Śakti or the female principle as primary factor in the creation and reproduction of the universe. According to Śāktas, Śakti is the primal mother from whom everything proceeds, who pervades everything and is coterminous with the Supreme Being himself, who is without the beginning or the end and is vaster than the universe.[104]

The reverence shown to the different goddesses as the wives of gods is different from the Śākta faith which is religion by itself as it places Śakti as the Highest power and the source of all beings and at the same time advocates specific form of worship. Some scholars consider the Śākta Faith as an off-spring of Śaivism. But there are others who take it as an independent cult of female principle having only faint relationship with Śaivism.

The Śākta Faith is quite popular in the Kathāsaritsāgara which refers to the principal goddess under several names such as Chaṇḍi, Chāmuṇḍā, Maṅgalā, Tripurā, Jayā, Ekānaṁśā, Śivā, Durgā, Nārāyaṇī, Sarasvatī, Bhadrakālī, Mahālakṣmī, Siddhā, Gāyatrī, Mahārājñī, Revatī, Vindhyavāsinī, Umā, Kātyāyanī,[105] Sārikā,[106] Śarvāṇī,[107] Ambikā,[108] etc. The critical eye will see that these are not merely names, but indicate different goddesses who owed their conception to different historical conditions, but who are afterwards identified with the one goddess by the usual mental habit of the Hindus.[109] The large number of names of the goddess and the diversity of her character (benignant, awful, cruel, horrible) also render it probable that she is a combination of many deities.

The Śāktas try to establish their superior position over other sects by describing Śakti as foremost of all other gods including Śiva, Viṣṇu and Brahmā. They hold that Śiva, Skanda,Brahmā and Vasiṣṭha praise her.[110] The gods, sages and men always obtain their desired objects from her.[111]

The goddess, often called Bhagavatī Durgā,[112] is held as the upholder of the three worlds.[113] She is the principle of life in creatures. The world moves by her.[114] She, as the ruling power of Śiva, governs the three worlds, and inspired by her they live and move.[115] She is held as the refuge of those who are bent upon final beatitude.[116]

The goddess is always seen fully armed and well guarded. She bears a sword, a club, a bow, arrows and a spear in her hands.[117] She has a dark complexion. She wears skulls and skeletons.[118] She is shining[119] and terrible to look at.[120] It is difficult to behold her.[121] She is known for her loud laughter.[122]

She is a symbol of power. With her eighteen mighty arms, she destroys terrible Dānavas.[123] She kills the Asuras with her trident and strikes the haughty Daityas.[124] She kills the Asura Mahiṣa[125] and the Dānava Ruru.[126] She employs her power for the protection of the world.[127] Kālarātri is the invincible Chaṇḍikā.[128] It is believed that she was originally created by Viṣṇu, when the sea was churned for nectar, in order that she might tear into pieces the chiefs of the Dānavas, who wished to steal the heavenly drink.[129]

The goddess is described as living on the Vindya hills[130] and on the mount Kailāsa.[131] Like Śiva, she is associated with Gaṇas.[132]

The goddess is highly adored in the Kathāsaritsāgara. The king Parityāgasena,[133] Vararuchi,[134] Indīvarasena, Vīravara,[135] Guṇāḍhya Niśchayadatta and his three friends, Sundarsena[136] and many others are among her devotees. Devotees comfort themselves by putting all faith in her.[137] They believe that the goddess removes their calamities,[138] grants boons,[139] bewilders the wicked persons[140] and can even restore dead person to life.[141] It is also observed that devotion to her destroys hunger, thirst and fatigue.[142]

The goddess is invoked for help[143] and for attaining desired objects.[144] She is known for her exceeding readiness to manifest herself to her votaries.[145]

In the text, there are references to temples of Chaṇḍikā,[146] Kātyāyanī[147] and Mātṛkas.[148] A temple of Chaṇḍikā appears to be terrible with a long waving banner of red silk like the tongue of Death eager to devour the lives of animals.[149] At another place it is said that a temple of Chaṇḍikā looks like the mouth of Death, the flame of the lamp being its lolling tongue, the range of bells being its row of teeth, to which the heads of men cling.[150] Temples of the goddess contain an inner sanctuary.[151]

Construction of such temples is considered to be a work of great merit. The king Śūdraka establishes a temple of Chaṇḍi in the vicinity of his palace.[152]

Some of the temples of Chaṇḍikā are constructed outside towns.[153] Such temples provide a peaceful atmosphere for worship and penance. Devotees go to these temples for worshipping the goddess. For instance, Puṣkarākṣa sees an empty temple of Chaṇḍikā, goes there and worships her.[154] The Brāhmaṇa Govindaswāmin spends the day in Banārasa in a temple of Chaṇḍikā outside the town, engaged in worshipping the goddess.[155] Chaṇḍamahāsena goes to the temple of Chaṇḍikā and worships her.[156]

Setting up of an image of the goddess is considered to be an act of great religious merit. The father of Anaṅgamañjarī sets up an image of the goddess Chaṇḍi near a tank.[157] Devotees worship an image of the goddess. Anaṅgamañjarī worships the image.[158]

Devotees believe that the goddess can best be pleased by songs. Puṣkarākṣa pleases her by devoutly singing on a lyre in her honour.[159]

Devotees believe that the goddess, pleased by fast and penance of her devotees, grants them their desired objects. The king Parityāgasena propitiates her to obtain a son, and performs penance.[160] In order to obtain a wife, the killing Chaṇḍamahāsena pleases the goddess with austerities.[161] The prince Indīvarasena,[162] Yaśovarman[163] and Marubhūti[164] also undertake a severe penance for pleasing the goddess.

Devotees like Guṇādhya,[165] Jīvadatta[166] and Yaśovarman[167] resort to the shrine of Vindhyavāsinī for performing penance. There is a story of a man who goes to the shrine and performs penance in order to obtain wealth.[168] Nāgasvāmin,[169] Simhaprākrama[170] and Vararuchi[171] also pay a visit to the holy shrine. The very frequent references to this famous shrine of Durgā are probably accounted for by the proximity of the regions peopled by forest tribes.[172]

Devotees walk round an image of the goddess.[173] They please her by the offerings of animals.[174] Various living creatures are offered day and night in the temple of Vindhyavāsinī which therefore resembles the palace of the god of Death.[175]

A primitive method of worshipping a deity is by human-offerings. Human-offerings are made to the goddess. Sacrificing the head to Durgā suggests self-castration in order to identify with the mother.[176] A.Barth opines that perhaps we ought to view these practices of human-offerings as derived, by contact or by heritage, from the bloody rites of the aboriginal tribes.[177]

Several passages of the Kathāsaritsāgara describe the blood-thirsty orgies in honour of Devī. For instance, Vīravara goes with his family to a temple of Chaṇḍi at night and cuts off his son's head and offers it to the goddess.[178] The king Śūdraka also wants to cut off his head as an offering to her so that she may confer favour on him.[179] Guṇakara sees in the temple of the goddess Vindyavāsinī, a corpse of a man who has offered himself, and who holds in his hand a sword that has pierced his throat. He also decides to offer himself to the goddess in order to please her.[180] Dhavala, thinking that people worship the goddess with various sacrifices of living creatures, wants to obtain salvation by sacrificing himself to her.[181] The prince Anichchhasena pleases the goddess with offerings of his head.[182] Simhagupta wants to cut off his head before the goddess in order to ensure Sātavāhana's happiness.[183] The king Mahāsena goes to the temple of the goddess, clips pieces of his own flesh and offers a Homa with them.[184] Naravāhanadatta makes up his mind to appease Kālarātri by offering his head.[185] A mendicant also thinks that he can please the goddess by sacrificing himself.[186]

Besides, voluntary human offerings, the Kathāsaritsāgara shows that the robbers and wild Bhillas make offerings of human-beings to the goddess, and for this purpose they bring people to her temple. Robbers lead Jīmūtavāhana to a temple of Chaṇḍikā in their village with the view that he might serve as a creature of offering.[187] A large army of brigands binds Śrīdatta, carries him off to a village and takes him to an awful temple of Chaṇḍi to offer him up to the goddess.[188] Some followers of the Śavara king take the innocent Chandrasvāmin to the village and fetter him, in order to be offered as a victim.[189] The Śavaras observe auspicious marks on the person of the king Kanakavarṣa and take him to their king Muktāphala so that he may offer him as a victim to the goddess.[190] The king of the Śavaras takes him to the temple of Devī to offer him up.[191] A Bhilla ties a man firmly to a tree, in order that he be next day offered to the goddess.[192] The two sons of the fisherman think that they must sacrifice their father's murderer Śaktideva the next morning in front of her. They bind him and take him off to the awful temple of Chaṇḍi.[193]

Those persons who are to be sacrificed to the goddess are provided with good garments and food. Śivadatta is continually served with garments and food by the Śavara chieftain because the latter intends to offer him as a victim to the goddess.[194]

The fourteenth day of a month is considered to be sacred for human-offerings to the goddess. On this day, victims are taken to her temple.[195]

Drinking wine at the time of worship is considered to be sacred. It is under this pretext that Vāsavadattā gives the superintendent of the elephants with all the elephant - drivers, a supply of wine and makes them drunk.[196]

Vārāṇasī is considered as a sacred place for worshipping the goddess. A great merchant comes to this city for offering worship to her.[197]

Śakti is especially worshipped in her fierce form. The orgies of the Tāntrikas are held to propitiate her.

The Saura Faith[198]

In the Kathāsaritsāgara, there are scanty references to the worship of the Sun as the Highest Reality. He is referred to as the Supreme Lord of creatures. He is said to remove the internal and external darkness of his devotees. He is Viṣṇu, in the sense that he pervades the three worlds. He is Śiva, in the sense that he is the treasure-house of blessings.[199] He is also identified with Prajāpati.[200]

The Kathāsaritsāgara refers to the worship of the Sun. Mṛgāṅkadatta[201] and the Brāhmaṇa Chandrasvāmin invoke him.

The Śākta is the most popular of all the Faiths discussed in this chapter. The sectarian tendencies are clearly marked in case of the Vaiṣṇava, Brāhma, Śākta and the Saura Faiths. The Vaiṣṇavas consider Viṣṇu as the Highest Reality and the creator of the universe. The Virāṭa form of Viṣṇu as described in the Kathāsaritsāgara, exactly resembles that of the Vedic Puruṣa. In the text, concept of Viṣṇu as the Supreme Reality is similar to the Upaniṣadic concept of the Brahman. The concept of Brahmā includes the ideas of creation and fate. The Śāktas hold Śakti as the Highest Reality. Human-offerings are made to the goddess with the belief that she becomes pleased by such acts. Like the Śaiva Faith, the Śākta Faith too is influenced by Tāntricism. Though the text contains a few references to the worship of Sūrya as the Highest Reality, the Sauras identify it with Viṣṇu, Śiva and Prajāpati.

Footnotes Of Chapter II

1. "Worship of Vishṇu as a solar deity dates back from the early Vedic times. Although some of the Brāhmaṇas of the Vedas already saw the progress which the solar Viṣṇu had made in the imagination of the people, and although they contain the germ of several legends, which at the later time, became fully developed, the really mythological character of this god, as the basis of the divine worship, belongs the epic poem - the Rāmāyaṇa and Mahābhārata and to the Purāṇas."

Goldstücker,Theodore; Sanskrit and Culture, p.37.

2. तां तामृद्धिं सुराः प्राप्तस्त्वत्प्रसन्नेक्षणेक्षिताः ।

KSS. 9.4.38

3. देवानां साहायः सर्वदा हरिः ।

KSS. 8.5.15.

4. ब्रह्मा ते नाभिकमले स्वाध्यायोद्यन्मृदुध्वनिः ।
तद्भूतानेकचरणोप्येष षट्चरणायते ॥

KSS. 9.4.32.

This shows the belief of the Vaiṣṇavas that as Viṣṇu is the support of Brahmā, he is superior to the latter.

5. भक्त्योपगीयमानं च गन्धर्वैर्नारदादिभिः ॥
प्रणम्यमानं देवैश्च सिद्धैर्विद्याधरैस्तथा ।

KSS. 9.4.25-26.

6. सर्वज्ञ

KSS. 3.3.8.

7. नमस्ते दिव्यहंसाय सन्मानसनिवासिने ।
सततोदितनादाय पराकाशविहारिणे ॥

KSS. 9.4.30.

8. तुभ्यं नमोऽतिसर्वाय सर्वाभ्यन्तरवर्त्तिने ॥

KSS. 9.4.31.

9. The Ṛg Veda (10.90.3-4)shows that the entire world is only one fourth of the Divinity whereas His three- fourths are above it.

Cf.also इदं विज्णुर्विचक्रमे त्रेधा निदधे पदम् ।
समूढस्य पांसुरे स्वाहा ॥

Vājasaneyī Saṁhitā, 5.15.

The passage states that Viṣṇu pervaded the world with His three strides and His fourth stride reached out into the world beyond that ordinary eyes cannot penetrate.

10. Cf. व्यापित्वात्सर्वभूतानां विष्णुरित्यभिधीयते ।

Padma Purāṇa,

Uttara Khaṇḍa, 265-74.

Cf. also- एतत्सर्वं जगद् व्याप्तं मया त्वव्यक्तमूर्तिना ।
अतो मां मुनयः प्राहुर्विष्णुं विष्णुपरायणाः ॥

Ibid., Bhūmi Khaṇḍa, 38.15.

and- विष्णुर्विशतेर्वा व्यश्नोतेर्वा ।

Nirukta, 12.2.

11. X.90.

12. Ṛg Veda X, 81.3.
Cf. also-Śvetāśvatara upaniṣad, III.3.

13. भूमिपादो द्युमूर्धा त्वं दिक्श्रोत्रोऽर्केन्दुलोचनः ।
ब्रह्माण्डजठरः कोऽपि पुरुषो गीयसे बुधैः ॥

KSS. 9.4.33.

14. त्वत्तो धामनिधेश्चासौ भूतग्रामो विजृम्भते ।
नाथ स्फुलिङ्गसङ्घात इव प्रज्जवलतोऽनलात् ॥
पुनश्च प्रविशत्येव त्वामेव प्रलयागमे ॥
दिनान्ते विग्रहवात इव वासमहाद्रुमम् ।
सृजस्युल्लसितः स्वाशांस्त्वमेतान् भुवनेश्वरान् ।
अनन्तवेलाक्षुभितस्तरङ्गानिव वारिधिः ॥

KSS. 9.4.34-36.

15. गुणातिक्रान्तरूपाय ।

KSS. 9.4.31.

16. विश्वारूपोऽप्यरूपस्त्वं विश्वाकर्मापि चाक्रियः ।
विश्वाधारोऽप्यनाधारः कः स तत्त्वमवैति ते ॥

KSS. 9.4.37.

17. KSS. 3.3.29.

18. KSS. 6.1.143.

19. KSS. 2.2.40.

20. KSS. 12.6.87.

21. हरिः क्षीराम्बुधिस्थितः ।

KSS. 3.3.8.

22. शेषशय्यागतं हरिम् ।

KSS. 17.2.103.

23. गुरुडारूढः । KSS. 7.4.58. पक्षिराजरथः । KSS. 8.4.48.

24. पद्माङ्कितोत्सङ्गः ।

KSS. 7.4.58.

25. धृतचक्रायुधो देवः ।

KSS. 8.4.48.

26. KSS.9.4.25.

The Chakra is taken as the symbol of the Sun-god with whom Viṣṇu was originally identified and is believed to light the path of the devotees in this world of ignorance. It also represents the wheel of time. The Śaṁkha is taken as a symbol of banishing all fears of the devotees and as proclaiming victory. It is the remover of Avidyā or ignorance. The Gadā is the destroyer of Adharma or unrighteousness. The Padma or the lotus is sacred to Lakṣmī. For different interpretations of Viṣṇu's weapons vide Pai, D.A., Monograph of Religious Sects of India among Hindus, p.57; Rao, T.A. Gopinatha; Elements of Hindu Iconography, Vol.I, part I, pp.293,295.

27. KSS. 3.5.110.

28. परित्राणाय साधूनां विनाशाय च दुष्कृताम् ।
धर्मसंस्थापनार्थाय सम्भवामि युगे युगे ।।

Śrīmadbhagavadgītā, IV.8.

29. "The doctrine of incarnation preserved the basic unity of the different divine manifestation while furnishing a variety of personalisation with a differential appeal to different temperaments."

Krishna Chaitanya, A New
History of Sanskrit Literature, p.222.

Viṣṇu's characteristic benevolence in the Vedic mythology seems to have developed into the doctrine of his Avatāras for the good of humanity. According to R. G.Bhandarkar (Vaiṣṇavism, Śaivism and Minor Religious Systems, p.2), the conception of the incarnations of Viṣṇu is in the opposite direction of the idea that one God, for instance Agni, is the same as Varuṇa, Mitra, Indra and Aryaman (Ṛg Veda, V.3,1-2). If these several gods are one, one god may become several. This led to the conception of incarnations or Avatāras.

30."Viṣṇu's ten chief incarnations appear to symbolize a kind of evolution of organic life."

Monier-Williams,M. Hinduism, p.104.

31. 14,1,2,11.

32. 7,1,5.

33. II.110,3.

34. I.4.1 ff.

35. I.4.59 ff.

36. Sṛṣti Khaṇḍa, 3.21-47.

37. XII, 349,37; 399.77-90; 399.104.

38. महावराहो भगवान्महार्णवमिवाविशत् ।

KSS. 9.4.221.

39. सौकर्योद्यतया मूर्त्या दक्षनन्दो वसुंधराम् ।
इमां हरिरिवोद्धृत्य यो बभार चिरं भुजे ॥

KSS. 12.26.4.

"Probably the tortise and the boar were originally popular theriomorphic deities worshipped by the masses (including Brāhmaṇic families), and were afterwards elevated by the same

Brāhmaṇas to a higher rank by assuming them to be forms of some recognized god." Encyclopaedia of Religion and Ethics, Vol. II, p.81.

40. The notion of the Vāmana (Dwarf) incarnation of Viṣṇu may have developed from the myth in the Ṛg Veda in which three steps of Viṣṇu with which he measured the three worlds are referred to (इदं विष्णुर्विचक्रमे त्रेधा निदधे पदम् Ṛg Veda, i.22.16).

Vide also - Ṛg Veda, i.154.1; Taittirīya Saṁhitā, 2.1. 31; Aittareya Brāhmaṇa, II.1.3.1; Śatapatha Brāhmaṇa, I.2,5,1-7 वामनो ह विष्णुरास; Taittirīya Brāhmaṇa, 1,6, 15; 3,1,2.

Compared with the three giant steps of Viṣṇu, his body might have appeared dwarfish.

41. – – – – – – विष्णोः सूकररूपस्य
– – – – – – जातस्यैव न किं हरेः ।
चकम्पे चरणाक्रान्ता वसुधा वामनाकृतेः ॥
तदैव वृद्धिं गत्वा च तेन न किं पदम् ।
द्युलोके – – – – – – – – – – ॥

KSS. 18.5.223, 229-230.

42. KSS. 11.1.34.

For incarnation of Viṣṇu as Vāmana Cf. Rāmāyaṇa, 1,29,5 ff, 3,61,24; 6,59,38; Mahābhārata, Vana-Parvan 484; Matsya Purāṇa, Chapter 246.

43. KSS. 12.21.3.

Cf. Rāmāyaṇa, 1,76,17; 7,17,35; 7.27,14 ff; Māhābharata, 3,151,7.

44. KSS. 12.36.4.

For incarnation of Viṣṇu as Narasiṁha
Cf. वज्रनखाय विद्महे तीक्ष्णदंष्ट्राय धीमहि
तन्नो नारसिंहः प्रचोदयात् ।

Taittirīya Āraṇyaka, X.1.6-7.

Cf also - Māhābhārata, 3,272,56; Viṣṇu Purāṇa, 1.2.32; Padma Purāṇa, Sṛṣti Khaṇḍa, Chapters 42-43; Bhāgavata Purāṇa, VII.8,12 ff.

45. KSS. 2.4.146.

46. KSS. 10.7.55.

47. The word 'Vaiṣṇava' (a devotee of Viṣṇu) occurs in the text (KSS. 3.3.4; 7.2.10).

48. KSS. 12.4.117.

49. KSS. 12.4.200.

50. KSS. 2.4.146.

51. KSS. 12.6.87.

52. KSS. 6.6.50.

53. भक्तवत्सलः ।

KSS. 7.4.58.

54. भक्तकल्पमहीरुह ।

KSS. 9.4.29.

55. स भक्तानां योगक्षेममवेक्षते ।

KSS. 8.6.78.

56. अभीष्टदायिने ।

KSS. 9.4.29.

57. भगवान्स हि सद्भक्तमिहामुत्र च रक्षति ।

KSS. 8.1.153.

58. KSS. 4.2.189.

59. KSS. 12.6.68.

60. KSS. 7.2.115; 12.4.95.

61. KSS. 2.4.174.

62. भक्त्या च देवस्य हरेर्मथुरावर्त्तिनः कृते ।
हस्तेऽस्याब्जगदाशङ्खचक्रान्हेममयान्ददौ ॥

KSS. 2.4.146.

63. KSS. 12.4.200.

64. KSS. 7.2.115.

65. KSS. 12.4.201.

66. KSS. 3.3.29.

67. कृतप्रतिष्ठस्तत्रास्ते भगवान्हरिरब्धिना ।
आषाढशुक्लद्वादश्यां तत्र यात्रोत्सवे सदा ॥
आयन्ति सर्वद्वीपेभ्यः पूजायै यत्नतो जनाः ॥

KSS. 5.3.34.

68. KSS. 7.5.36-38.

69. तत्र तीर्थवरे स्नात्वा पञ्चरात्रोपवासिनाम् ।
नारायणानुचरतादायनी स्नायिनां नृणाम् ॥
KSS. 6.7.30.

70. – – – – स ययौ पादन्यासोद्भवं हरे ।
तीर्थं क्रमसरो नाम त्रिविक्रमकृतं पुरा ॥
यदध्यासितमभ्यर्णपर्वताग्रनिवेशिभिः ।
शृङ्गाकारैस्त्रिभिर्देवैर्ब्रह्मविष्णुमहेश्वरैः ॥
येन विष्णुपदेनान्या काश्मीरेषु सुरोपमा ।
सृष्टाविषुवती नाम वितस्ता मत्सरादिव ॥
KSS. 12.9.95-97.

71. KSS. 5.3.3-4.

72. Śvetadvīpa is described in the Māhābharata (XII,335, 6-12) as the island which exists north of the ocean of milk and lies 32,000 Yojanas from Meru. A few scholars have tried to identify it with a land of "white men" in the North, inhabited by Westorian Christians.

Cf. Kannedy, J., Journal of the Royal Asiatic Society, 1907,481 ff and Grierson, Encyclopaedia of Religion and Ethics, Vol.II, p.549.

According to A. Barth, Śvetadvīpa is a sort of Atlantis situated in the extreme north, beyond the sea of milk.

The Religions of India, p.193.

73. "She is the Hindu counterpart of the Greek goddess of beauty, Venus Aphrodite."

Thomas, p., Epics, Myths and Legends of India, p.58.

74. लक्ष्मी पद्महस्ता । KSS. 16.3.91.

75. KSS. 3.4.204; 6.2.53.

76. विचित्रकमलोत्पत्तिधामाम्बुधिम् ।
KSS. 12.8.67.

जलधेरुद्गतां श्रियम् – – – ॥
KSS. 2.6.68.

77. प्राङ्मन्थादर्णवस्येव कमला कुक्षिकोटरे ।

KSS. 2.3.80.

78. कमलां निर्मथ्यापहृतां सुरैः ॥

KSS. 7.8.18.

79. KSS. 12.2.78.

80. KSS. 2.2.10.

81. The concept of Brahmā goes back to the Vedic period.
Cf. ब्रह्मा देवानां पदवीः कवीनामृषिर्विप्राणां महिषो मृगाणाम् ।

Ṛg Veds, 9.96.6.

82. KSS. 17.2.98.

83. ब्रह्मास्त्रमेतदन्येन नास्त्रेण प्रतिहन्यते ।
विना पाशुपतं रौद्रमस्त्रम् – – – – – – ॥

KSS. 17. 2. 21.

This shows that Brahmā, though held as superior to many other gods, decidedly holds an inferior position to Śiva.

84. Here Brahmā is mentioned only as the creator of the world. For the concept of Fate vide pp. 157-159 infra.

85. ब्रह्मा देवानां प्रथमः संबभूव ।
विश्वस्य कर्त्ता भुवनस्य गोप्ता ॥

Muṇḍaka Upaniṣad, 1.9.

Cf. also Gopatha Brāhmaṇa, i.1; Bṛhadāraṇyaka Upaniṣad, 1.4, Chhāndogya Upaniṣad, vi.2; Praśna Upaniṣad, 1.4; vi.3; Aitareya Upaniṣad, 1.1; Śvetāśvatara Upaniṣad, vi.1.

86. KSS. 9.5.11; 10.4.51; 12.20.5.

87. यादृशो यः कृतो धात्रा भवेत्तादृश एव सः ॥

KSS. 10.6.124.

88. KSS. 7.1.35.

89. KSS. 8.7.19.

90. KSS. 2.1.24.

91. KSS. 17.2.75

92. KSS. 3.6.63.

93. KSS. 3.6.63. "Brahmā is Chaturmukha not as having four faces but as being omniscient."
Hopkins,E.W., Epic Mythology, p.97.

94. KSS. 3.6.66. 95. KSS. 8.7.43.

96. KSS. 8.7.54. 97. KSS. 2.1.76.

98. KSS. 17.2.47. 99. KSS. 3.1.138.

100. The Egyptian Horus, like Brahmā of the Hindu triad, was born of lotus. Thomas,P., Epics, Myths and Legends of India, Introduction, p.4.

101. KSS. 8.3.60-61.

102. For another reason of the downfall of Brahmā worship vide Padma Purāṇa Sṛṣti Khaṇḍa 16.130-35; 17. 152-53.

103. The origin of the Śākta Faith is traced to the pre-Vedic period.

Cf. "The different objects belonging to the Mohenjodaro civilisation may not supply positive and direct proof about the existence of Śakti-worship of a developed type at such an early date, yet there is sufficient indirect evidence regarding its beginning."

Banerjea,J.N., Pauranic and
Tantric Religion, p.112.

Cf. Also - "It is difficult to say to what extent the pre-Vedic culture of India contributed to the conception of a mother goddess of the type now familiar to us as Śakti, but that the cult of the Mother Goddess was fed by indigenous and aboriginal beliefs is almost certain judging by the qualities with which she was invested at a later time."

Majumdar,R.C. and Pusalkar,A.D.,
The Classical Age, p. 445.

P.Thomas observes that mother cults and myths, fairly universal among mankind, are of very ancient origin and most of them can be traced to the matriarchal phase of social development when women held a better position in society than men (Epics, Myths and Legends of India, p.54)

R.P.Chanda traces the origin of the Śākta Faith from Dravidian people.

Cf. "As a matter of fact the Śakti or Mother Cult which presupposes a matriarchal society is supposed to have originated with the Dravidian people among whom mother- kin is still found to be prevalent."

Indo Aryan Races, p.156.

B.C.Majumdar has also traced Śākta Faith to a non-Aryan source (vide Journal of the Royal Asiatic Society, 1906, pp.355 ff.)

For a brief history of the Śākta Faith, vide Bhandarkar, R.G., Vaiṣṇavism, Śaivism and Minor Religious Systems, pp.203 ff; Banerjea,J.M., Pauranic and Tantric Religion, p.114.

104. Payne,E.A., the Śāktas, p.63.

105. नमस्ते चण्डि चामुण्डे मङ्गले त्रिपुरे जये ।
एकानंशे शिवे दुर्गे नारायणि सरस्वती ।
भद्रकालि महालक्ष्मि सिद्धे – – – – ॥
त्वं गायत्री महाराज्ञी रैवती विन्ध्यवासिनि ।
उमा कात्यायनी च त्वं – – – – – – – ॥

KSS. 9.3.170-72.

Cf. Mahābhārata (Bhīṣma Parvan, 23.5,6,9,11; Virāṭa Parvan, 6.14,17,7) which clearly mentions the worship of Śakti under different names viz. Kumārī, Kālī, Mahākālī, Chaṇḍi, Chāmuṇḍā, Kātyāyanī, Kāntāravāsinī and Umā.

106. KSS. 12.6.116.

107. KSS. 12.13.49.

108. KSS. 7.8.116.

109. Bhandarkar, R.G., Vaiṣṇavism, Śaivism and Minor Religious Systems, pp.143-44

110. संस्तुतासि च तनैव देवेनैवं त्रिशूलिना ।

KSS. 9.3.170.

स्कन्दो वसिष्ठश्च ब्रह्माद्यास्त्वां च तुष्टुवुः ॥

KSS. 9.3.173.

111. स्तुवन्तस्त्वां च भगवत्यमरा ऋषयो नराः।
ईप्सिताभ्यधिकान्कामान्प्राप्तश्च प्राप्नुवन्ति च ॥
KSS. 9.3.174.

112. KSS. 7.3.43.

113. KSS. 7.3.46; 12.11.90.

114. त्वं प्राणशक्तिर्भूतानां त्वयेदं चेष्टते जगत्।
KSS. 9.3.166.
Cf. also - KSS. 15.1.99.

115. KSS. 7.3.45.

116. KSS. 12.11.91.

117. भुजानां चक्रवालेन संघाटितदिगन्तरा।
खड्गखेटककोदण्डशरशूलादिधारिणा ॥
KSS. 9.3.169.
Cf. also - KSS. 12.11.90.

118. कालि, कपालिनी, कङ्कालिनी।
KSS. 12.11.92.
चामुण्डे, करङ्कमालाकुले।
KSS. 9.2.159.

119. धृतभास्करकिरणे। KSS. 12.11.91.

120. विकराले। KSS. 9.2.159.

121. दुरालोके। KSS. 9.2.159.

122. अट्टाट्टहासहसिते। KSS. 9.2.159.

123. अष्टदशदोर्दण्डखण्डितोच्चण्डदानवाम् ॥
KSS. 12.13.27.

124. दारितोद्दामदैत्येन त्रिशिखेनास्रवर्षिणा।
शमितासुरसंतापे - - - - - - - - - ॥
KSS. 12.34.303.

125. पादपद्मतलाक्षिप्तमहिषासुरमर्दिनीम्।
KSS. 12.13.28.

Cf. also- महिषासुरसूदनि । KSS. 7.3.46.
and महिषासुरमारिणि । KSS. 12.11.90.
Cf. Mārkaṇḍeya Purāṇa, Chapter 82.

126. दारिणि रुरुदानवस्य । KSS. 12.11.90.

127. स्रवन्महिषकण्ठास्रधाराभिस्त्रिशिखात्रिभिः
आश्वासितत्रिभुवने दुर्गारुपे नमोऽस्तु ते ॥
रुरुरक्तभृतभ्रान्तकरस्थितकपालया ।
नृत्यन्त्या त्रिजगद्रक्षापात्रयेव जितं त्वया ॥
KSS. 15.1.100-1

128. कालरात्रिं च चण्डिकामपराजिताम् ।
KSS. 15.1.70.

129. एषा चोत्पादिता पूर्वं विष्णुनामृतमन्थने ।
दारणी दानवेन्द्राणाममृतं हर्तुमिच्छताम् ॥
KSS. 15.1.90.

130. विन्ध्यवासिनी ।
KSS. 9.3.72.

131. शर्वपर्वतवासिनी ।
KSS. 9.3.72.

132. KSS. 12.28.86.

133. KSS. 7.8.116.

134. KSS. 12.3.12.

135. KSS. 9.3.166-74; 12.11.90-93.

136. KSS. 12.34.302.

137. KSS. 7.8.103.

138. हरणे दुरितान्धकारवृन्दाम् ।
KSS. 12.11.91.

139. वरदा । KSS. 1.6.79;
वरप्रदा । KSS. 16.1.45.

140. KSS. 1.3.41.

141. KSS. 9.3.180; 12.11.102-3; 12.28.89; 16.1.45.

142. KSS. 7.8.103.

143. KSS. 9.2.159.

144. KSS. 7.8.170.

145. सांनिध्योत्कर्षशालिनी ।

KSS. 12.11.50.

146. KSS. 12.2.113.

147. KSS. 12.14.45,47,50.

148. KSS. 18.4.207.

149. – – – – चण्डिकागृहम् ॥
विलोलदीर्घया घोरं रक्तांशुकपताकया ।
जिघत्सतः पशुप्राणान् कृतान्तस्येव जिह्वया ॥

KSS. 4.2.62-63.

150. दीपज्वालाचलज्जिह्वं घण्टालीदन्तमालया ।
व्यासक्तवीरशिरसा घोरं मृत्युमुखं यथा ॥

KSS. 12.34.301.

151. KSS. 1.3.39.

152. KSS. 12.11.50.

153. KSS. 5.2.86.

154. KSS. 12.2.113.

155. KSS. 5.2.86.

156. KSS. 2.3.13.

157. KSS. 12.28.29.

158. KSS. 12.28.29.

159. उपवीणयति स्मैतां देवीमत्र स्वगीतकैः ॥

KSS. 12.2.115.

160. KSS. 7.8.56.

161. KSS. 16.2.26.

162. KSS. 9.2.168.

163. KSS. 9.4.168.

164. KSS. 14.4.84.

165. KSS. 1.7.224.

166. KSS. 9.2.244.

167. KSS. 9.4.160-62.

168. KSS. 10.10.101.

169. KSS. 14.4.23.

170. KSS. 1.6.78.

171. KSS. 1.5.27.

172. Ocean, Vol.IX, Foreword, p.viii.
Vide also - Ocean, Vol.I, p.9, fn. i.
As Vindhya - Vāsinī, the dwellers in the Vindhyas, she is (now) worshipped at a place of that name where the Vindhyas approach the Ganges near Mirzapur.
Dowson, John, A Classical Dictionary of Hindu Mythology and Religion, p.87.

173. KSS. 7.8.175.

174. लोकः पशूपहारेण प्रीणाति वरदामिमाम् ।
KSS. 1.6.79.

175. तस्या उपाहृतानेकनानाजीवमहर्निशम् ।
प्राविशं भवनं देव्याः कृतान्तसदनोपमम् ॥
KSS. 12.5.17.

176. Spratt,P., Hindu Culture and Personality, p.70.

177. The Religions of India, p.204.

178. KSS. 9.3.148-49, 164; 12.11.66,68,70,93.

179. KSS. 12.11.99.

180. KSS. 12.5.18-19.

181. KSS. 12.13.29-31.

182. KSS. 7.8.178.

183. KSS. 1.6.156.

184. KSS. 2.3.37.

185. स्वमूर्धोपहारेण तामर्चितुमियेष सः ॥
KSS. 15.1.103.

186. KSS. 3.4.161.

187. KSS. 4.2.62,64,66.

188. KSS. 2.2.189.

189. KSS. 9.6.25.

190. KSS. 9.5.220.

191. KSS. 7.8.178.

192. KSS. 10.5.158.

193. KSS. 5.3.142-44.

194. भगवत्युपहारत्वे यत एवासि कल्पितः।
अत एव सदा वस्त्रैर्भोगैश्चोपचर्यसे ॥

KSS. 2.2.143.

195. प्राप्तायां च चतुर्दश्यामत्र राजाज्ञया ततः।
ते सर्वेऽप्युपहार्थमनीयन्ताम्बिकागृहम् ॥

KSS. 12.34.300.

196. KSS. 2.5.15.

197. KSS. 5.2.113.

198. Worship of the Sun can be traced to the Vedic period. (Ṛg Veda, 1.50; 4.30; 5.29; 6.51; 7.36, 60-61, 63; 10.37) For worship of the Sun vide Bhandarkar, R.G., Vaiṣṇavism Śaivism and Minor Religious Systems, p.217.

199. तुभ्यं परापराकाशशायिने ज्योतिषे विभो।
आभ्यन्तरं च बाह्यं च तमः प्रणुदते नमः।
त्वं विष्णुस्त्रिजगद्व्यापी त्वं शिवः श्रेयसां निधिः ॥
सुप्तं विचेष्टयन्विश्वं परमस्त्वं प्रजापतिः ॥

KSS. 9.6.29-30.

Cf. एष ब्रह्मा च विष्णुश्च रुद्र एष हि भास्करः।

Sūrya Upaniṣad, p.55.

200. KSS. 12.35-37.

201. KSS. 9.6.28-34.

Chapter III

DIVINE FAMILY

The psychological instinct creates in human mind the belief in the existence of various divinities. The two main feelings to which the origin of this belief is ascribed are fear and wonder. It is quite conceivable that man might cultivate the divinity through fear of the latter's displeasure and an elaborate system of ceremonies and beliefs might arise from the desire to avert his anger.[1] Beliefs of the Hindus about the divine family, as mentioned in the Kathāsaritsāgara, are given below.

The Gods

The gods are considered as active and kind-hearted beings who take interest in human affairs. They are kind to their votaries, look after their safety and fulfil their desires. They are the givers of boons.[2] Their grace is looked upon as extremely beneficial and effective.[3] Even the most difficult tasks can be successfully accomplished if gods are propitious.[4] Just as boon is the expression of their favour and the bestower of every desired object, curse is the expression of their anger which is aroused by some one's immoral act. Curses pronounced by many gods are referred to in the text.[5] Such references amply prove that god's annoyance can destroy one's happiness and cause higher beings to be thrown to the lower births.[6]

Beliefs in the communication of truth to man from a divine source is common in every religion. In the Kathāsaritsāgara, it is maintained that gods show their awareness of human affairs by uttering a divine or heavenly voice.[7] They rejoice in the festivity of men by showering flowers and beating drums.[8] They are highly pleased when some one performs a good[9] or brave act.[10] Compared with human-beings, they are believed to be supremely blessed[11] and immortal.[12] No human thought can grasp their exact nature.[13]

The society of the Kathāsaritsāgara believes in the existence of various gods. The sectarian gods of the Hindus have already been dealt with in the previous chapters. The other gods, referred to in the Kathāsaritsāgara are mentioned now.

Indra

The position enjoyed by Indra in the Vedic period is no more granted to him in the Kathāsaritsāgara. He is assigned a very subordinate position only. He is described as receiving orders form Viṣṇu with reverent mind.[14] His forces gain more confidence by the favour of Śiva.[15] He seeks the help of human kings in his war against Asuras. For instance, Purūravas goes to heaven invited by Indra to assist him in his war against Dānavas.[16] Indra asks Sahasrānīka for aid in his war against Asuras.[17] The king Merudhvaja also extends him all the help.[18]

Indra is more closely connected with human beings than any other god. The earthly kings are described as attending his assembly.[19] They participate in the functions held by Indra to celebrate his victory over his foes.[20]

Indra is not without limitations. Many charges of adultery and false love are often levelled against him. He is called the lover of Ahalyā.[21] He is not free from jealousy. Once when he hears that the god Kārttikeya is defending gods, he becomes annoyed. He has the impression that his kingdom is being taken away from him and being jealous, he goes to the extent of fighting with Kārttikeya.[22] He sends heavenly nymphs to disturb the penance of great ascetics. Disguised as a Brāhmaṇa, he comes to Tapodatta in order to prevent him from asceticism.[23] He dispatches heavenly nymphs to tempt Kāla who is engaged in muttering prayers.[24]

Many names and attributes of Indra are found in the Kathāsaritsāgara.

He is called Vajrin,[25] Devarāṭ,[26] Maghavan,[27] Vāsava,[28] Śatakratu,[29] Śatamakha,[30] Surapati,[31] Śakra[32] and Śachipati.[33] Being the sworn enemy of Vṛtra, he is often termed as Vṛtrārī[34] of Vṛtravairī.[35]

Thunderbolt and Airāvata are as it were two gems of Indra.[36] Airāvata is his elephant on which he mounts.[37] Uchchaiḥśravas is his divine horse. The horse is supposed to resuscitate the dead.[38] The story of the generous Dānava Namuchi shows that as soon as gods kill Asura, the horse Uchchaiḥśravas immediately restores him to life.[39]

Indra is held as the god of conquest and is known for his fights with Asuras.[40] He is fond of observing wars.[41] He cuts off the wings of the mountains with his thunderbolt.[42]

Indra is always surrounded by gods in his court.[43] He dwells in his city called Amarāvatī.[44] The doors of his palace are decorated by elephants of gods and the garden of Nandana is attached to it to add to its beauty.[45]

Jayanta is Indra's son.[46] Rambhā his dancer,[47] Mātali his charioteer and messenger[48] and Bṛhaspati his minister.[49]

Worship of Indra was far more popular in the Vedic Age than in the later period. In the Kathāsaritsāgara, Indra does not receive any direct worship, though a festival is held in his honour.[50]

Agni

Fire is held as the consumer of oblations to gods and manes.[51] It is personified as the god Agni[52] who is also called Vaiśvānara.[53] The god of fire is the giver of boons[54] and is invoked for getting a son.[55] The 'story of the brave King Vikramatuṅga' and the 'story of the Brāhmaṇa Vidūṣaka' point out the belief that the god of fire becomes pleased with one's courage.[56]

Yama

The Ṛg Veda describes Yama as the god of death but does not

associate him with the task of the punishment of the wicked. Yama becomes the judge of the dead in the later mythology. In the Kathāsaritsāgara, Yama is conceived as the judge of the dead. He is a stern god with noose in his hand.[57]

It is held that there is an abode of Yama where he receives from Chitragupta the account of the good and bad deeds of the deceased persons. If a person has done both good and bad deeds, Yama asks him what he wants first heaven or hell? If the person wants heaven first, Yama orders his chariot to be brought and the person mounting on it is sent to heaven.[58]

Kāma[59]

Like Eros of the Greeks and Cupid of the Latins, Kāma is the Hindu god of love. He is one of the most pleasing and remarkable creations of Hindu fiction.[60]

The influence of Kāma on Devas and Asuras, who cannot evade his decree, is accepted in the Kathāsaritsāgara.[61] Kāma exercises his influence even on Śiva.[62] The thunderbolt and other weapons of gods are blunted before his arrows of flowers.[63]

He has many names and these sum up his nature and personality. In the Kathāsaritsāgara, he is called Kāma[64] (longing), Smara[65] (mind-disturber), Madana[66] (insolent), Manobhava[67] (mind born) and Anaṅga[68] (limbless). He is armed with bow and arrows which are made up of flowers and that is why he is named as Puṣpachāpa,[69] Kusumāyudha,[70] Kusumaśara[71] and Puṣpeṣu.[72] His arrows are odd in number (Asama-sāyaka).[73]

Kāma conquers the world[74] and his order is hard to resist.[75] He is known for his beauty.[76] It is believed that he makes fun of ugly people.[77] Rati and Prīti are described as his wives.[78]

The 'story of the birth of Kāmadeva' is given in the Kathāsaritsāgara.[79] It is held that the god is born from the mind of Brahmā. As soon as he is born, he enquires of Brahmā – whom shall I make mad (Kaṁdarpayāmi). Therefore Brahmā names him 'Kandarpa' and advises him not to attack Śiva. But, Kāma tries to disturb Śiva's austerities and therefore, he is burnt up by him.[80] On Pārvatī's request, Śiva decrees that Kāma be born in the mind of creatures. Rati performs penance for the revival of her husband.

The worship of Kāmadeva is prevalent in the Kathāsaritsāgara.[81] The god is generally worshipped by young girls at the time of marriage with the view of happy married life.[82]

There are temples of Kāmadeva. People go to such temples to offer worship to the god. Naravāhanadatta beholds an all-loving temple of Kāmadeva. He enters the temple and worships the god.[83]

The spring festival is celebrated is honour of Kāma. It is variously named as Madhūtsava,[84] Vasantotsava[85] or Vasantasamayotsava.[86] It is held in the spring season and its chief purpose is merry-making. Royal dignitaries enjoy this festival. The King Dharmadhvaja of Ujjayinī, goes to the palace garden accompanied by his wives to enjoy himself at the arrival of the spring festival. In this festival,[87] the King Sātavāhana also visits the garden on the banks of the Godāvarī along with his wives for entertainment.[88] Princes and ministers also participate in this mood of great festivity. The prince Naravāhanadatta is noticed enjoying this festival in garden alongwith his ministers.[89] Besides the Royalties, the common people also whole-heartedly take part in it. Prince Naravāhanadatta is amused to behold the jubilant citizens who dance non-stop on spring festival.[90] The king Yaśodhana of Kanakapura goes out to see the joyous festival o' spring in his city.[91] Citizens of Pāṭaliputra are seen in a mood of great jubilation on the night of the spring festival.[92] Śrīdatta goes with his friends to witness some festival rejoicing in a garden on occasion of this festival.[93] Maidens also take part in it. Śaśiprabhā goes to a garden with her attendants to see a procession of people celebrating the spring festival.[94] The festival is celebrated in gardens of palaces or public gardens and a festival procession is also taken out as a part of this ceremony.

Kuvera

Kuvera is the god of wealth. In the Kathāsaritsāgara, he is called as Rājarāja[95] (King of Kings), Dhanādhipati[96] or Dhanādhyakṣa[97] (Lord of wealth) and Dhanadeśvara[98] (Bestower of wealth). Yakṣas are associated with him.[99]

It is believed that Kuvera creates troubles in the austerities of those who aspire to his status. He sends a divine lady to obstruct Viśvāmitra in his penance because the latter wants to acquire his rank.[100]

Alakā on Kailāsa, is situated in the eastern direction. It is called the city of Kuvera who is named as Alakāpati.[101] The city is known for its prosperity.

The Other Gods

The other gods referred to in the Kathāsaritsāgara are Aśvins,[102] Dharma,[103] Vāyu,[104] Varuṇa,[105] Tvaṣṭṛ, Bhaga, Aryaman and Pūṣan.

The Groups of Deities

Ādityas, eight Vasus[106] and Lokapālas[107] are the groups of deities who are also mentioned in the text. The Lokapālas[108] are invoked to prove one's innocence. For instance, Yaugandharāyaṇa calls the guardians of the world to prove his faithfulness and purity of the queen Vāsavadattā before the King Udayana.[109]

The Presiding Deities (Adhidevatā)

There are references to the presiding deities of the moon,[110] army,[111] city, house, forest and garden.

The Goddesses

Besides Pārvatī,[112] Lakṣmī[113] and Śakti,[114] the Kathāsaritsāgara refers to the belief in the existence of the following goddesses:

Sarasvatī

She is the goddess of learning. She is like a bee that dwells on the lake of the great poet's mind.[115] Her form is the word.[116] She is like a lamp that illuminates countless objects.[117] She wears white garments[118] and is free from longing.[119]

The worship of goddess Sarasvatī is realistically presented in the Kathāsaritsāgara. The poet Somadeva himself invokes her.[120] Udayana asks Vāsavadattā to bring the requisites for the worship of Sarasvatī.[121]

The thirteenth day of the bright fortnight is considered to be sacred for the worship of the goddess. There is a reference to the shrine of Sarasvatī where the wives of the principal courtiers of Siṁhākṣa go once on the thirteenth day of the bright fortnight to make a pilgrimage.[122]

Sāvitrī or Gāyatrī

The goddess Sāvitrī or Gāyatrī wears rosary of Akṣa beads and carries Kamaṇḍalu in her hand. She is held as kind to her votaries.[123]

The Other Goddesses

Goddesses known as Gaṅgā,[124] Kṣiti,[125] Nirti,[126] Kīrtti[127] and Jayā are also mentioned in the text. People believe in the destructive nature of goddess of Pestilence (Sarvasaṁhāriṇī Mārī). They being terrified by this all destroying goddess, implore the protection of god and remain devoutly muttering prayers to ward off calamity.[128]

The Associates of Gods

Bṛhaspati is called as the preceptor of gods (Suraguru,[129] Amaraguru).[130] He is known for his intellect[131] and policy.[132]

In the Kathāsaritsāgara, Chitragupta[133] is held not only as the associate of Yama[134] but also of Brahmā and Rudra.[135] He alone records the good and evil deeds of men[136] and presents the entire record of the dead to Yama.[137]

Worship of Chitragupta is a striking feature in the Kathāsaritsāgara. A thief worships him thinking that he delivers his devotees,[138] of course, by hiding their sins from Yama.

The word 'Viśvakarman' which seems to have been originally an epithet of any powerful god, as of Indra and Sūrya, in course of time, came to designate a personification of the creative power.[139] In the Kathāsaritsāgara, Viśvakarman is the architect of gods. He is especially associated with Brahmā.[140] Brahmā is the creator of the world and Viśvakarman is his appropriate helper in his task of creation.

The Divine-Seers[141]

Nārada is called Devarṣi who belongs to the highest class of divine seers.[142] He is the messenger of gods.[143] He plays on all the musical instruments in the court of Indra.[144] He is a seer of great lustre.[145] His words are never false.[146] He is expert in indirectly predicting future prosperity.[147]

Kaśyapa is another divine seer referred to in the text. He is held as the cause of the origin of Devas and Asuras.[148]

Vālakhilyas are the divine personages mentioned in the text which does not give any detail about them.

The Divine Races.

Many divine-races, who possess superhuman powers, are generally held as the attendants of gods. Belief is the existence of the following divine-races finds place in the Kathāsaritsāgara.

The Gandharvas[149]

They form a divine race.[150] The Kathāsaritsāgara represents them as the celestial singers who wonder about in the air. It is believed that they come to the earth being attracted by human beauties. Sometimes, they become friendly to human beings and appear before them whenever remembered. A Gandharva becomes a friend of Mṛgāṅkadatta and tells him that he will appear to him when he thinks of him.[151]

The birth of a Gandharva in this mortal world is assigned only to the influence of curse. For instance, a Gandharva becomes an elephant Śvetaraśmi by the curse of a hermit.[152] The daughter of the Gandharva Padmaśekhara is also born as a mortal due to a curse.[153]

The abode of the Gandharvas is variously described.[154] The Kathāsaritsāgara describes them as living on the Malayāchala.[155] Their city is inaccessible to men.[156] It has been depicted as very beautiful with magnificent castles and abundance of every kind of wealth. It is believed that the jewelled palace of this city has pillars of precious stones. Luxurious couches and splendid thrones are placed on its pavement of costly mosaic. There is a magnificent heavenly garden, planted with trees and creepers of gold, and full of hundreds of tanks adorned with costly stones. The splendid city of the Gandharvas is called more beautiful than the world of moon.[157]

The Apsarasas

According to the Kathāsaritsāgara, the Apsarasas originated from the ocean of milk and it was Viṣṇu who entrusted them with the help of Indra.

These heavenly nymphs[158] are held as the divine dancers[159] who participate in the festivals of Indra.[160] Rambhā is one of the celestial dancers whose preceptor is Tumburu.[161]

The Apsarasas are extremely voluptuous. They are held as the most beautiful creations of the creator.[162] Apsarasas Surbhidattā,[163] Alaṁbuṣā, Urvaśī,[164] Tilottamā and others are the embodiment of beauty. They can kindle the flame of love, even in the hearts of sages. The great hermit Gautama fails to resist the charm and temptations of Rambhā.[165]

Many supernatural powers are attributed to the Apsarasas. They can travel through the air,[166] and can assume any shape. They do not land on earth. Unlike human beings, they do not wink their eyes.[167] They are described as the most helpful and affectionate to the people whom they never fail to oblige.[168]

The belief that the Apsarasas fall in love with human beings, is quite ancient.[169] In the Kathāsaritsāgara, it is maintained that though nymphs normally shun the company of men, still, sometimes, they do fall in love with human-beings.[170] This departure from their basic attitude towards men is mostly due to the influence of some curse for their past misbehaviour. The Apsarasas Surabhidattā,[171] Kaliṅgasenā[172] and Mṛgāvatī[173] are born as mortals due to the curse of Indra.

Apsarasas are subject to this law that when a mortal child is conceived they must abandon it and go afar. Bound by this law, it may be cited that Menakā leaves Śakuntalā in the hermitage of Kaṇva.[174]

The Kinnaras[175]

Kinnaras are the celestial singers. They are known for their music.[176] Their dwelling place Himavat is ever resounded by their songs.[177] They are held as the spirits of the air.[178]

The Gaṇas

The Gaṇas are the superhuman attendants of Śiva[179] and Pārvatī though they are associated with Devī also in the text.[180] Both Śiva and Pārvatī keep strict control over their Gaṇas. Any breach of discipline is punished by their expulsion from Kailāsa.

It is believed that lord Śiva sends his Gaṇas to safeguard the interests of his devotees. Śiva, propitiated by Devadatta, commands his Gaṇa Pañchaśikha to help him in the satisfaction of his cherished desire.[181] Yaugandharāyaṇa tells Udayana that Śiva has commissioned a Gaṇa to protect Naravāhanadatta.[182]

The position of a Gaṇa is a privileged one. It can best be attained by the special favour of Śiva. Devadatta manages to attain this position by grace of Śiva.[183]

The Gaṇas are also called'Pramathas' in the text. For instance, Puṣpadanta and Mālyavān are called Pramathavaras.(i.e. the excellent Pramathas).[184] The chief of the Gaṇas is called Gaṇeśa.[185] Nandī is also described as their lord.[186]

It is held that the Gaṇas shave their heads in such a way that five locks are left hanging. They put necklace of skulls round their necks and strip off their clothes. They paint one side of their body with black colour and the other one with red lead.[187]

The Gaṇas are described as the inhabitants of the Mount Kailāsa.[188]

There are clear references in the text which testify that people show great respect to the Gaṇas. A king honours Sundaraka thinking that he is a Gaṇa of Śiva.[189] Similarly Sātavāhana welcomes Guṇāḍhya because he is an incarnation of a Gaṇa.[190]

Birth of the Gaṇas on the earth is generally ascribed to the influence of some curse. The Gaṇas Puṣpadanta and Mālyavan are born on the earth on account of the curse of Pārvatī.[191] Similarly the Gaṇas Piṅgeśvara and Guheśvara becomes swans by the curse of Pārvatī.[192]

The Yakṣas

They are the attendants of Kuvera.[193] Some of them are regarded as his friends. A Yakṣa named Sāta is called a friend of Kuvera.[194]

Yakṣas are mentioned along with Guhyakas and Kūṣmāṇḍas. Sometimes, the words Guhyaka and Yakṣa are used as synonyms in the text. Both these words are used for the Yakṣa Sāta.[195]

Yakṣas are the pious spirits. They are not allowed to associate themselves with the Rākṣasas who are the evil spirits. The Piśācha Kāṇabhūti was once a Yakṣa who selected the Rākṣasa Sthūlaśiras as his friend. The lord of wealth was forced to intervene and banished him to the forests of the Vindhya mountains.[196]

The Yakṣas are dressed in heavenly ornaments.[197] They are the inhabitants of Kailāsa.[198]

Yakṣas face many problems in their lives. They share the joys and sorrows of life.[199] They are subject to curses. For instance, the Yakṣa Supratīka becomes Piśācha by the curse of Kuvera.[200] Another Yakṣa is transformed into a lion by the curse of Kuvera.[201] The Yakṣa Virupākṣa is born on the earth due to the curse of Kuvera.[202] Another Yakṣa is born as a man owing to the curse of his master.[203] Thus, the birth of Yakṣas as mortals is generally attributed to the influence of some curse.

Yakṣas are held as the treasure-guarding spirits.[204] The Yakṣa Virupākṣa is appointed as chief guardian of a rich treasure.[205] Another Yakṣa tells the King Udayana that the treasure which he has so long guarded belonged to him as it was buried by his forefathers. He asks him to take possession of it.[206] In this way, the Yakṣas are believed to be the givers of wealth.[207]

Sometimes, the Yakṣas are also depicted as tree-spirits. A mendicant hears from within a tree a conversation of a Yakṣa and his wife.[208]

Yakṣas are worshipped. There is a holy shrine of the powerful Yakṣa Maṇibhadra where people go and make petitions offering various gifts in order to obtain blessings.[209]

The Kūṣmāṇḍas

Kūṣmāṇḍas form a divine race along with Yakṣas and Guhyakas. But, the Kathāsaritsāgara does not give any other information about them.

The Vidyādharas

The Vidyādharas belong to a divine race of supermen. The word 'Vidyādhara' means' possessors of the redeeming knowledge'. It is believed that the Vidyādharas are the possessors of some attainments (Vidyās or Siddhis) viz., flying through the air, assuming any from, knowing all human secrets and restoring dead person to life.

The Vidyādharas are the creation of popular imagination. The concept of Supermen is undoubtedly a popular reflection of the high mystical ambition of transcending the mundane world. We can recognize easily enough in them a contamination of the old ideas of the Gandharvas with notions derived from the mysterious powers of Hindu seers and ascetics and Buddhist saints.[210]

The Vidyādharas are considered as the spirits of the air. Many references in the text point at the belief that the Vidyādharas can fly up into the air. The Vidyādharas Madanavega[211] and Chitrāṅgada[212] are seen flying in the sky. In a former birth, Jīmūtavāhana was a sky-roaming Vidyādhara.[213] The Vidyādhara maidens Anurāgaparā,[214] Prabhāvatī[215] and Vegavatī[216] can move upward in the sky. An old Vidyādharī has been described as descending from the sky.[217]

It is believed that these Vidyādharas can assume any form. A Vidyādhara King cleverly transforms himself into the form of the King of Vatsa.[218] The Vidyādharī Vegavatī is described as deliberately taking Madanamañchukā's shape.[219] She assumes, by the power of her knowledge, a terrible form of Bhairava also.[220] The Vidyādharī Tārāvatī takes the form of a bee to hide her real identity.[221]

But no change of identity is permanent. It is totally lost during sleep. The Vidyādhara King Madanavega, who assumes the form of Udayana, while sleeping is found in his own form because he has lost his power of changing form due to sleep.[222] Similarly, the Vidyādharī Vegavatī, who takes the shape of Madanamañchukā when asleep loses the power of disguising herself by magic.[223]

The Vidyādharas are primarily the successful penetrators of all secrets. The Vidyādhara Hemaprabha knows by his supernatural power that his daughter has come to see Naravāhanadatta.[224] Kāñchanaprabhā knows by her Vidyā that Alaṅkāravatī has gone to the temple of Śiva.[225]

The Vidyādharas can even restore dead person to life.[226] They possess various other superhuman powers. The Vidyādhara king Dharmaśīla produces water in the hallow of-hand by virtue of his Vidyā. Immediately there is produced there an altar of gold, covered with a heavenly cloth and a pavilion composed of various jewels.[227]

They are conceived as a deceitful race.[228] They produce delusion by their power. The Brāhmaṇa Vidūṣaka beholds a heavenly palace and inside it a lady of heavenly beauty with a heavenly retinue. Her name is Bhadrā. When she disappears at the close of night, Vidūṣaka immediately finds himself in the empty temple of the goddess, in which he has been before and no Bhadrā and no palace. This is all due to the Vidyādharī Bhadrā's power.[229]

Vidyādharas can conceal others by virtue of their power. Vidūṣaka is concealed by the power of a Vidyādharī.[230]

There are various ways of attaining the position of a Vidyādhara. It is believed that the resolute souls having pleased Śiva either in this or in a former birth obtain by his favour the rank of a Vidyādhara.[231] The world of the Vidyādharas can be attained by propitiating a Vetāla[232] also. It can also be attained by the power of the magical sword which can be acquired by an extraordinary act of foeticide.[233]

The Vidyādharas are described as fond of wearing ornaments. They wear a diadem, a bracelet[234] and a necklace.[235] They also keep a sword in their hands.[236]

They are devoted to music and dance and their females are of extraordinary beauty.[237] They are the worshippers of Śiva. The King of the Vidyādharas named Vajraprabha pleases Śiva with austerities and obtains boon from him.[238] The Vidyādhara Madanavega, standing on his one foot and observing fast, performs penance for pleasing Śiva.[239] Many Vidyādharas assemble on the great mountain Ṛṣabha from all quarters on the fourteenth day of the lunar fortnight to worship Śiva.[240] The Vidyādhara maidens worship Śiva on the fourteenth and the eighth days of both the fortnights.[241]

Besides worshipping Śiva, the Vidyādharas adore fire also. A prince of the Vidyādharas named Piṅgalagāndhāra has become yellow with continually adoring fire.[242]

Some of the Vidyādharas are seen engaged in sacrificing and muttering prayers. Sūryaprabha and others see that Vidyādharas have lighted fires in the fire-cavities, and are engaged in sacrificing and some are occupied with muttering prayers.[243]

Vidyādhara's wealth has been described at various places in the Kathāsaritsāgara. The palaces of their golden city gleam with fabric of gold. The city has charming garden, the lake of which has steps made of jewels.[244] The city of the Vidyādhari Kāñchanaprabhā is adorned with many palaces of gold and thus though it is on the Himālayas, it makes the beholder feel that he is looking on the peaks of the mount Meru.[245] The palace of the Vidyādharaī Chandraprabhā is glittering with pillars of precious stones, and has walls of gold.[246] The city of the Vidyādhara Hemaprabha is all of gold and it is gleaming with golden ramparts.[247] Chandrapura is the city of the Vidyādharas about which it is maintained that Viśvakarman made wonderful and of unparalleled magnificence as if dissatisfied with the city of gods. The splendour of the gardens of the city is inconceivable. The trees of the gardens are of glittering jewels, and have this peculiarity that one tree produces a great many flowers of different kinds. These are rendered charming by the blending of the notes of various birds and with the sounds of heavenly songs. These are full of many slabs of precious stones. There is a slab of emerald at the foot of a Pārijāta tree. Wonderful are the splendours of the Vidyādharas, since they possess such a garden in which enjoyments present themselves unlooked for, in which servants are birds, and the nymphs of heaven keep a perpetual concert.[248]

The kings of the Vidyādharas are appointed by Śiva and sometimes by Devī too. Even some of the mortals become kings of the Vidyādharas. Naravāhanadatta, though a mortal, is appointed by Śiva as the emperor of the Vidyādharas. Sūryaprabha, a mere mortal, becomes the ruler of the southern division of the territory of the Vidyādharas.[249] The goddess gives Devadatta the rank of the king of the Vidyādharas.[250]

The pattern of the government of the Vidyādharas is considered to be similar to that in the great cities on the earth. They have their kings[251] and ministers. They live in their city[252] and keep a strong army.[253] They are fond of Dharma. In the world of the Vidyādharas there exists a court of the Vidyādharas to protect Dharma.[254]

The land of the Vidyādharas is different from the land of the Siddhas and the land of mortals. It is considered to be inaccessible to men.[255]

Many references in the text seem to show that the Vidyādharas live on hills and by their supernatural powers get divine attributes. The mount Himavat is described as haunted by them.[256] There are two divisions of their territory on the Himālayas, the northern and the southern. Both extend over many peaks of the range. The northern division is on the other side of Kailāsa but the southern is on this side of it.[257] To reach the last retreat of the empire of the Vidyādharas it is necessary to cross the mountain through an underground passage, that of Triśīrṣa.

Many kings of the Vidyādharas are described as ruling over some place in the Himālayas.[258] Many hills are associated with the Vidyādharas. For instance, Vidyutprabha is the lord of the hill of Kālañjara. Urdhvaroman dwells in the great mountain Vankaṭaka. Vikrośana is the king of the hill Dharṇīdhara. The home of the Vidyādhara Indramālin is the mountain Līlā. Kākaṇḍaka has his dwelling in the mountain Malaya. Darvāha is the lord of the hill Niketana, Dhūrtavayayana of the mountain Añjana, Varāhasvāmin of the mount Kumuda and Medhāvara of Ḍuṇḍhubhi. Kācharaka is the lord of the mountain Kuraṇḍa. Ḍiṇḍimālin's home is the hill of Pañchoka. Vibhāvasu is the king of the mountain Jayapura and Dhavala, the ruler of Bhūmituṇḍika.[259] Vidyādhara kings Chitrapada and others rule over mount Malaya.[260]

The Vidyādharas are closely associated with human beings. They are believed to participate in their prosperity and adversity. They are deeply involved in human affairs. Sometimes, their maidens fall in love with human beings. A Vidyādhara maiden is captivated by the beauty of Niśchayadatta.[261] A Vidyādharī named Bhadrā is attracted by the virtues of Vidūṣaka.[262]

Generally, the Vidyādhara maidens are not supposed to associate themselves with the mortals.[263] The Vidyādharas get annoyed when any Vidyādharī lives with a man. The Vidyādharī Yogeśvarī tells Bhadrā that the Vidyādharas are angry with her because she has decided to live with a man.[264]

The fall of Vidyādharas on this mortal world is attributed to the influence of some curse. A prince of the Vidyādharas named Vajravega is born in the world of mortals due to the curse of his father.[265] The Vidyādharī Aśokamālā is cursed by her father and is born as a woman.[266] The Vidyādhara king Kāñchanavega, by the curse of Gautama, is reduced to the condition of serpent.[267] A Vidyādhara becomes a mortal by the curse of a hermit.[268] A Vidyādhara maiden Māyāvatī becomes a female elephant on account of a curse.[269] Jīmūtavāhana who was a Vidyādhara becomes the son of a merchant due to the curse of Śiva.[270] The Vidyādhara Chitrāṅgada is born as a lion in consequence of a curse of Nārada.[271] Both Aśokadatta and Vijayadatta are the Vidyādharas fallen on the earth by the curse of sages.[272] The three Vidyādhara sisters are born on the world of mortals due to the curse of a hermit.[273] The Vidyādhara Padmasena with his two wives and brother is born on the earth due to the curse of his father Muktāsena.[274] Kanakarekhā is born on the earth due to the curse of a hermit.[275] Sthūlabhuja,[276] Anaṅgarati,[277] Hiraṇyākṣa,[278] and Hemaprabhā[279] originally belong to the Vidyādhara race but have now fallen to the earth due to curses. A Vidyādhara becomes a camel by the curse of the hermit Vijitāsu.[280] Muktāphalaketu and Saṁyataka are also born as men owing to a curse.[281]

There is a remarkable belief that attracted by the beauty of women, the Vidyādharas fell from their status. Many Vidyādharas are deprived of their positions as divine beings have been cursed for their weakness for women. Even a minor moral lapse can deprive a Vidyādhara of his position. In ancient times, most of the Vidyādhara emperors, puffed up with the attainment of their high rank, abandoned the right path, and fell from their position, blinded with passion.[282]

The Siddhas

They are supernatural beings enjoying great occult powers. They are mentioned along with gods and Vidyādharas[283] though, sometimes with Piśāchas also.[284] They can fly through the air.[285] They can change their forms. A pair of Siddhas has been described as roaming about the sky in the shape of a pair of swans.[286]

The Siddhas possess divine knowledge. They are called omniscient. They can predict the future. They applaud brave warriors. When Samarabhaṭa is killed by Bhīmabhaṭa, the Siddhas praise the victorious person.[287]

Their maidens, sometimes, perform penance. The daughter of the king of the Siddhas, named Devaprabhā, performs a very severe penance.[288]

Like the Vidyādharas, the Siddhas are also described as living on various mountains. The Ṛṣabha mountain,[289] Udayādri[290] and Malaya mountain are associated with them. There is a city called Kārkoṭaka on the shore of the eastern sea, and beyond that there is a sanctifying stream named Śītodā. Near Śītodā is a great mountain named Udaya, the land of the Siddhas. The Vidyādharas cannot invade this land of the Siddhas. The Vidyādharī Yogeśvarī asks Bhadrā to go to that place so that she may not be attacked by the Vidyādharas.[291]

The Enemies of Gods[292]

A belief in every type of demoniacal influence is an essential ingredient of the Hindu Faith. The idea of the existence of various gods creates in Hindu mind the concept of their powerful enemies whom they ultimately conquer. The Asuras are in general held as a 'a Suras', the ungodly.[293]

Asura is the common word used for both Daityas (descendants of Diti) and Dānavas (descendants of Danu). In the Kathāsaritsāgara, there is no clear difference among the concepts of the Asura, Daitya and Dānava. The three terms are used as synonyms in the text. Maya is called an Asura[294] as well as Dānavendra.[295] In the 'story of the king Chaṇḍamahāsena', all the three words are used for Aṅgāraka. Similarly, Trailokyamālin is called Daityarāja[296] or Daityendra,[297] Asureśvara,[298] Asurādhipa[299] or Asurapati[300] and Dānavādhipa.[301]

The Asuras are held as very huge in their appearance. The Asura Maya looks like a mountain in the night, for his hair gleam on his black lofty head like the potent herbs upon the mountain peaks and his crimson robe resembles the flowing streams of cinnabar.[302] The Daitya Aṅgāraka is depicted as of adamantine frame.[303]

Asuras are the opponents of gods. The Asura Yaṁdaṁṣṭra and others come to fight Indra. Two terrible Dānavas named Ghaṇṭa and Nighaṇṭa come to impede Prajāpati in his task of creation.[304] Asuras obstruct sacrifices[305] and, thus, debar gods from their share of offerings.

Daityas get angry with another Daitya who helps gods. When the Daitya Maya builds the palace for Indra, the other Daityas are annoyed with him, thinking that he has become a partisan of gods.[306]

The Daityas, Dānavas and Ādityas are regarded as the sons of the sage Kaśyapa by his wives Diti, Danu and Aditi respectively. There is no enmity among them in the beginning. The 'story of the generous Dānava Namuchi' reveals that the excellent Dānava Namuchi is devoted to charity and is very brave, and does not refuse anything to anybody – even to his enemy. He practises asceticism as a drinker of smoke for ten thousand years, and obtains a favour from Brahmā that he should be made unvulnerable against iron, stone and wood. Then he frequently conquers Indra and makes him flee. So the sage Kaśyapa entreates him and causes him to make peace with the gods. Then the Devas and Asuras, as their enmity is at an end, they deliberate together, and go to the ocean of milk and churn it, with the mountain Mandara. Many things come out of the sea in consequence of its churning. Viṣṇu and the other gods receive Lakṣmī and other things as their shares. Namuchi gains the horse Uchchaiḥśravas. The other gods and Asuras receive other various shares appointed by Brahmā. Amṛta comes up at the end of the churning, and the gods steal it. So a quarrel again takes place between them and the Asuras.[307]

The Asuras are generally held as less powerful than the gods. It is maintained that the Asuras are slain in battle by the Suras but not Suras by Asuras.[308] The Asuras who transgress law fall a prey to the discus of

Viṣṇu.[309] There is a curious belief that the Asuras, who were slain by Śiva and Viṣṇu were born on the earth in the form of Mlechchhas.[310]

Some of the Dānavas are described as even more powerful than the gods. The Dānava named Prabala conquers Indra a hundred times.[311] The two terrible Dānavas named Ghaṇṭa and Nigaṇṭa are invincible even by gods.[312]

Though Asuras, Daityas and Dānavas are generally held as the enemies of gods, some of them are depicted as their worshippers also. The Daitya Aṅgāraka is a devotee of Śiva.[313] On the fourteenth day of a month the Daitya ladies worship Śiva in the form of Hāṭakeśvara in a holy bathing-place called Pāparipu.[314] A Daitya maiden worships Pārvatī.[315] The king of the Daityas named Vidyutprabha performs penance for hundred years, along with his wife, in order to please Brahmā.[316]

The Asuras possess many supernatural powers. They can fly through the air, sink into the sea and go to the Pātāla.[317] Somaprabhā, the daughter of the Asura Maya, travels invisible through the air.[318]

The Asuras are known for their Māyā. The Asura Maya is called the chief of the Yogins.[319] The Asura Vidyuddhvaja resorts to Māyā and ascends the sky with his whole army.[320] The Asura maiden Somaprabhā makes a heavenly garden by her magic power. [321]

Asuras possess many articles of magic. The Asura Maya and his two sons possess three articles of magic viz., the vessel, the stick and the shoes.[322] The inexhaustible magical vessel supplies whatever is required.[323] Whatever is written with the stick comes out to be true.[324] By putting on the shoes, one gains the power of flying through the air.[325] Asura maiden Somaprabhā possesses a divine fruit capable of making one free from old age.[326] An Asura maiden gives to a Brāhmaṇa a sword which confers the power of flying in the air.[327]

It is believed that the Asuras can assume any from at their will but put off their unnatural form while sleeping. The Daitya Aṅgāraka who assumes the form of a boar sleeps only in his original form.[328]

Asuras are considered as very brave. The two Asuras named Sunda and Upasunda are hard to overcome because they surpass the three worlds in valour.[329]

Generally speaking, the Asuras are of destructive nature. They destroy holy places, temples and hermitages.[330] But some of them are very religious. A Dānava named Namuchi is very generous. Austerities of the Daitya Vidyuddhvaja represent a severe way of asceticism. Asura maidens perform penance. The Asura maiden Svayamprabhā is engaged in severe vow of mortification.[331]

Asuras love beautiful ladies. The Asura Andhaka hopes to win the love of Pārvatī.[332] Brahmā employs the artifice of sending the Daitya Atāpin to Nandana asking him to go there and witness a very curious sight. When he goes there he sees only the foot a woman, which is of wonderful beauty, and so he dies of an insane desire to see the rest of her body.[333]

Sometimes, the Daityas carry off beautiful ladies and entrust them with various tasks. The Daitya king Aṅgāraka carries off hundred princesses from the places of kings and appoints them as attendants to his daughter Aṅgāravatī.[334]

It is believed that Asuras, generally, do not want to give their daughters to human beings in marriage.[335] But, sometimes, they do so under divine influence. For instance, the goddess Chaṇḍikā blesses the king Mahāsena with the daughter of the Asura Aṅgāraka[336] and the king later marries her.[337]

Asuras are mostly held as the inhabitants of Pātāla. The Asura Aṅgāraka lives in Pātāla.[338] Śrīdatta beholds the Asura maiden Vidyutprabhā and other maidens there.[339] But, some of the Asuras prefer to live outside it. The Asura Maya lives on the Vindhya mountain.[340]

Their dwelling place Pātāla is described as a place of great beauty with magnificent castles and abundance of every kind of wealth. The seven Rasātalas of the Dānavas have splendid palaces adorned with various types of jewels. Their palaces are rendered delightful by gardens that gratify every wish, and have in them lakes of heavenly wine, with many ladders of precious stones.[341] The palace of the Asura Maya possesses curiously jewelled terraces.[342] The garden of the city of the Asuras has tanks studded with golden lotuses. It has trees bearing fruits as sweet as nectar. It is full of birds of golden variegated plumage and seems to have pillars of bright gems. It gives the illusion of a wall where there is no wall and of an unobstructed space where there is actually a wall. Where there is water, it presents the appearance of dry land and where there is dry land, it bears the semblance of water.[343]

The Lower Mythology

At all times in India there has been under the higher mythology of gods and great demons a lower mythology of spiritualised matter.[344] Almost all the branches of sciences – zoology, botany, mineralogy and geography –as they existed then in Ancient India, were employed into the service of religious superstition. In the Kathāsaritsāgara also, some animals, trees, rivers and oceans are thought to be permeated by divinity. The belief appears to rest on the conception of the unity of life in nature.

Animal Divinities

Animals are divinities partly by birth, partly because they are forms of demoniac or divine powers, and partly because they are the life givers of any community.[345]

Belief in the sanctity of the cow is a very prominent feature of the Hindu Faith.[346] Cow is the symbol of the animal world.[347] The divinity of the cow rests on the element in the totemism which consists in the deification of that class of animals which provides livelihood. The slaughter of cows was probably prohibited for the advancement of agriculture at a time when this was a toilsome occupation and men had to be compelled to take to it and leave off their ancient habit of killing cattle and feeding on their meat.[348] Cow was declared sacred at an early period. Had it not been so, this useful animal might have been exterminated in times of a famine. Thus, this religious belief had its origin in a wise foresight.[349]

According to the Kathāsaritsāgara, the cow is adorable in all the three worlds.[350] The wickedness of the act in the form of eating the flesh of a cow is inconceivable.[351] Nothing can atone for this sin. It is believed that one gets birth on the earth in a very low family on account of this sin. For instance, Bindumati is condemned to be born in the race of fishermen on account of a trivial, although an unconscious offence against the sacredness of the cow.[352]

Horses were the object of worship even among the early Aryans[353] owing to their great importance in the time of war. In the Kathāsaritsāgara, the excellent horses are said to be possessed of divinity.[354] They are worshipped. Udayana worships the horse who carries him to the Vindhya hills.[255]

Serpents are held as divinities[356] because they are emblematic of eternity.[357] In this worship, serpents, owing to their hurtfulness, are naturally regarded as having a demoniac nature which has to be propitiated.[358]

Serpents are held as sacred in the Kathāsaritsāgara. They are regularly worshipped. Naravāhanadatta worships snakes in a Nāgavana.[359]

Divine Tress, Groves, Rivers and Ocean

The age old belief in the divinity of trees is also found in the Kathāsaritsāgara. Trees are worshipped due to their divine character. Mṛgāṅkadatta bows down to the tree of Gaṇeśa.[360] The prince takes bath, worships it and walks around with his right hand towards it.[361] Somadatta sees big Aśvattha tree and declares that he is a faithful votary of the being who resides in it. He does Pradakṣiṇā of the tree, bows before it and makes an oblation to it.[362] Devadatta also daily worships a tree.[363]

Grimm in his Teutonic Mythology connects the description of wonder maidens sitting inside hallow trees or singing on the branches with tree worship. Such descriptions are also found in the Kathāsaritsāgara. For instance, Guhachandra hears a sweet music from Nyagrodha tree and sees a heavenly maiden.[364]

Climbing on the sacred trees is considered to be a sin. It is said that friends of Mṛgāṅkadatta find a sacred tree to Gaṇeśa and climb it to pluck fruits and are turned down into fruits themselves by the curse of the god.[365]

Rivers are invested with divinity because these are the source of fertility and purification. Worship of rivers is prevalent in the Kathāsaritsāgara. Vararuchi worships the goddess of the river Ganges.[366] Belief in the divinity of rivers is at the root of pilgrimage to these sacred rivers.[367]

The Kathāsaritsāgara refers to the worship of an ocean. Offerings are made to an ocean in order to please its divinity. For instance, the merchant Skandhadāsa worships the sea with jewels, when his ship is suddenly stopped.[368]

Thus, the Kathāsaritsāgara contains beliefs about a large divine family consisting of gods, goddesses, associates of gods, divine seers, divine races and enemies of gods. Even some animals, trees, groves, rivers and ocean are considered to be the visible manifestations of the divine spirit. The post-Vedic gods are assigned better position than the Vedic gods. There is no great change in the beliefs about the mythological characters of various gods and goddesses.

Footnotes Of Chapter III

1. Toy, C.W., Introduction to History of Religion, pp.3-4.

2. Cf. KSS.1.6.79,82,163; 1.7.97; 2.2.13-14; 3.4.315- 16; 4.2.67, 116, 189; 6.5.11; 6.7.213; 7.1.73,75; 7.4. 70; 8.2.381; 8.3.218; 8.6.242-43; 9.3.165; 10.3.11; 12. 2.80; 12.13.45; 15.2.73; 16.1.45; 17.2.5,117.

3. अमोधो देवतानां च प्रसादः किं न साधयेत् ॥

KSS. 12.2.76.

4. इत्थं सुदुष्करमपि स्वरसेन कार्यम् ।
सिद्धयत्यनुग्रहवतीष्विह देवतासु ॥

KSS. 12.2.184.

5. Cf. KSS. 1.1.59; 1.7.113; 2.6.26; 4.2.57,59; 6.1.70; 6.8.35,77; 7.7.23; 9.5.177-78; 12.6.43; 12.22.85; 17. 1.135.

6. Cf. KSS. 1.1.59,63; 1.7.113; 2.1.26-29; 2.2.42; 4.2. 57-59; 6.1.71; 6.8.35,77-78; 12.6.43,426; 17.1.135-36.

7. Cf. KSS. 2.3.14-15; 3.4.162; 6.8.242; 7.4.68-69; 9. 2.162; 9.3.150; 9.4.216; 9.6.34,36; 12.2.85-86; 12.11. 71,74,101; 12.21.45-46; 12.23.75-76.

8. Cf. KSS. 2.2.214; 4.3.74,92; 6.8.110-11,117-18,258; 9.6.278; 12.13.190; 18.1.48.

9. Cf. KSS. 4.2.225; 9.6.163; 12.27.121-22.

10. Cf. KSS. 8.3.77; 8.5.61; 14.4.113; 17.3.11; 17.5. 89.

11. एकान्तसुखिनो देवा मनुष्या नित्यदुःखिताः ।

KSS. 1.1.47.

12. त्रिदशास्त्वमराः । KSS. 9.6.262.

13. अचिन्त्यगतयश्च सुराः । KSS. 6.6.191.

14. KSS. 3.3.14.

15. KSS. 7.3.1.

16. KSS. 3.3.18.

17. KSS. 2.1.13.

18. KSS. 17.5.9.

19. KSS. 6.4.43; 17.5.17-18.

20. KSS. 2.1.19.

21. अहल्याकामुकः । KSS. 6.1.70.

22. KSS. 3.6.91.

23. KSS. 7.6.15.

24. KSS. 8.2.89.

25. KSS. 6.1.58.

26. KSS. 3.6.93.

27. KSS. 8.2.391.

28. KSS. 2.1.16.

29. KSS. 3.6.89.

30. KSS. 3.6.68.

31. KSS. 8.7.54.

32. KSS. 8.1.37.

33. KSS. 3.3.139.

34. KSS. 6.1.62.

35. KSS. 3.6.93
Cf. Ṛg Veda, i.32; Mahābhārata, iii.100; xii. 281 ff.

36. KSS. 2.3.42.

37. KSS. 17.2.60.

38. KSS. 8.7.119.

39. KSS. 8.2.224.

40. KSS. 2.1.13; 3.3.18.

41. KSS. 8.5.2.

42. KSS. 2.6.13; 12.1.22; 13.1.206; 12.27.11.
Cf. Ṛg Veda, IV. 54.5; Maitrāyaṇī Saṁhitā, 1,10,13; Vājasaneyī Saṁhitā, 1,1,74.

43. KSS. 1.6.67.

44. KSS. 2.3.31; 12.2.36; 17.2.73; 18.1.11.

45. KSS. 18.2.128-29.

46. KSS. 18.2.235.

47. KSS. 17.3.87.

48. KSS. 2.1.13.

49. KSS. 12.19.5.

50. KSS. 1.4.3; 2.3.75.

"The festival occurred after the rains had ceased and when New year's eve was celebrated." Macdonell,A.A., Epic Mythology, p.126.

51. हव्यकव्यभुक् । KSS. 3.4.135.

52. KSS. 8.7.34.

53. KSS. 1.7.44.

54. अग्निर्वरदः KSS. 7.1.75.

55. KSS. 6.1.164.

56. KSS. 3.4.313; 7.1,69-70.

57. पाशहस्त KSS. 8.2.93.

58. KSS. 12.5.353-57.

59. The origin of the concept of Kāma (Kāmadeva) can be traced to the Vedic mythology. The Atharva Veda invokes him as the personification of desire (IX.2) and conceives him as the god of sexual love (III.25).

60. Goldstücker,Theodore, Sanskrit and Culture, p.59.

61. सुरासुरदुरुल्लङ्घ्यमन्मथाज्ञा ।
KSS. 6.2.80.

62. KSS. 3.1.2; 6.1.2.

63. जितं स्मर शरैर्येषु पौष्पेष्वपि पतत्स्विह ।
वज्रादीन्यपि जायन्ते कुण्ठितान्येव तद्भृताम् ॥
KSS. 12.1.3.

64. KSS. 3.6.70.

65. KSS. 3.6.63.

66. KSS. 3.6.62.

67. KSS. 3.6.71.

68. KSS. 6.8.40.

69. KSS. 2.6.29.

70. KSS. 3.6.60.

71. KSS. 5.3.279.

72. KSS. 6.2.58.

73. KSS. 3.1.2.

74. KSS. 3.1.2; 6.7.59.

75. KSS. 12.28.38.

76. KSS. 12.4.68.

77. नूनं विरूपैरधिकं हासनैः क्रीडति स्मरः ।

KSS. 3.6.119.

78. KSS. 3.4.27.

79. KSS. 3.6.62-66,70-71.

80. KSS. 3.6.382; 8.2.237; 12.31.41; 15.1.13.
Cf. Rāmāyaṇa, I,23,10 ff; Kālidāsa, Kumārasambhavam, Canto V.1.

81. KSS. 6.1.2; 16.1.37.

82. अत्र स्थिताः कामदेवं विवाहेऽर्चन्ति कन्यकाः ।

KSS. 13.1.128.

83. KSS. 11.1.16.

84. KSS. 1.4.35.

85. KSS. 1.4.49.

86. KSS. 1.6.108.

87. KSS. 12.18.6.

88. KSS. 1.6.108-9.

89. KSS. 6.9.6.

90. KSS. 9.4.58.

91. KSS. 12.24.25.

92. KSS. 1.4.35.

93. KSS. 2.2.87.

94. KSS. 12.22.6.

95. KSS. 2.6.31.

96. KSS. 1.2.19.

97. KSS. 6.8.79.

98. KSS. 1.2.22.

99. KSS. 1.6.97.

100. KSS. 2.2.76.

101. KSS. 6.8.258.

102. KSS. 8.7.31.

103. KSS. 1.1.7.

104. KSS. 8.7.37.

105. KSS. 9.6.260.

106. KSS. 8.7.32.

The Vedic list enumerates them as Fire, Earth, Wind, Air, Sun, Sky, Moon and Stars and the Pauranic list as - Fire, Earth, Wind, Day or Water or Sāvitr̥, Dawn-Light, Glory (Brightness), Moon and Pole-star.

107. KSS. 8.4.45.

108. The Lokapālas or the guardian deities of the eight directions are Indra (East), Agni (South East), Yama (South), Sūrya (South West), Varuṇa (West), Vāyu (North West), Kuvera (North) and Soma (North West). Sometimes, Nirti is substituted for Sūrya and Pr̥thivī or Śiva especially in his form Īśāna for Soma.

109. KSS. 3.2.118.

110. KSS. 1.7.61.

111. KSS. 7.1.23; 8.7.23.

112. Vide pp. 23-25 supra.

113. Vide pp.51-52 supra.

114. Vide pp. 53-57 supra.

115. कवीन्द्रमानसाम्भोजनिवासभ्रमरी।

KSS. 13.1.13.

116. सहृदयानन्दशब्दमूर्तिसरस्वती।

KSS. 13.1.13.

117. निःशेषपदार्थोद्योतदीपिका।

KSS. 1.13.3.

118. शुक्लाम्बरधरा

KSS. 1.3.9.

119. KSS. 9.1.205.

120. KSS. 1.1.3; 13.1.3.

121. KSS. 2.4.62.

122. KSS. 10.10.30.

123. KSS. 14.1.30.

124. KSS. 12.7.31,132.

125. KSS. 9.3.132.

126. KSS. 8.7.36.

127. KSS. 8.4.47.

128. KSS. 2.4.183-84.

129. KSS. 17.2.72.

130. KSS. 17.2.128.

131. KSS. 1.5.124; 17.1.23.

132. KSS. 6.7.163.

133. "He belongs in fact entirely to the post epic period." Hopkins,E.W., Epic Mythology, p.113.

134. KSS. 18.2.198.

135. कायस्थो हि करोत्येको व्यापारं ब्रह्मरुद्रयोः ।
KSS. 12.5.323.

136. तद्यो लिखति जन्तूनामेकः सुकृतदुष्कृते ।
KSS. 12.5.322.

137. KSS. 12.5.353-55.

138. KSS. 12.5.322,325.

139. Dowson, John,, A Classical Dictionary of Hindu Mythology and Religion, p.363.

140. KSS. 3.1.136.

141. "The inclusion of the Ṛṣis among the deities is a late development of orthodox Brāhmaṇism." Mackenzie, Donald A., Indian Myth and Legend, p.102.

142. KSS. 3.3.8-9.

143. KSS. 3.1.127. ff.

144. KSS. 18.2.131.

145. KSS. 4.1.18; 8.2.12.

146. KSS. 3.2.52.

147. भंगिसूचनविधौ विशारदो नारदः ।
KSS. 3.1.148.

148. KSS. 8.2.395.

149. The appearance of the Gandharvas is quite obscure. The following views of scholars about it may be noted –

They are purely mythical beings. Barth,A., The Religions of India, p.28.

They are of half bird like half horse-like appearance. Hopkins,E.W., Epic Mythology, p.153.

They are half-man half bird. Thomas, P., Epics, Myths and Legends of India, p.69.

150. Cf. Amarakoṣa 1/1/11.

151. KSS. 17.2.82.

152. KSS. 7.2.13.

153. KSS. 17.2.125.

154. The Atharva Veda describes them as the dwellers of waters (2,2,3; 4.37,12)

Cf. "The Gandharvas do not live in heaven but inhabit the valley of the mythical mountains."

Thomas, P., Epics, Myths and Legends of India, p.69.

155. KSS. 7.2.131.

156. KSS. 4.2.4.

157. KSS. 17.4.13-18.

158. KSS. 4.3.79; 6.1.69; 18.2.110.

159. KSS. 18.2.130. Cf. Śatapatha Brāhmaṇa, 11, 6.1.

160. KSS. 3.3.19-20.

161. KSS. 3.3.20.

162. KSS. 17.3.36.

163. KSS. 6.1.68.

164. KSS. 3.3.5.

165. KSS. 6.6.104.

166. KSS. 6.2.19.

167. KSS. 6.2.61.

168. KSS. 6.2.59.

169. The Ṛg Veda (X.95) refers to the name of the Apsaras Urvaśī who falls in love with the earthly King Purūravas.

170. The nymph Rambhā falls in love with the human king Suṣeṇa. KSS. 6.2.68.

171. KSS. 6.1.71.

172. KSS. 6.2.95, 103; 6.4.7; 6.8.35, 52,120,139.

173. KSS. 2.1.26-29.

174. KSS. 6.8.33-34.

175. "Kinnaras are the mythical beings with the form of a man and the head of a horse."

Dowson, John., A Classical Dictionary of Hindu Mythology and Religion, p.158.

"In shape, they are akin to the Gandharvas." Thomas, P., Epics, Myths and Legends of India, p.69.

176. KSS. 9.4.56.

177. KSS. 9.2.9.

178. KSS. 8.7.100.

179. KSS. 3.6.87.

180. KSS. 12.28.86.

181. KSS. 1.7.76.

182. KSS. 5.1.8.

183. KSS. 1.7.105.

184. KSS. 1.1.63.

185. KSS. 8.7.178.

186. KSS. 8.2.42.

187. KSS. 2.4.168-70.

188. KSS. 17.1.19.

189. KSS. 3.6.175.

190. KSS. 1.8.31.

191. KSS. 1.1.63.

192. KSS. 17.1.135-36.

193. KSS. 1.2.8.

194. KSS. 1.6.97.

195. KSS. 1.2.18-19.

196.KSS. 1.2.18-19.

197. KSS. 10.1.27.

198. KSS. 12.6.434.

199. KSS. 12.6.434.

200. KSS. 1.1.59.

201. KSS. 2.2.42.

202. KSS. 6.8.77-78.

203. KSS. 12.6.426.

204. "They are guardians of hidden treasure like the dwarfs and giants of Teutonic legends."

Mackenzie, Donald, A., Indian Myth and Legends, p.68.

205. KSS. 6.8.68.
206. KSS. 3.4.41-42.
207. KSS. 3.6.45.
208. KSS. 8.3.199.
209. अस्मद्देशे पुरस्यान्तर्मणिभद्र इति श्रुतः ।
पूर्वैः कृतप्रतिष्ठोऽस्ति महायक्षः प्रभावितः ।
तस्योपयाचितान्येत्य तत्रत्याः कुर्वते जनाः ।
तत्तद्वाञ्छितसंसिद्धिहेतोस्तैस्तैरुपायनैः ॥
KSS.2.5.165-66.
210. Keith, A.B., A History of Sanskrit Literature, p.270.
211. KSS. 6.7.195-96.
212. KSS. 4.2.144.
213. KSS. 4.2.56.
214. KSS. 7.3.30.
215. KSS. 14.2.83.
216. KSS. 14.1.78.
217. KSS. 6.7.188.
218. KSS. 6.7.170.
219. KSS. 14.1.42-43.
220. KSS. 14.1.88.
221. KSS. 12.2.96.
222. KSS. 6.7.178.
223. KSS. 14.1.62.
224. KSS. 7.1.146.
225. KSS. 9.1.51.
226. KSS. 15.1.145.
227. KSS. 9.1.220-21.
228. मायी विद्याधरजनः ।
KSS. 14.3.37.
229. KSS. 3.4.212,239-40.
230. KSS. 3.4.227.
231. KSS. 5.1.16.
232. KSS. 5.3.243.
233. KSS. 5.3.268.
234. KSS. 5.1.9.
235. KSS. 6.7.211.
236. KSS. 5.1.9.

237. Cf. Mahābhārata, 4,9,15.
238. KSS. 8.1.6-8.
239. KSS. 6.4.10-11.
240. KSS. 5.3.65-66.
241. KSS. 12.19.132.
242. KSS.14.2.73.
243. KSS. 8.3.55.
244. KSS. 5.3.285.
245. KSS. 9.2.11.
246. KSS. 5.3.44.
247. KSS. 7.1.151-52.
248. KSS. 17.4.80,82-83,85-88.
249. KSS. 5.1.5, 6.4.67, 8.1.9-13.
250. KSS. 5.3.253.
251. KSS. 6.4.2.
252. KSS. 17.3.90.
253. KSS. 7.1.141.
254. KSS. 14.2.156-57.
255. KSS. 5.3.49.
256. KSS. 1.1.13; 4.2.17; 7.1.20; 15.2.18.
257. KSS. 14.3.65-66; 15.1.61.
258. Cf. KSS. 7.8.198; 8.1.5-6; 9.1.15; 9.2.69; 9.2.169-70; .0.3.9; 10.3.86; 10.9.57-58, 72, 221.
259. KSS. 8.5.42, 49-55, 63-64.
260. KSS. 8.5.97.
261. KSS. 7.3.14.
262. KSS. 3.4.216-17.
263. KSS. 6.4.5.
264. KSS. 3.4.232-33.
265. KSS. 10.9.68.
266. KSS. 9.2.62.
267. KSS. 10.5.319.
268. KSS. 10.9.232.
269. KSS. 2.5.35.
270. KSS. 4.2.57-59.
271. KSS. 4.2.136-42.
272. KSS. 5.2.282-86.

273. KSS. 5.3.58,60.
274. KSS. 7.8.211.
275. KSS. 5.3.105,169.
276. KSS. 9.2.85.
277. KSS. 9.2.144.
278. KSS. 10.9.232.
279. KSS. 10.10.138.
280. KSS. 12.2.108.
281. KSS. 17.1.142.
282. KSS. 16.3.13.
283. KSS. 9.4.26.
284. KSS. 1.8.4,6.
285. KSS. 3.6.179; 12.5.278.
286. KSS. 12.5.186.
287. KSS. 12.7.296.
288. KSS. 17.4.177.
289. KSS. 15.2.58.
290. KSS. 3.4.348.
291. KSS. 3.4.233-35.

292. Only the aerial demons viz. the Asuras, Daityas and Dānavas, being the enemies of gods, are included in the divine-family.

Cf. असुरदैत्यदैतेयदनुजेन्द्रारिदानवाः ।
शुक्रशिष्या दितिसुताः पूर्वदेवाः सुरद्विषः ॥

Amarakoṣa 1/1/1/.

Cf. also - "Asuras are demons of the first order in perpetual hostility with the gods and must not be confounded with the Rākṣasas or imps who animate dead bodies and disturb sacrificies." Monier-Williams, M., A Sanskrit English Dictionary, p.121.

293. Hopkins, E.W., Epic Mythology, p.46. Belief in the existence of the enemies of gods can be traced to the Vedic period. The tenth book of the Ṛg Veda represents Asuras as the class of celestial demons who are the serial foes of the gods. The Indra-Vṛtra myth of the Vedas is also interpreted as representing the hostility of Devas and Asuras.

294. KSS. 8.2.3.
295. KSS. 8.2.5
296. KSS. 17.5.70.
297. KSS. 17.5.80.

298. KSS. 17.5.72.

299. KSS. 17.5.167.

300. KSS. 17.5.196.

301. KSS. 17.5.73.

302. KSS. 8.2.4.

303. KSS. 2.3.54.

304. KSS. 18.2.229.

305. KSS. 17.5.50.

306. KSS. 6.3.13.

307. KSS. 8.3.216 ff.

308. निहता हि सुरैः संख्येष्वसुरा नासुरैः सुराः ।

KSS. 8.2.147.

309. KSS. 8.2.374.

310. KSS. 18.1.19. Enmity of Aryans with the non-Aryans is at the root of such beliefs.

311. KSS. 8.3.237.

312. KSS. 18.2.229.

313. KSS. 12.2.53.

314. KSS. 17.5.154-56.

315. KSS. 12.14.80.

316. KSS. 17.2.3-4.

317. KSS. 17.5.14-15, 53.

318. KSS. 6.2.100; 6.4.144.

319. KSS. 8.2.20.

320. KSS. 17.3.73-74.

321. KSS. 6.8.142.

322. KSS. 1.3.47.

323. KSS. 1.3.50.

324. KSS.1.3.50.

325. KSS. 1.3.49.

326. KSS. 6.3.55.

327. KSS. 9.6.219.

328. KSS. 2.3.53-56.

329. KSS. 3.1.135.

330. KSS. 17.5.14-15; 18.2.229.

331. KSS. 6.3.52-53.

332. KSS. 17.1.77-78, 80.

333. KSS. 14.2.64-65.

334. KSS. 2.3.54.

335. KSS. 17.6.5.

336. KSS. 2.3.39-40.

337. KSS. 2.3.74.

338. KSS. 16.2.34.

339. KSS. 2.2.53.

340. KSS. 6.3.51.

341. KSS. 17.5.105-6. Cf. also - 12.19.92,101; 8.2.129, 131,135-36, 152.

342. KSS. 8.2.339.

343. KSS. 6.3.58-60.

344. Hopkins, E.W., Epic Mythology, p.3.

345. Hopkins, E.W., Epic Mythology, p.12.

346. The cow is considered to be sacred from the Vedic times (vide Ṛg Veda, 8.90.15-16; Vājasaneyī Saṁhitā, 4.19,20; Atharva Veda,12,4.5). Her sacredness becomes established by the time of Epics (vide Mahābhārata,5,36,66;13,66,43 – पशुत्वाद्धिनिर्मुक्ता गावः) Purāṇas (Padma Purāṇa,V.XIV. 122-90 and Smṛtis (Āpastamba, i,30,20,22; i.31; 6-12; Gautama, ix.12, 23-24; Manu, IV.39; Yājñavalkya, i.133).

347. Radhakrishnan, S., The Heart of Hinduism, p.19.

348. Thomas, P., Epics, Myths and Legends of India, p.128.

349. Monier-Williams, M., Hinduism, p.32.

350. वन्द्यास्त्रिजगतोऽप्येता याः घेनवः।

KSS. 5.3.159.

351. KSS. 5.3.160,171.

Cf. Āpastamba Dharma Sūtra, i.26, 1; Gautama Dharma Sūtra,xxii.18; Manu Smṛti, xi.108; Yājñavalkya Smṛti, iii.263.

352. KSS. 5.3.161.

353. Cf. Ṛg Veda, IV. 33.

354. दैवतं हि हयोत्तमः।

KSS. 3.4.100.

355. KSS. 3.4.98-100.

356. From remote antiquity, the sacred character has been ascribed to the serpents. Mohenjodaro seals (Marshall, Mohenjodaro and Indus Civilization Plate cxvi, cxviii) show human devotees with hooded snakes behind them. For the divine character of serpents cf. –

नमोऽस्तु सर्वेभ्यो ये के च पृथिवीमनु ।
ये अन्तरिक्षे ये दिवि तेभ्यः सर्पेभ्यो नमः ॥
या इषवो यातुधानानां ये वा वनस्पतीरनु ।
ये वाऽवटेषु शेरते तेभ्यः सर्पेभ्यो नमः ॥
ये वामी रोचने दिवो ये वा सूर्यस्य रश्मिषु ।
येषामप्यसु सदस्कृतं तेभ्यः सर्पेभ्यो नमः ॥

Yajurveda Saṁhitā, XIII.6-8.

Vide also - Atharva Veda, VIII.8.16; 10,19; IX.2,22; X.4; Taittiriya Saṁhitā, i.5.4,1; Chhāndogya Upaniṣad, ii.21,1; vii,2,2; Āśvalayana Gṛhya Sūtra, ii,1,9-14; iv.8, 27,28; Prāśara Gṛhya Sūtra, Kaṇḍa II, Kaṇḍikā ,14.

W.Crook has shown that even now Nāga-worship exists in Kaśmīra, Punjab, Uttara Pradeśa, Madhya Bhārata, Bengal, Assam and in almost every part of South India (Religion and Folklore of Northern India, pp.383-99).

357. Monier-Williams, M., Hinduism, p.169.

358. Macdonell, A.A., Vedic Mythology, p.153.

359. ततो नागवने तत्र नागानभ्यर्च्य स्वयम् ।

KSS. 6.8.188.

360. KSS. 12.35.2

361. KSS. 12.33.54.

362. KSS. 3.6.26-27.

363. KSS. 5.3.209.

364. KSS. 3.3.106-8.

365. KSS. 12.35.92-93.

366. KSS. 1.5.56.

367. For details vide pp. 119-122 infra.

368. KSS. 3.4.295; 12.34.178.

Offerings to sea are still common among tribes on the coast. For details vide Ocean, Vol.vii,p.146.

Chapter IV

RELIGIOUS PRACTICES

The ritual aspect of religion consists of worship when it assumes a specific form and is regulated by definite observances and ceremonies. The performance of religious practices psychologically satisfies the person possessing a religious bent of mind. The present chapter analyses the ritual aspect of the Hindu Faith.

Fire-Worship[1]

Fire-worship is the most ancient form of Hindu worship. Fire symbolizes the vital spark, the principle of life in the animate and the inanimate.[2] Because of the inherent importance of fire in all Hindu ceremonials and its utility in daily life, it is held in great veneration by all the classes of Hindus.

The Kathāsaritsāgara refers to the worship of fire.[3] Fire is generally pleased with circumambulation.[4] Belief in the fire worship gives rise to the idea of performing elaborate sacrifices.

Sacrifices[5] (Yajña and Homa)

Sacrifice springs from a deep rooted impulse of the religious nature. In its religious connotations, the sacrifice is an act manifesting affection and gratitude towards the gods through which the man expresses his gratefulness to them for the benefits which he has reaped and hopes to obtain others in the future – either in this life or after death.[6] The basic idea behind the performance of a sacrifice is the supposed actual nourishment of the gods by the offerings of human beings. The gods are pleased with offerings in a sacrifice so that they may give plenty in return. The idea of expiation is also attached to the performance of a sacrifice.

Faith in the efficacy of sacrifices is found in the Kathāsaritsāgara. It is held that the constitution of the universe will be broken up if there is no god and sacrificer.[7] The oblation offered in the fire by the Brāhmaṇas nourishes the dwellers in heaven. But, when the sacrifices are not performed, the world of gods is exhausted by the cutting of their share of the sacrifice.[8]

A pilgrimage is approved by the wise only for a man who cannot, according to the scriptures, attain happiness by performing the actions enjoined by the Vedas. But, it is of no avail to a person who can acquire merit by giving offerings to the gods, the manes, the fire and who can perform vows and Japa.[9]

A sacrifice is considered to be purifying and rewarding. A Brāhmaṇa offers sacrifice with Bilva fruits with the belief that when the god of fire is pleased, Bilva fruits of gold will emerge out of the fire's cavity.[10] There is a belief that the heavenly nymphs, who have been cast down by some curse, live as wives in the houses of righteous men as a reward for their performance of sacrifices and other religious acts.[11]

If a sacrifice is obstructed, it is believed that the sacrificer will certainly sink down to hell.[12]

Purity of mind is considered to be essential in offering oblations. If a person gives oblation to fire with impure motives, he will suffer as a consequence.[13]

Royal persons and common men believe in performing sacrifices. Royal families appoint domestic priests for this purpose. Vāsavadattā has a domestic priest Śāntikara. She appoints the two sons of Piṅgalikā as the domestic priests of her son Naravāhanadatta.[14]

Popularity of sacrifices is clearly pointed out in the Kathāsaritsāgara. Even Dakṣa Prajāpati is believed to have performed a sacrifice. Many

Brāhmaṇas are engaged in sacrifices. The Brāhmaṇas Yaśaskara,[15] Devaswāmin[16] and Padmanābha[17] offer many sacrifices. Yajñadatta collects wealth for the sake of sacrifice only.[18] Though a boy, Mahipāla is occupied in the rites of the sacred fire.[19] Piṅgalikā is called so, because from her childhood her eyes have been reddened by the smoke of the burnt offerings.[20] Kālanemi performs Homa.[21] Sūryaprabha also performs Homa with lotuses and ghee.[22] Vīravara daily nourishes the fire with clarified butter.[23]

Many sacrifices are referred to in the Kathāsaritsāgara. Pious men of the hermitage of Kaśyapa offer Agnihotra oblations.[24] Aśvamedha is one of the most ancient and important sacrifices.[25] In the Kathāsaritsāgara, there is a reference to Aśvamedha sacrifice in connection with Janamejaya.[26] Lava is caught by Lakṣmaṇa for a human sacrifice (Naramedha or Puruṣamedha) which is to be performed by Rāma.[27] Putreṣthi sacrifice is performed for obtaining a son. It is said that a certain king who has no sons, begets a son named Jantu by performing this sacrifice.[28] The King Ugrabhaṭa is blessed with sons on account of this sacrifice performed by the priest Yajñasvāmin.[29] Rudrayajña is already mentioned under Śaiva rituals.[30] Sarpasatra sacrifice is performed by Janamejaya.[31]

Temple Worship[32]

There is no country in the world where so many shrines dedicated to gods and goddesses under different forms, images, symbols, and names, meet the eye as in India.[33] Idols or images are the symbols invented to aid the memory and the imagination of a common man. An image may be regarded in two aspects : as a symbol merely bringing close to the sense the spiritual idea of divinity, and serving to stimulate the prayerful thought of the worshippers; or it may be venerated as the indwelling abode of the divinity in which he habitually resides or into which, by spells and blood-offerings, he may be compelled to enter.[34] Idolatory is the representation of the abstract by the concrete, of the remote by the proximate, and of the principal by the agent. The thinking Hindu does not forget the instrumental character of idol worship.[35]

In the Kathāsaritsāgara, there are frequent references to temples. The words Devakula,[36] Devāgāra,[37] Devagṛha,[38] Devatāgṛha,[39] Mandira,[40] Suramandira[41] and Surasadma[42] are used to denote a temple.[43] There are references to many temples in the cities of Vārāṇasī[44] and Lāṭa.[45] Flags flutter on these temples.[46]

Construction of a temple is considered to be a meritorious task. Kings and rich people get the temples built for their own glory. The King Āryavarman causes the construction of a beautiful temple all made of gold.[47] The King Indradatta gets a great temple built at the holy bathing place of Pāpaśodhana.[48] Temples are generally constructed near water, or gardens or outside cities.[49] It appears that such places for constructing temples are chosen with a definite purpose. Water is essential for taking bath before performing worship. Flowers of a garden are offered to a deity. The temples are built outside cities to provide a peaceful atmosphere for worship and asceticism.

Many characters of the Kathāsaritsāgara have faith in the temple-worship. Alaṅkāravatī goes to many temples along with her mother.[50]

It seems that some of the old temples have lost their sanctity. They have become meeting-places for lovers at night.[51]

Sacred Prostitution[52]

The term used for a sacred prostitute is Devadāsī which implies that such a woman dances before a deity and that she is a public prostitute. These lewd women, who make a public traffic of their charms, are consecrated in a special manner to the worship of the divinities.[53]

There are numerous theories which try to give the true explanation of the religious practice of sacred prostitution.[54]

The Kathāsaritsāgara provides us with some important data about the practice of Devadāsī. Some of the courtesans in the text serve as a temple dancers. Rūpaṇikā of Mathurā and Sundarī of Kāñchanapura are temple dancers. Rūpaṇikā is a prostitute and a temple dancer. She is a courtesan who goes to a temple to perform her duty at the time of worship. Her mother is a courtesan. Rūpaṇikā too is primarily a courtesan who makes money by her profession. Her dancing activity in a temple is only a side duty.[55] The account of Sundarī shows that the public does not hesitate to approach such sacred prostitutes. Īśvaravarman approaches Sundarī as soon as her dance is over in a temple.[56]

There is a practice that such temple dancers can be married and given the legal status of a wife. The 'story of Unmādinī' shows the belief that a Devādasī severs all connection with her past life. All her bonds are shattered and she can be taken as a wife. A commander-in-chief tells the King Devasena that he will repudiate Unmādinī in a temple, then his lord can take her because there is no sin in accepting a temple-woman.[57]

The 'story of Unmādinī' clearly shows that the practice of dedicating woman to a temple is not held in high esteem. The King tells his commander-in-chief that if he repudiates his wife Unmādinī to a temple, it will be an unrighteous act.[58]

The Other Religious Practices

Prayer,[59] Nāmasaṁkīrtana,[60] dance, instrumental performances,[61] kneeling on the ground,[62] circumambulation,[63] flower-offerings,[64] gift offerings,[65] animal and human offerings,[66] drinking wine[67] and observing fast[68] are popular modes of worship already referred to in the previous chapters. The other religious practices of the Hindus are mentioned below.

Deva-Jāgaraṇa

A number of people spend night in front of a temple in devout vigils before a 'Yātrā'[69] (festive procession).

Japa

The practice of Japa has its origin in the theory of the power of the word. It can be traced back to that remote period when the primitive man attributed good and evil power to the word.[70]

The Kathāsaritsāgara refers to the religious practice of Japa. There are ascetics who perform Japa for a long time in an inaudible voice.[71]

Japa is considered to be very rewarding. It is believed that the world of the gods called Śiva can be attained by performing Japa. It is said that a Brāhmaṇa gives the fruit of half of his Japa to the King Ikṣvāku. By means of this, the King obtains access to all the worlds, and the muttering Brāhmaṇa obtains the world of the gods called Śiva.[72]

Vows

Various vows are undertaken for the purity of one's mind and achievement of desires. The King Mahendrāditya observes various vows in order to obtain a son.[73] There is a reference to the vow Upoṣaṇa. The Brāhmaṇa Bhavaśarman undertakes this vow which consists in speaking of the truth, the observing of strict chastity, the circumambulating of the images of the gods (Pradakṣiṇā), eating only at the time when ascetics do, restraint of the mind, and patience.[74] It is believed that one will become god in heaven by undertaking this vow.[75]

Bali

Offering Bali is considered to be a religious act. Devadāsa and his wife take only that food which remains after offering to gods, manes and guests.[76]

Penance

Belief in the efficacy of undertaking penance is clearly expressed in the Kathāsaritsāgara. Good fortune[77] and happiness[78] are considered to be the result of penance. There is nothing that cannot be accomplished by performing penance.[79] Penance is capable of even upsetting the world.[80] It helps in the attainment of heaven.[81] It can even shatter the bonds of mundane existence[82] and bestow eternal bliss (Mokṣa).[83]

Many stories of the Kathāsaritsāgara contain belief in the power of asceticism. A young hermit sends the King Suṣeṇa to heaven by virtue of a part of his asceticism just as the Chāṇḍāla Triśaṅku was carried to heaven by Viśvāmitra.[84] The King Chirāyus attains eternal bliss by asceticism.[85] Niśchayadatta and Somasvāmin also, having performed many austerities, attain final beatitude.[86]

Purity of mind is considered to be essential in performing Tapa. It is believed that one's asceticism is exhausted by one's sins.[87] Moreover, if a person performs it with anger, he is hurled down from his rank.[88]

Austerities are undertaken with different purposes.[89] Tapodatta goes to perform asceticism for the acquisition of knowledge.[90] Virūpaśarman begins to practice severe penance through desire for beauty and wealth.[91] The hermit Viśvāmitra performs austerities in order to attain the position of the god of wealth.[92] Padmāvatī keeps performing penance in order to ensure the success of Muktāphalaketu.[93]

People go to forest,[94] ascetic groves[95] or some sacred place of pilgrimage[96] for undertaking penance.

There are various modes of practising penance. The kings Hemaprabha[97] and Parityāgasena[98] sit on the Darbha grass and observe fast. The king Mandāradeva restrains his senses, eats little and sleeps on the Darbha grass.[99] Naravāhanadatta sleeps on the ground, takes bath in early morning and eats fruits only.[100] A merchant's son also lives on roots and fruits.[101]

There is a more severe mode of practising penance. Devadatta first eats leaves, and afterwards feeds only on smoke.[102] The King Ajara, in his previous birth, hangs with his feet on a banyan tree and that way performs penance until he dries up his body.[103] The hermit Maṅkaṇaka also performs penance with his feet upwards.[104]

The study of the Kathāsaritsāgara reveals that women and Śūdras also have the right to perform penance. The Kings Parityāgasena,[105] Karpūraka,[106] Sāgaravarman[107] and Vīradeva[108] perform penance in the company of their wives. A Brāhmaṇa from the Deccan[109] and a merchant's son[110] also perform penance with their wives. Women by themselves also resort to penance. Padmāvatī[111] and the wife of the Brāhmaṇa Padmanābha[112] go to perform penance. The story of the two ascetics, one a Brāhmaṇa and the other a Chāṇḍāla shows that even the Chāṇḍālas have a right to perform penance.[113]

Pilgrimages (Tīrthayātrā)[114]

A Tīrtha is supposed to wash away ill luck and sin and bestow upon the bather beauty and fortune.[115] According to the Kathāsaritsāgara, Tīrthas impart an everlasting purity.[116] One's sins are washed away by going to these places. The Brāhmaṇa Harisvāmin decides to visit all the holy places to wash away all his sins.[117] Jīvadatta says that he will go to holy places to wash his sins.[118] Guṇaśarman tells Agnidatta that he will wander around holy places and wash off the stains of sin contracted ever since his birth.[119] The 'story of the gambler Ṭhiṇṭhākarāla' shows that the sins of the gambler are washed away by bathing in holy places.[120]

It is believed that visit to a holy place gives Sadgati to a person who has met with an accidental death. Kālanemi's brother is desirous of visiting places of pilgrimage for the Sadgati of his wife who has died of a snake-bite.[121]

Many other characters of the Kathāsaritsāgara viz; Devasena,[122] the Brāhmaṇaś Agniśarman[123] and Saṅgamadatta,[124] the King Chandraprabha[125] and Devadarśana[126] also believe in going on a pilgrimage.

Visit to sacred places is especially recommended in young age. It is said that one should visit the sacred places while one is young and strong. For, who knows what will take place hereafter because the body perishes in a moment.[127]

In the Kathāsaritsāgara, many cities, bathing places, shrines and other places are considered to be sacred. Vārāṇasī,[128] Ujjayinī,[129] Vilāsapura,[130] Dhāreśvara,[131] Kaśmīra[132] and Mathurā[133] are the sacred cities already referred to in the previous chapters. Some other cities are also considered to be sacred by pilgrims.

Gayā is a sacred place of pilgrimage.[134] The pilgrims offer Piṇḍa to their ancestors at Gayā. Gayā-śirah[135] is the interior part of Gayākṣetra. Gayākūpa in which Piṇḍas are offered to one's ancestors is in the south-west of Gayāśiraḥ. It is believed that the hand of a deceased person comes out from the Gayākūpa to receive a Piṇḍa.[136] Dharmāraṇya[137] is a sacred place in the east of Boddha Gayā.

Kanakhala in Haridwāra is a sanctifying place of pilgrimage.[138] It is held that here, at the point where the Ganges issues forth from the hills, the sacred stream was brought down from the mount Uśīnara by Kāñchanapāta, the elephant of the gods, after having broken the mountain.[139]

Prayāga is a sacred place where the confluence of the Ganges and Yamunā shines for the welfare of men.[140] Pilgrims visit this city. The king Chandraprabha along with Brāhmaṇas and priests, comes here.[141] The king Sāgaravarman also comes here with his wife Anaṅgaprabhā.[142]

Some bathing places are considered to be sacred. The Brāhmaṇa Chandrasvāmin comes to bathe in the holy tank of Anantahrada.[143] The holy waters of the lake Pampā in Karnāṭaka are sanctifying.[144] There is a reference to the holy bathing place of Pāpaśodhana where people come to bathe in the holy water.[145] Puṣkara is a celebrated tank about five miles from Ajmer.[146] It is a place of pilgrimage. Kāla goes to this holy bathing place.[147] There is a great purifying tank of clear waters called Śaṅkhahrada. People from all the countries come here for taking bath.[148] It is believed about the lake Ṭiṭibhasaras that a certain chaste woman named Ṭiṭibhi, being falsely accused by her husband, in her helplessness invoked the goddess Earth and the Lokapālas, and they produced this Saras in her justification.[149]

There are many holy shrines where pilgrims come from all over the country.[150] Kailāśa,[151] Badarikāśrama,[152] Siddhiśvara, Gokarṇa[153] and Ratnakūṭa[154] are the other sacred places of pilgrims.

Bathing in a holy water of a Tīrtha is considered to be sacred. Upakośā, anxious for Vararuchi's success, bathes every day in the Ganges.[155]

Fast, Japa and austerities are undertaken on the places of pilgrimage. The King Chandraprabha fasts for three nights at Vārāṇasī.[156] The Brāhmaṇa Kāla performs Japa day and night at Puṣkara.[157] The King Amaradatta performs penance at Vārāṇasī.[158] At Kanakhala, a certain Brāhmaṇa from the Deccan, performs austerities in the company of his wife.[159] The wife of the Brāhmaṇa Padmanābha goes to a Tīrtha to perform penance.[160] The bank of the Ganges is considered to be a suitable place for performing asceticism.[161] The king Vīradeva, alongwith his wife Padmāvati,[162] performs austerities on the bank of the Ganges. The King Sāgaravarman alongwith his wife Anaṅgaprabhā, undertakes austerities at Prayāga.[163]

Badarikāśrama is also resorted to for practising penance. Devadatta[164] and Sundarasena[165] go there with this purpose.

There are various shrines where people go for performing penance.[166]

Fasting at the sacred places of pilgrimage is rewarding. It is held that the water of Pañchatīrthi possesses the power of enabling those men who bathe in it and fast for five nights to become followers of Nārāyaṇa.[167]

Personal purity is essential for pilgrims. The 'story of the two ascetics, one a Brāhmaṇa, the other a Chāṇḍāla' shows the belief that one should observe fast, at a Tīrtha, only with a pure mind because according to the purity or impurity of a man's heart is without doubt the fruit which one receives. According to this story, two ascetics remain for same length of time fasting on the banks of the Ganges. The Brāhmaṇa, being overpowered with hunger, and seeing some Niṣādas come that way bringing fish and eating it, thus reflects in his mind 'Oh ! happy in the world are these fishermen for they eat to their fill the fresh meat of fish.' But the other, who is a Chāṇḍāla, thinks that moment he sees these fishermen, 'out on these destroyers of life and devourers of raw flesh. So why should I stand here and behold their faces.' Saying this to himself, he closes his eyes and remains buried in his own thoughts. Later on, both die of starvation. The Brāhmaṇa is eaten by dogs on the bank while the Chāṇḍāla is destroyed in the water of the Ganges. The Brāhmaṇa not having disciplined his spirit is born in the family of a fisherman. The Chāṇḍāla who possessed self-control, and whose mind was not marred by passion, is born as a King in a palace on that very bank of the Ganges.[168]

Religious Suicide[169]

The phenomenon of suicide has been observed through the ages in all cultures with different beliefs. In our country, a righteous man is not afraid of death and welcomes it at a Tīrtha for obtaining higher rewards in the next world.

Attainment of high position is expected in the next world by committing religious suicide. It is believed that if one consumes one's body with austerities at the bank of some holy water, one will never endure the misery of poverty in the next life.[170] The King Udayana says that he will abandon his perishable body at the mount Kāliñjara and will obtain the imperishable mansion.[171] His ministers and queen Vāsavadattā also think that by doing so, they will obtain a high position in the next world.[172]

Those who leave their bodies on a Tīrtha are attributed with the power of remembering their previous births. It is said that Lāvaṇyamañjarī remembers her previous birth because she abandoned her life in a holy bathing place.[173]

Various modes of committing religious suicide are mentioned in the Kathāsaritsāgara. Some people abandon their bodies by performing severe asceticism at a sacred place of pilgrimage while others drown themselves in the waters of some holy river. The King Sūryaprabha abandons his body in performance of severe asceticism at Vārāṇasī.[174] Sāgaravīra goes to the river Ganges, intending to leave his body by means of penance.[175] The King Udayatuṅga goes to the Ganges to lay down his body.[176] Śīladhara, seeing that his body is emaciated by long penance, flings himself into the Ganges.[177] The father of Vasudatta goes to the Ganges with his wife to leave his body.[178] Lohajaṅgha also sets out for some holy place of pilgrimage, in order to leave his life there.[179]

Badarikāśrama is also resorted to for committing religious suicide. Vararuchi goes to this place for committing suicide.[180]

Sometimes, Yoga is practised for committing suicide. Guṇāḍhya[181] and Vararuchi[182] leave their bodies through Yoga.

Entering fire is another way of committing suicide. A Brāhmaṇa, along with his two wives, enters fire.[183]

Some of the ascetics hang with their feet on a banyan-tree and this way perform asceticism until they dry up their bodies and abandon them. The King Ajara performs such asceticism in his previous birth.[184]

The practice of ending one's life by throwing oneself from a precipice is also mentioned in the Kathāsaritsāgara. Vasudatta flings himself from a hill-side with his wife and friend.[185] The King Udayana, his queens, Yaugandharāyaṇa and other ministers hurl themselves from a cliff.[186] The King Sahasrānīka, accompanied by his ministers and his wife, ascends the Himālaya to prepare for their last journey.[187]

Festivals

The people believe in celebrating various religious festivals. Besides, festivals in honour of Viṣṇu, Indra, Kāma and Gaurī,[188] the Kathāsaritsāgara refers to the festival called 'Udakadānotsava'. The people of Ujjayinī celebrate this festival of offering water every year. It is held that long ago when Chaṇḍamahāsena killed the Daitya Angāraka, just before he expired he said, 'If that man who has thus slain me when thirsty, does not every year offer water to my manes, his five ministers shall perish.'[189] Therefore, the King Chaṇḍamahāsena offers water every year to the manes of Angāraka and all the people of Ujjayinī celebrate the festival.

The ritual aspect of the Hindu Faith points at the performance of various religious practices belonging both to the Vedic and the non-Vedic traditions. Performance of sacrifices is, sometimes, considered to be more beneficial than going on a pilgrimage. Temple-worship is in vogue. Though the practice of Devadāsī is quite popular, it is not held in high esteem. Undertaking penance is considered to be an effective way of pleasing gods and getting desired objects from them. Importance of Tīrthas in washing one's sins is fully accepted. Religious significance is attached to committing suicide at sacred places of pilgrimage. Religious festivals are celebrated with full faith.

Footnotes Of Chapter IV

1. The worship of fire dates back to the Indo-Iranian period. Both the Iranians and Indians worship fire under the different names of Agni and Ātar. Fire is personified as the god 'Agni' as early as the Vedas.

Vide Macdonell, A.A., Vedic Mythology, pp.88-100.

2. Mackenzie, Donald. A., Indian Myth and Legend, p.19.

3. KSS. 3.4.317.

4. KSS. 3.2.81.

5. Belief in the performance of sacrifices goes back to remote antiquity. TheBrāhmaṇas of the Vedas contain information about the application of various hymns to particular sacrifices.

6. Barth, A., The Religions of India, p.36.

7. यष्टव्ययाजकाभावाद् भज्यंते च जगत्स्थितिः ॥

KSS. 7.7.18.

8. भूलोकाद्देवलोकश्च शश्वदाप्यायते प्रभो ।
ब्राह्मणेर्हुतमग्नौ हि हविस्तृप्त्यै दिवौकसाम् ॥
म्लेच्छाक्रान्ते च भूलोके निर्वषट्कारमङ्गले ।
यज्ञभागादिविच्छेदाद्देवलोकोऽवसीदति ॥

KSS. 18.1.21-22.

9. तीर्थयात्रा तवेष्टा वा तच्छस्ता तस्य सा बुधैः ।
सम्पत्तिर्विधिवन्न स्याद्वैदिके यस्य कर्मणि ॥
अन्यथा देवपित्रग्निक्रियाव्रतजपादिभिः ।
गृहे या पुण्यनिष्पत्तिः साध्वनि भ्रमतः कुतः ॥

KSS. 8.6.224-25.

10. KSS. 7.1.56,61-62.

11. एवं यागप्रदानादिसुकृतेः शुभकर्मणाम् ।
दिव्याः शापच्युता नार्यस्तिष्ठन्ति गृहिणीपदे ॥
KSS. 3.3.133.

12. KSS. 12.15.9.

13. KSS. 2.2.12.

14. KSS. 4.1.125,130.

15. KSS. 13.1.19.

16. KSS. 12.25.3.

17. KSS. 12.20.34.

18. यज्ञार्थभृतसंपदः ।
KSS. 4.1.109.

19. KSS. 9.6.40.

20. KSS. 4.1.122.

21. KSS. 2.2.10.

22. KSS. 8.3.90.

23. KSS. 12.11.19.

24. KSS. 16.1.98.

25. Cf. Ṛg. Veda, i,162-63; Śatapatha Brāhmaṇa, iii.1-5; XIII.; Taittirīya Brāhmaṇa, iii, 8-9.

26. KSS. 8.1.123.

27. KSS. 9.1.101.

28. KSS. 2.5.58.

29. KSS. 12.7.42-48.

30. Vide p.21 supra.

31. KSS.6.4.41

32. It is not certain when this temple or image-worship came into existence. Scholars hold different opinions about the beginning of this worship.

Cf. "Idols seem not to have been known in the age of the Vedas; at all events they first begin to be referred to in the later additions of the Brāhmaṇas and in the Sūtras".

Macdonell,A.A., Article in the Encyclopaedia of Religion and Ethics, Vol.12,p.610.

"The worship of idols in India is a secondary formation, a later degradation of the more primitive worship of ideal gods."

Max Muller, Chips from a German Workshop, i.38.

"The physical description given in the Veda of the gods, both great and small, is sometimes so precise, there are so many traits in it bordering on fetichism, and a very decided tendency to represent the deity by symbols, and, on the other hand, the human being, as soon as he conceives of his gods under a definite form, is so irresistibly tempted to realise that form in sensible objects, that it is difficult to believe that Vedic India did not worship images."

Barth, A., The Religions of India, p.60.

33. Monier Williams, M., Hinduism, p.165.

34. Farnell, Evolution of Religion, p.42 ff.

35. Radhakrishnan, S., The Heart of Hinduism, p.11.

36. KSS. 2.2.30.

37. KSS. 4.2.77.

38. KSS. 1.4.102.

39. KSS. 3.4.158.

40. KSS. 11.1.16.

41. KSS. 1.7.69.

42. KSS. 5.2.228.

43. For the temples of different divinities vide pp.19-20,24,26,50,54-55,78 supra.

44. KSS. 17.1.18.

45. KSS. 12.7.140.

46. सुरसद्मध्वजपटैर्मरुत्ता नमितोद्धतैः ।

KSS. 17.1.18.

For the description of various temples vide pp.19,20, 24,50,54-55 Supra.

47. KSS. 3.4.319.

48. KSS. 6.8.11.

49. For situation of temples vide pp. 20,26,55 Supra.

50. KSS. 9.1.44. For details of temple or image worship vide pp.20,28,54,55,78 Supra.

51. KSS. 6.4.76.

52. The origin of the sacred prostitution in India is wrapped in mystery. The term 'Rūpadāsī' mentioned in the Arthaśāstra of Kauṭilya is explained by scholars like Louis Renou (The

Civilization of Ancient India, p. 129) as 'Devadāsī'. Neither the religious nor the secular or legal literature before 600 A.D. clearly refers to the sacred prostitution. Kālidāsa (Meghadūta, 1.35) refers to dancers at the Mahākāla temple of Ujjain. R.C. Mazumdar (The Classical Age, p. 573) holds that Devadāsīs were maintained at the great temple of Mahākāla at Ujjayinī in Kālidāsa's time. The cult of 'Devadāsī' was widely prevalent by the time of the composition of the Kathāsaritsāgara (cf. Kalhaṇa, Rājataraṅgiṇī, IV.36-37; Kṣemendra, Deśopadeśa, III, IV; Narmamālā, II). For sacred prostitution in India and other countries vide Ocean, Vol.I, Appendix IV.

53. Vide - Dubois, J.A., Hindu Manners, Customs and Ceremonies, pp.585-87.

54. Vide - Ocean, Vol.I, Appendix IV, p.268 ff. Cf "The Vedic god Indra is depicted as being very fond of wine, women and dance. The system of Devadāsis probably originated from Indra worship" (Nadkarni, Vithal. C., Devadāsīs - Married to God and Mammon of India, The Illustrated Weekly of India, Vol. xcvi.50 Dec.14-20, 1975, p.11).

55. KSS. 2.4.78 ff.

56. KSS. 10.1.74-77.

57. त्यजामि तां देवकुले स्वीकरोतु ततः प्रभुः ।

KSS. 3.1.76.

Cf also - अथवा तां त्यजामीह देव देवकुले ततः ।
न दोषो ग्रहणे तस्यास्तव देवकुलस्त्रियः ॥

KSS. 12.24.37.

58. नाहं परस्त्रीमादास्ये त्वं वा त्यक्ष्यसि तां यदि ।
ततो नंक्ष्यति ते धर्मो दण्ड्यो मे च भविष्यसि ॥

KSS. 3.1.78.

59. Vide pp. 20,24,28,50,55,80 supra.

60. Vide p.20 supra.

61. Vide pp. 20,24,28,55 supra.

62. Vide p. 21 supra.

63. Vide pp. 20,56 supra. 64. Vide pp. 20,24 supra.

65. Vide p.50 supra. 66. Vide pp. 56-57.

67. Vide p.57 supra.

68. Vide pp. 21,25,?8,55 supra.

69. ततस्तत्रैव देवाग्रे दृष्ट्वा जागरणागतान्।
रात्रौ यात्रोत्सवे लोकान् – – – – – ॥

KSS. 2.4.177.

70. The Mahābhārata (XII.326.122 – नित्यं जप्यपराः) refers to the Pāṇḍavas engrossed in regular Japa. The Purāṇas (Cf. Nīlamata, V.1049, 1101, 1104) also lay emphasis on the efficacy of Japa.

71. KSS. 14.1.25. 72. KSS. 8.2.111.

73. KSS. 18.1.15.

74. सत्याभिभाषणं ब्रह्मचर्यं देवप्रदक्षिणम्।
भोजनं भिक्षुवेलायां मनसः संयमः क्षमा ॥

KSS. 10.7.83.

75. KSS. 10.7.77.

76. देवपित्रतिथिप्रत्ताशेषं प्रमितमश्नतोः।

KSS. 6.1.92.

77. तपोऽधीना हि सम्पदः।

KSS. 1.3.24.

78. तपोऽधीनानि हि श्रेयांसि।

KSS. 6.4.10.

79. न हि किंचित्तपसासाध्यमस्ति।

KSS. 17.4.174.

80. KSS. 17.2.20. 81. KSS. 12.5.259.

82. KSS. 9.2.313.

83. KSS. 7.3.242; 7.7.55.

84. KSS. 6.2.88, 90,92.

85. KSS. 7.7.55.

86. KSS. 7.3.242.

87. कामं तस्य रिपोः प्राप्तो दुष्कृतेस्तपसः क्षयः ॥
KSS. 17.2.96.

88. KSS. 12.7.31.

89. For austerities as means of pleasing gods and getting desired objects from them, vide pp.21,25,26,28,51,55 supra.

90. KSS. 7.6.14.

91. KSS. 7.6.27.

92. KSS. 2.2.76.

93. KSS. 17.3.57.

94. KSS. 10.9.14; 12.6.410.

95. KSS. 1.5.105; 7.6.27.

96. KSS. 12.20.52. Vide also - p.121.

97. KSS. 7.1.97.

98. KSS. 7.8.56.

99. KSS. 12.34.219.

100. KSS. 14.3.81.

101. KSS. 10.9.14.

102. KSS. 1.7.53.

103. KSS. 7.6.102.

104. KSS. 6.6.99.

105. KSS. 7.8.56.

106. KSS. 7.9.144.

107. KSS. 9.2.388.

108. KSS. 12.16.8.

109. KSS. 1.3.6.

110. KSS. 10.9.14.

111. KSS. 17.5.1.

112. KSS. 12.20.52.

113. KSS. 6.1.123.

114. Particular sanctity is attached to rivers and waters even in the Ṛg Veda (6.61; 7.95; 7.47; 10.9; 10.30). The religion of the Brāhmaṇas also regards Tīrthas as sacred. From the period of the

Mahābhārata, these pilgrimages occupy a prominent place in the religious life of our country.

115. Cf. Mahābhārata, 3,47,29; 82,43 ff.

116. नित्यशुद्धानि तीर्थानि ।

KSS. 12.19.21.

117. भ्रमामि तावत्तीर्थानि क्षपायाम्यघसंचयम् ।

KSS. 12.20.25.

118. पूर्वपापवशादेतद्दुःखमापतितं मम ।
तत्क्षालनाय यास्यामि तीर्थन्युज्झितमत्सरः ॥

KSS. 9.2.239.

119. तत्परिभ्रम्य तीर्थानि प्रक्षाल्याजन्मकिल्बिषम् ।

KSS. 8.6.218.

120. KSS. 18.2.194-96.

121. कालनेमेरथ भ्राता तीर्थार्थी सर्पभक्षिताम् ।
भार्यामुद्दिश्य विगतभयो देशान्तरं ययौ ॥

KSS. 2.2.16.

122. KSS. 18.4.20.

123. KSS. 6.7.53.

124. KSS. 9.6.207.

125. KSS. 12.26.73.

126. KSS. 12.6.70. Cf also 1.6.78; 9.2.243; 10.5.97.

127. यावच्च यौवनं राजंस्तावद्गम्यानि धीमता ।
अविश्वास्ये शरीरे हि सगंमस्तैः कुतोऽन्यदा ॥

KSS. 12.19.22.
Cf also 12.26.70-71.

128. Vide p.18 Supra.

129. Vide p.18 Supra.

130. Vide p.18 Supra.

131. Vide p.18 Supra.

132. Vide p.50 Supra. 133. Vide p.119 Supra.

134. KSS. 12.26.84. 135. KSS. 12.26.86.

136. KSS. 12.26.87-88. 137. KSS. 12.26.87.

138. तीर्थं कनखलं नाम गङ्गाद्वारेऽस्ति पावनम् ।

KSS. 1.3.4.

139. KSS. 1.3.5.

140. गङ्गायमुनयोर्वाहो यातः सुगतये नृणाम् ॥

KSS. 12.26.81.

141. KSS. 12.26.73-74,80. 142. KSS. 9.2.386.

143. KSS. 9.6.121. 144. KSS. 14.3.9.

145. KSS. 6.8.11-12.

146. Dowson, John, A Classical Dictionary of Hindu Mythology and Religion, p.250.

147. KSS. 8.2.83. 148. KSS. 13.1.86-87.

149. KSS. 9.1.78-79.

150. Vide p.17 Supra. 151. Vide p.118 Supra.

152. KSS.3.3.26. 153. Vide p.51 Supra.

154. Vide p.119 Supra. 155. KSS. 1.4.28.

156. KSS. 12.26.84. 157. KSS. 8.2.83.

158. KSS. 12.36.236-37. 159. KSS. 1.3.6.

160. KSS. 12.20.52.

161. KSS. 1.3.10; 6.1.123; 6.2.26; 9.2.295; 10.10.97.

162. KSS. 12.16.8 163. KSS. 9.2.386, 388.

164. KSS. 1.7.52.

165. KSS. 9.2.313.

166. Vide p.51 Supra.

167. KSS. 6.7.30.

168. KSS. 6.1.123-32.

169. Though suicide is condemned in the period of the Vedas, Brāhmaṇas and Smṛtis (vide Vājasaneyī Saṁhitā, 40.3; Śatapatha Brāhmaṇa, 10.2.6.7; Āpastamba Dharma Sūtra, i.28.17; Manu Smṛti, V.89; Yājñavalkya Smṛti, iii.154; Gautama Smṛti, 14.1; Vasiṣṭha Smṛti, 23.14-15), the religious practice of committing suicide was in voage in the Gupta period.

170. इदानीं च तनुं तीर्थे तपसा दाहयाम्यहम् ।
येन निधर्नतादुः खभागी न स्यामहं पुनः ॥

KSS. 12.29.22-23.

171. तस्मात्कालञ्जरगिरौ गत्वा देहमशाश्वतम् ।
त्यक्त्वेमं साधयाम्यत्र यथोक्तं शाश्वतं पदम् ॥

KSS. 16.1.70.

172. KSS. 16.1.72.

173. KSS. 12.2.164.

174. KSS. 12.26.61-62.

175. KSS. 9.2.342.

176. KSS. 12.5.89-90.

177. KSS. 12.7.34.

178. KSS. 4.2.155.

179. KSS.2.4.106.

180. KSS.1.5.132.

181. KSS. 1.8.34

182. KSS. 1.5.141.

183. KSS. 12.6.418.

184. KSS. 7.6.102.

185. KSS. 4.2.165.

186. KSS. 16.1.83.

187. KSS. 2.2.217; 6.4.59.

188. Vide p.18 Supra.

189. KSS. 16.2.25, 57-61.

Chapter V

SOME RELIGIOUS CONCEPTS AND ETHICAL VIRTUES

Belief in the following religious concepts is clearly traced in the Kathāsaritsāgara.

Afterworld

The belief about the abode of the dead, the world after death,[1] is common in the text. It is held that a dead person is led off by Death to the hall of Yama.[2] At one place it is mentioned that black men, with nooses in their hands, with flaming eyes, tall, with upstanding hair, terrible, darkening the whole horizon with their shadows, lead the dead person to the abode of Yama.[3] Yama listens from Chitragupta to the account of the good and bad deeds of the deceased person and announces the award accordingly.[4]

It is believed that a dead person will get the same thing to eat from the men with maces in the afterworld which he has given in charity in this world. There is a story of the King Vinītamati who sees in a dream that he goes to the other world where being hungry he asks for some food. Then some men with maces in their hands give him numerous grains of hot sand which he had once given to a hungry Brāhmaṇa.[5]

It is also believed that a person passing into the afterworld forgets all about his relationship with the people in this world.[6]

Heaven and Hell[7]

Belief in heaven is widespread in the Kathāsaritsāgara.[8] It is held that one obtains a right to perpetual residence in heaven by virtue of his good deeds[9] and severe asceticism.[10] A wicked person cannot go to heaven.[11] The door of heaven is opened on the morning of eleventh day (Ekādaśī).[12]

Heaven is held as the abode of all happiness. Persons living in it have nothing left to be desired.[13] One who has tasted its pleasures cannot take delight in any other thing.

Heaven is considered to be temporary-paradise where duration of stay is in proportion to the good deeds of a person. Vararuchi says that the joys of heaven are perishable as one falls from heaven after one's merits are exhausted.[14]

Surabhi[15] or Kāmadhenu[16] is the wish-yielding cow of paradise. It is believed that Pṛthu brought her from heaven to the earth. By taking her milk, he returned to heaven though he had fallen from it.[17]

Kalpavṛkṣa of Kalpavallī[18] is the wish-yielding tree of paradise. It is held as the giver of progeny[19] and the bestower of prosperity. Even Indra cannot do any harm to him who possesses the wish-yielding tree.[20]

A beautiful description of the Kalpavṛkṣa is given in the Kathāsaritsāgara. The wish-yielding tree is decorated with boughs glittering with gold, which are adorned with sprays of coral and bears lovely fruits and flowers.[21] Garuḍa sits on its branch.[22]

The garden of Nandana is situated in heaven.[23] Ganges also flows through it.[24]

In the Kathāsaritsāgara, there are references to the hell Avīchi[25] and the hell Andhatāmisra.[26] The hell Avīchi is assigned to a person by his sins.[27]

It is held that one goes to hell on account of one's evil actions.[28] The task of sending various beings to hell or heaven is assigned to Yama.[29]

Concept of Sin

People being afraid of final judgment in the afterworld, perform good acts and abstain from wrong doings, so that they may go to heaven and not to hell. They become afraid of committing sins.[30]

Many sins are referred to in the Kathāsaritsāgara. To kill others is considered to be a sin.[31] Killing of a hermit[32] or of a woman[33] is a big sin.

Even giving troubles to others is a sin. A merchant's wife is dejected because she considers it a sin to become the cause of the tearing out of a prince's eyes.[34]

Committing suicide is another sin. It is believed that tortures of hell come to him who commits suicide.[35] Such a person suffers more severe pain in the next world than what he does here.[36]

To behold an unchaste woman is another sin.[37] Morality in sexual matters is always stressed. It is a sin to carry away or lay a violent hand on other's wife.[38] It is said that one shall endure sorrow for committing sin in the form of carrying off the wives of others.[39] This sin causes great misery in the next world.[40] It is always a sin to have illicit relations with one's master's or preceptor's wife.[41] To repudiate one's wife is also called a sin.[42]

Curse and Boon

Curse is an expression of anger which is believed to destroy one's happiness. Boon, on the other hand, is an expression of favour and promises prosperity and good luck.

Belief in the power of curse and boon is expressed at various places in the Kathāsaritsāgara.[43] Even some of the human beings are attributed with the power of pronouncing curse. People are always afraid of a curse, thinking that it will do them some harm. The king Suśarman being afraid of a curse gives his daughter Śrī to the Brāhmaṇa Devadatta.[44] The King Yaśaḥketu agrees to keep the girl fearing a curse from the Brāhmaṇa Manaḥsvāmin.[45] A barber says that he will not kill Kadalīgarbhā as her father, who is a sage, will pronounce curse.[46]

Beliefs founded on Astrology and Astronomy

Astrologers command respect in the society of the Kathāsaritsāgara. People believe in their proclamations. The 'thief's story' shows that astrologers predict that the child should be a thief. As he grows up, his father being apprehensive of the prophecy, starts instructing him diligently in Dharmaśāstra.[47]

Sometimes, people are seen showing their blind reverence even for pseudo astrologers. For instance, the Brāhmaṇa Hariśarman by means of an artifice displays an assumed knowledge of Astrology. Once, he steals a horse. His wife describes him as a wise man skilled in Astrology. Hariśarman draws all kinds of pretended diagrams and says that the horse has been placed by thieves on the boundary line south of some place. Many men run and bring the horse quickly praising the discernment of Hariśarman. The pseudo-astrologer is honoured by all men as a sage.[48]

When something is stolen, people resort to astrologers for knowing its whereabouts. Much wealth is carried off by a thief from the palace of the King Sthūlabhuja. The king quickly summons Hariśarman on account of his reputation for his knowledge of Astrology.

Astrologers are consulted for knowing the conformity of horoscope for marriage. The king Mahāvrāha asks astrologers to find out with which of the four suitors Anaṅgarati has conformity of horoscope. All the suitors accept to wait for three months as advised by the astrologers.[49]

Auspicious days and lucky moments are asked from astrologers.[50] These are ascertained by considering the position of heavenly bodies.

Auspicious Day

An auspicious day is ascertained for commencing any important work. Kings march against their enemies on the day which is considered to be auspicious. On the auspicious day, the king of Vatsa marches against Brahmadatta.[51] On an auspicious day, a hero gives orders that the imperial troops should march out towards the city of Gaurimuṇḍa.[52] Somaprabha also marches out on an auspicious day, with his forces, for the conquest of the regions.[53]

A journey is commenced on an auspicious day. Īśvaravarman sets out on an auspicious day, with a caravan, with the object of journeying to Svarṇadvīpa.[54] Mṛgāṅkadatta sets out, on an auspicious day for Ujjayinī.[55] Naravāhanadatta sets out for the Ṛṣabha mountain on an auspicious day.[56] Sundarasena sends Mandāravatī off from Haṁsadvīpa by sea on an auspicious day.[57]

Pilgrimage is also undertaken on an auspicious day.[58]

Important ceremonies too are performed on auspicious days. People believe in performing marriage ceremonies on auspicious days only. Somaprabha says that he will marry Makarandikā on an auspicious day.[59] Jīmūtavāhana gets married on the auspicious day fixed by astrologers.[60] On an auspicious day, Anaṅgadaya gives Śrīdarśana his daughter Anaṅgamañjarī.[61] The king Vikramāditya marries on a fortunate day the daughter of the king of Siṁhala.[62]

Auspicious day is fixed for the coronation ceremony. On such a day, Bhīmabaṭa gives to Śaṅkhadatta, the kingdom of Lāta.[63] Coronation of Naravāhanadatta too is performed on an auspicious day.[64] Suṣeṇa tells Sūryaprabha that his coronation should take place on the third day at the mountain Ṛṣabha,[65] for that will be an auspicious day.

Harvesting and such other undertakings are started on auspicious days. Somadatta desires to practise husbandry, and goes to a forest on a lucky day to find a piece of ground suitable for the purpose.[66]

People believe in commencing study on auspicious days. The minister Gunaśarman says to the king Mahāsena that he will begin teaching lyre to the queen on an auspicious day.[67]

Sacred vows are undertaken on auspicious days.[68]

Auspicious or Favourable Moment (Lagna)

Not only an auspicious day but an auspicious or favourable moment is also ascertained before starting any important work.

For expeditions, kings ask astrologers about favourable moments. Sūryaprabha fixes upon a moment pointed out by astrologers on the seventh day for marching out for war.[69] The king Pṛthvirūpa sets out on his expedition, after ascertaining a favourable moment.[70] In an auspicious moment, Naravāhanadatta performs the ceremony for good fortune before setting out for a battle with Mandaradeva.[71]

The 'story of the King Chamaravāla' confirms the belief that if a person sets out on an expedition in an unfavourable moment, he will be defeated. According to this story, five kings secretly ask astrologers for a favourable moment for their expedition. The astrologers, not seeing a favourable moment say, 'There is no favourable moment for you this year. Under whatever circumstances you set out on your expedition, you will not be victorious'.[72] Despite their advice, the kings start their campaign and in consequence they have to suffer a defeat at the hands of the King Chamaravāla.

Lagna is ascertained before setting out on a journey. King Chandraśekhara makes his daughter Chandravatī board a ship in a lucky moment.[73] The King Udayana asks his astrologers to decide an auspicious hour for journey to Lāvāṇaka.[74]

A favourable moment is sought for performing marriage. Yaugandharāyaṇa quickly ascertains an auspicious moment for the marriage of Udayana and Padmāvatī.[75] He asks the King Udayana to consult astrologers and marry Kaliṅgasenā at an auspicious time.[76] The King Udayana summons astrologers and asks for the favourable moment for the marriage of Naravāhanadatta.[77] The King Ratnādhipati asks astrologers about a favourable time for his marriage with Rājadattā.[78] Sumeru fixes up an auspicious moment for the marriage of his daughter Kāmachuḍāmaṇi.[79] The father of Alaṅkāravatī says to his wife Kāñchanaprabhā that when a year passed, there will be an auspicious moment for the marriage of their daughter.[80] Śuddhapaṭa after ascertaining the auspicious moment gives his daughter Madanasundarī to Dhavala.[81] Astrologers fix an auspicious Lagna for the marriage of Mṛgāṅkadatta.[82] A favourable moment is also fixed for the marriage of the king Kanakavarṣa and Madanasundarī,[83] Kamalākara and Haṁsāvalī,[84] Saudāminī and Aṭṭahāsa.[85]

There are many other instances in the Kathāsaritsāgara which show that people believe in performing marriages in auspicious moments. The marriage of Madanasena takes place in an auspicious moment.[86] Sundarasena marries Aṅgāravatī in an hour fixed by astrologers.[87] The king Vikramāditya also marries the daughter of the chief of the Bhillas in an auspicious hour.[88]

It is believed that if a favourable moment is fixed for marriage, the couple will remain happy throughout life. It does not matter whether an auspicious moment is near or far off. The chamberlain of Kaliṅgasenā asks astrologers to fix a favourable moment for the marriage of Kaliṅgasenā with Udayana, so that couple may be happy all their lives. Although the astrologers fix a distant date for the marriage, all of them agree to it in the interest of the couple.[89] The king Mahāsena also asks astrologers when a favourable time will come for the marriage of his son. When they answer that the time will come in three months, all on both sides remain eagerly expecting the auspicious time.[90]

The 'Story of the King Ratnādhipati and the elephant Śvetaraśmi' shows the belief that if marriage is performed in an unfavourable constellations, the bride will prove unchaste. According to this story, astrologers tell the King Ratnādhipati that if he marries Rājadattā in the present position of the constellations, she will be unchaste.[91] The king does not listen to them and marries her in an unfavourable moment. Later on, she is proved unchaste. The king believes that his wife has become so, as he has not acted according to the advice of astrologers and married her in an inauspicious moment.[92]

Influence of Planets

The planets are regarded as having considerable amount of influence on the human beings, not only at the moment of their birth, but during the whole of their lives also. The basis on which such a theory could rest is the belief that gods and heavenly bodies are one and the same, so that if the heavens could be correctly read, the will of the gods could, thereby, be determined.[93]

The Kathāsaritsāgara contains the belief that malignant planets, seven in one place, oppress people.[94]

ETHICAL VIRTUES

The practical aspect of religion need not consist in ritual only. It consists in ethical conduct too. Ethical virtues are manifestations of a refined spirit without which no spiritual development is conceivable.[95] Every religion prescribes them for raising the spiritual level of its followers.

The principles of Brāhmaṇism enumerated in the 'story of the Buddhist merchant Vitastādatta and his Brāhmaṇic son Ratnadatta' show that due importance is given to ethics in the Hindu Faith which consists in avoiding passion and other evils and in possessing truth and compassion.[96]

The Kathāsaritsāgara contains fundamental beliefs about the following ethical virtues which are entertained by the society as having real and permanent foundation.[97]

Righteousness

Importance of righteousness is fully recognized in the Kathāsaritsāgara. It is held that it is better to live with righteousness even for a moment than with unrighteousness for millions of Kalpas.[98] Neither enjoyment nor heaps of wealth accompany one into the other world, but Dharma is the only friend that never moves a step from one's side.[99] It brings happiness in both the worlds.[100] Even a slight act of righteousness bears great fruit.[101]

All the riches depend on righteousness only.[102] It is believed that the wealth earned with righteousness never destroys and the wealth earned with unrighteousness is perishable like a drop fallen in the water.[103] The wealth, which men desires to gain by cheating their neighbours, or by robbing them, does not remain for a long time. The poison-trees of wealth, which are rooted in wickedness and bring forth an abundant crop of wickedness, are soon broken by the weight of their own fruit. All that is gained by that wealth in this world is the toil of acquiring it and other annoyances, and in the next world great suffering in hell -- a suffering that shall continue as long as the moon and stars endure.[104] Therefore, it is maintained that a man should endeavour to obtain wealth by righteousness.[105]

In the matter of Kāma pursuit also, it is held that it should be based on righteousness as the love which is not so, is simply the forerunner of the fire of hell.[106]

The city in which righteousness is never transgressed is considered to be inaccessible to the demon Kali.[107]

Benevolence

Giving benefit to all creatures is considered to be a work of great merit as it produces holiness and fame that bears witness for hundreds of Yugas.[108] The joy which one gets out of it continues for births after births and is considered to be superior to heaven, or even salvation.[109]

Jīmūtavāhana says to his father Jīmūtaketu that one gets fame by bestowing benefit to others and that no other wealth is comparable to it.[110]

It is believed that prosperity should be directed for the benefit of others. If prosperity is not used to give benefit to others, it is like lightening which flickers for a moment, pains the eye and disappears.[111] There is no use of a kingdom unless it is employed to give benefit to fellow creatures.[112] Even the enjoyments of heaven or liberation are of no use if these are devoid of giving benefit to others.[113] There is no use of the greatness of great ones, who have abundant courage and wealth if they do not put a stop to the sufferings of their neighbours as soon as they hear of them.[114]

Charity

It is believed that charity expiates one's sins[115] and averts misery in the next world.[116] An old lady says to the Brāhmaṇa Vidūṣaka that she gives to him all her belongings in order that her lot may not again be unfortunate in the next birth.[117] A person will get the same thing to eat in the other world which he has given in charity in this world.[118] The 'story of the bold gambler Ṭhiṇṭhākarāla' shows the belief that by giving charity to the knower of the Supreme Soul, one attains heaven.[119]

The 'story of the generous Indraprabha' shows the belief that those who are devoted to charity attain success.[120] It is maintained that even heavenly nymphs who have been cast down by some curses, live as wives in the houses of righteous men, as a reward for their good deeds, such as acts of devotion and charity.[121]

Believing in the importance of charity, people hold that a suppliant is not to be sent disappointed.[122] Tārāvaloka refusing nothings to suppliants thinks that it is better for him to live in the forest under trees, which give their fruits to be enjoyed by all.[123]

The gift is said to be of no avail if it contains even a single coin which belongs to a Brāhmaṇa.[124] The appointed order is that others should give and Brāhmaṇas should receive. It is considered to be the inversion of the due order if others receive and Brāhmaṇas give.[125] Only Brāhmaṇas and poor are considered to be fit for receiving charity.[126] Many references in the text show that people believe in giving charity to the Brāhmaṇas and the poor. For instance, Yajñadatta says to Putraka to give continually to Brāhmaṇas.[127] Udayana distributes among the Brāhmaṇas all kinds of wealth.[128] The king Hemaprabha gives ninety million of gold pieces to the Brāhmaṇas.[129] Naravāhanadatta bestows gifts on them.[130] The father of Alaṅkāravatī gives to Brāhmaṇas and the poor a myriad loads of gold and jewels.[131] The glorious prince Samudravarman gives by order of his parents, to the Brāhmaṇas numerous gifts of elephants, horses, gold and jewels.[132] The wife of Vīravara gives two hundred dināras by way of charity to poor Brāhmaṇas. Niśchayadatta gives money to the Brāhmaṇas, the poor and the helpless.[133] A courtesan also gives alms everyday.[134]

Almshouses are built for the Brāhmaṇas.[135] There are alms-houses where cooked food is distributed by the order of a king.[136] It is said that Tārāvaloka sets up almshouses for the distribution of food and other necessities.[137]

Self-Sacrifice

It is held that there is no use of life or courage unless it is employed to save others.[138] The idea of sacrificing one's life for saving others is present throughout the Kathāsaritsāgara. For instance, Satyavrata offers his body to save Śaktideva.[139] A Brāhmaṇa boy offers himself to save the life of a King.[140] Jīmūtavāhana sacrifices himself for the sake of a Nāga[141] believing that if he cannot save it by offering up his exceedingly perishable body, there will be no use of it.[142] Śivi offers his flesh with this very idea in his mind.[143]

Other Ethical Virtues

Compassion to creatures is highly extolled in the Kathāsaritsāgara. The 'story of the Chakra and the iron wheel' points at the belief that even one's sins can be washed away by possessing compassion for others.[144]

Non-injury to creatures too is held in high esteem. As all living creatures in the world fear death, they are not to be slain.[145]

Stress is laid on hospitality. Guests are to be pleased even at the cost of one's body that perishes in a moment.[146] The visit of a noble guest to a householder is considered to be the result of his merits done in a former state of existence.[147]

Purity of mind is essential because success or failure of a person depends on the purity or impurity of one's heart.[148] Importance of speaking truth is acknowledged in the text. It is said that there is no use of speech without truth.[149]

It is essential to conquer sixfold internal enemies because even hermits injure others when beguiled by them.[150] Anger is an evil and those who have conquered it can conquer the whole earth.[151] Good fortune comes spontaneous and unexpectedly to them.[152] They can gain even heaven.[153] Covetousness is an evil.[154] It does not give pleasure. It can only cause annoyance to those who cherish it.[155] Therefore, one should not direct one's thought to excessive hoarding.[156]

Discontent also does harm[157] as it produces, in both worlds, unbearable and unceasing grief. Therefore, it is emphasised that a wise man, who desires happiness, should establish his mind in contentment.[158]

Desire for worldly pleasures is condemned in the text. It deludes a person[159] and tortures him.[160] Men attracted by it cannot remain on the good path.[161]

Belief in the religious concepts helps in the uplift of the society of the Kathāsaritsāgara. The idea of final judgment in the after-world makes many people afraid of committing sins and encourages them to perform righteous actions. Frightened of the pains of hell and desiring the pleasures of heaven after their death, many people want to lead a virtuous life in this world. The belief in the powers of curse and boon too helps in raising their moral standards. Beliefs founded on Astrology and Astronomy reveal that some days and moments are considered to be more auspicious than others and all the significant works are performed on such days and moments which are declared lucky or favourable by astrologers. Influence of planets on human beings is given due consideration. The practical aspect of the Hindu Faith consists in ethical conduct also. Various ethical virtues are held as important for attaining spiritual development.

Footnotes Of Chapter V

1. KSS. 12.5.104, 338, 395.

2. KSS. 12.5.348.

3. KSS. 10.10.24-26.

4. KSS. 12.5.353-57. Vide p.77 supra.

5. KSS. 12.5.104-5.

6. KSS. 8.2.56.

7. Belief in the concept of heaven goes back to the Ṛg Vedic times (Cf. Ṛg Veda, 10,154-55; 1,125,5,10,107, 2). But belief in the torments of hell seems to be a later development in India (vide - Hopkins, E.W., The Religions of India, p.206).

8. KSS. 1.3.7; 2.1.4,19; 2.2.8; 2.4.164; 6.1.165; 6.2.68; 6.8.146; 7.7.20; 16.2.138.

9. KSS. 5.1.72; 9.2.14; 12.5.354; 12.6.80; 12.30.4.

10. KSS. 12.5.359.

11. KSS. 2.4.166.

12. एकादश्यां पुनः प्रातर्द्वारमुद्घाटते दिवि ।

KSS. 2.4.167.

13. KSS. 12.5.227.

14. पुण्यक्षयात्स्वर्गात्पतनम् ।

KSS. 9.3.118.

15. KSS 15.2.52.

16. KSS. 8.7.148.

17. KSS. 6.2.191-92.

18. KSS. 1.6.66; 9.2.21.

19. KSS. 4.2.23; 12.23.8.

20. KSS. 12.23.12-13.

21. KSS. 12.19.41-42; 12.33.20.

22. KSS. 2.4.141. S.A. Dange (The Genesis of the story of Jīmūtavāhana, Journal of the Asiatic Society of Bombay, New Series, 1959-60, Vol.34-35) has identified the Kalpavṛkṣa with the holy Nyagrodha.

23. KSS. 6.8.143. 24. KSS. 12.8.60.

25. KSS. 5.1.93. 26. KSS. 1.4.63.

27. KSS. 2.5.149.
"These hells of the later eschatology are really compartments of the general province of Yama and these are situated in the Vāyu Purāṇa, under the seven strata below earth's surface." Hopkins, E.W., Epic Mythology, p.111.

28. KSS. 5.1.94; 8.6.55.

29. KSS. 18.2.189-90. Vide also p.77 supra.

30. KSS. 6.4.46; 9.5.30. 31. KSS. 6.6.32-33.

32. KSS. 10.8.25-26. 33. KSS. 6.6.143.

34. KSS. 6.2.24. 35. KSS. 12.29.20.

36. इतः कष्टतरं दुःखममुत्र ह्यात्मघातिनाम् ।
KSS. 8.6.227.

37. KSS. 9.1.72-73. 38. KSS. 6.8.18; 9.2.255.

39. KSS. 9.2.175. 40. KSS. 8.6.55; 12.24.40.

41. KSS. 3.6.154. 42. KSS. 3.1.78.

43. For curses and boons of divine beings, vide p.74. supra.

44. KSS. 1.7.80. 45. KSS. 12.22.30.

46. KSS. 6.6.143. 47. KSS. 12.5.192.

48. KSS. 6.4.103-10.

49. KSS. 9.2.139, 141-42, 146.

50. "Belief in the importance of choosing such auspicious days and lucky moments for the performance of rites and ceremonies, both public and domestic, began to show itself very early in India and it grew and became deep-rooted, simultaneously with the growth of priest-craft and the elaboration of a complex ritual." Monier-Williams, M., Indian Wisdom, p.181.

51. KSS. 3.5.62.

52. KSS. 14.4.96-97.

53. KSS. 10.3.72.

54. KSS. 10.1.72.

55. KSS. 12.3.52; 12.6.1-3.

56. KSS. 15.2.47.

57. KSS. 12.34.164.

58. KSS. 12.26.73.

59. निश्चित्य परिणेष्यामि शुभेऽह्नि मकरन्दिकाम्।

KSS. 10.3.142.

60. KSS. 4.2.133.

61. KSS. 12.6.395.

62. KSS. 18.3.11.

63. KSS. 12.7.300.

64. KSS. 15.2.75-77.

65. KSS. 8.7.165.

66. KSS. 3.6.23.

67. कुर्मोऽत्र प्रारम्भं सुशुभेऽहनि।

KSS. 8.6.35.

68. KSS. 12.5.155.

69. KSS. 8.3.9.

70. KSS. 9.1.158.

71. KSS. 15.1.33.

72. KSS. 9.4.148-50.

73. KSS. 18.4 117.

74. KSS. 3.1.127.

75. KSS. 3.2.62.

76. KSS. 6.5.70.

77. KSS. 6.8.247.

78. KSS. 7.2.52-53.
79. KSS. 8.7.129.

80. KSS. 9.1.40.
81. KSS. 1.2.13,16.

82. KSS. 12.36.171.
83. KSS. 9.5.94, 96.

84. KSS. 12.4.126.
85. KSS. 12.6.36.

86. KSS. 12.17.27.
87. KSS. 12.34.378.

88. KSS. 18.4.77.

89. KSS. 6.6.2, 4, 9, 11, 14-16, 18, 20.

90. KSS. 12.34.118-19, 131.
91. KSS. 7.2.52-54.

92. KSS. 7.2.94.

93. Soper, E.D., The Religions of Mankind, p.102.

94. विभिन्नैः सप्तसंख्याकैरेकस्थानाश्रयैर्मिथः ।
सङ्घर्षात्तैरबाध्यन्त ग्रामा दुष्टैर्ग्रहैरिव ॥

KSS. 3.4.130.

95. Sharma, Ramashraya, A Socio-political Study of the Vālmīki Rāmāyaṇa, p.148.

96. ब्राह्मण्यमपि तत्प्राहुर्यद्रागादिविवर्जनम् ।
सत्यं दया च भूतेषु न मृषा जातिविग्रहः ॥

KSS. 6.1.22.

97. KSS. 3.6.149; 10.10.34; 12.27.107.
Cf. Ṛg Veda, X-117 and Manu Smṛti, IV.227-29.

98. वरं यद् धर्मपाशेन क्षणमेकं हि जीवितम् ।
परं न यदधर्मेण कल्पकोटिशतान्यपि ॥

KSS. 8.6.58.

99. KSS. 9.1.28.

100. KSS. 12.23.24.

Cf. नामुत्र हि सहायतार्थं माता पिता च तिष्ठतः
न पुत्रदारा न ज्ञाति धर्मस्तिष्ठति केवलः ॥
Manu Smṛti, IV.239.
Cf. also - धर्मः शर्मे परत्र नेह नृणाम् ।
Chaturvargasaṁgraha,1.3.

101. सम्यक् कृतोऽल्पोऽपि धर्मो भूरिफलो भवेत् ।
KSS. 6.1.108.

102. धर्ममूला हि संपदः ।
KSS. 12.5.156. Cf. also KSS. 8.2.159-60.

103. KSS. 3.5.50-51.
Cf. also निजधर्मार्जितानां हि विनाशो नास्ति सम्पदाम् ।
KSS. 3.5.14.

104. KSS. 13.1.116-18.
Cf.also अधर्मविषवृक्षस्य पच्यते स्वादु किं फलम् ।
KSS. 12.23.179.

105. Cf. अतो यतेत धर्मेण धनमर्जयितुं पुमान् ।
परित्यजेदर्थकामौ यौ स्यातां धर्मविवर्जितौ ।
Manu Smṛti, IV.176.

106. KSS. 1.3.64.

107. KSS. 12.24.3.

108. KSS. 12.23.20-23.

109. KSS. 12.27.121.

110. KSS. 4.2.27.

111. KSS. 4.2.28.

112. KSS. 12.5.173.

113. KSS. 12.23.152.

114. KSS. 12.7.124.

115. KSS. 12.5.106.

116. KSS. 10.5.216.

117. KSS. 3.4.271.

118. Vide p.134 supra.

119. KSS. 18.2.190.

120. KSS. 12.5.236.

121. KSS. 16.3.92.

122. KSS. 16.3.71.

123. KSS. 16.3.48-49.

124. KSS. 12.5.110.
125. KSS. 8.2.102.
126. KSS. 12.11.18.
127. KSS. 1.3.26.
128. KSS. 3.6.227.
129. KSS. 7.1.96.
130. KSS. 7.9.236.
131. KSS. 9.1.38.
132. KSS. 9.2.379.
133. KSS. 7.3.5.
134. KSS. 7.4.96.
135. KSS. 3.6.149.
136. KSS. 6.7.54.
137. KSS. 3.6.149.
138. KSS. 6.1.172.
139. KSS. 5.3.21.
140. KSS. 12.27.120.
141. KSS. 4.2.214, 219,232, 237, 240.
142. KSS. 12.23.130.
143. KSS. 1.7.92; 10.4.116.
144. KSS. 9.6.164.
145. KSS. 12.27.39-40. Cf. Manu Smṛti, II. 161.
146. KSS. 12.5.130. Cf. Manu Smṛti, III.100,105-6, IV.29.
147. KSS. 12.5.129.
148. KSS. 14.3.127.
149. KSS. 6.7.181.
150. KSS. 3.6.134.
151. KSS. 9.2.240. Cf. Manu Smṛti II.47-48.
152. KSS. 10.9.43.
153. KSS. 6.7.51.
154. KSS. 10.5.97.
155. KSS. 10.5.107.
156. KSS. 10.5.100.
157. KSS. 10.6.178.
158. KSS. 10.6.185.
159. KSS. 6.6.132.
160. KSS. 4.3.37.
161. KSS. 3.6.192.

Chapter VI

PHILOSOPHY

Religion and Philosophy are inseparable in the Hindu Faith. The superstructure of the Faith is built on the foundations provided by Philosophy. In the Kathāsaritsāgara, there are many views which are not purely philosophical. Sometimes, these appear as philosophico-religious and sometimes as philosophico-mythical. These views are noted under the following heads.

God

As noted earlier, the sectarian Faiths consider their respective deities as the Supreme God. Śiva, Viṣṇu, Chaṇḍikā and Sūrya are each separately called the ultimate cause of the world by their respective votaries.[1]

Trimūrti[2] of Brahmā, Viṣṇu and Śiva implies the unity of the three principles of creation, preservation and destruction and as such belongs more to the philosophical than to the popular religious belief.[3] All these three gods are the three forms of the one God and represent His threefold functions. They respectively represent the three states of the Upaniṣadic Brahman which are referred to as'of which all these beings are born','by which all these beings are sustained' and 'to which all these beings return and in which they rest'.[4] The three major aspects of the Supreme Being are personified in the concept of Trimūrti for the better understanding of the concept of God.[5]

The Kathāsaritsāgara clearly points out the belief that one should meditate on Brahmā, Viṣṇu and Śiva in the light of their unity. Until one perceives that these three are really one, one will always find successes that are gained by worshipping them separately as short lived and uncertain.[6]

The Soul

The belief in the transmigration of souls[7] controls the whole philosophical thought of the Hindus. It is the object of fantastical superstition as well as that of philosophical speculation.

In the Kathāsaritsāgara, the belief in the continuity of soul after death is quite obvious from many references to previous and next births.

The Kathāsaritsāgara refers to the previous birth.[8] Previous births of Sātavāhana[9] and Vāsavadattā[10] are mentioned in the text. The characters like Vararuchi,[11] Guṇāḍhya,[12] Jīmūtavāhana,[13] Karpūrikā[14] and Kanakarekhā[15] are depicted as the knowers of their previous births.

It is not easy to know one's previous birth. It is believed that a few seers perfectly acquainted with the highest truth know the previous birth on account of their good deeds.[16] Those persons who end their life by starvation on the holy place of Ganges are also believed to remember their previous birth.[17] The 'story of Lāvanyamañjarī' shows that owing to the virtue of her vow and the holy bathing place where she died, she remembers her previous birth.[18] On account of penance performed in a previous birth, and on account of devotion to Viṣṇu also one is believed to remember one's previous birth.[19]

There is a curious belief that if one is suddenly reminded of one's former birth and speaks it out, one is sure to die.[20]

Many characters of the Kathāsaritsāgara believe that there will be a next birth also after the fall of this mortal body.[21] Dharmavatī desires that may Vīravara be her husband in the next birth.[22] A merchant Vasudatta likes to have the same friend and wife in his future birth.[23] Śaśāṅkavatī prays to Gaurī that may Mṛgāṅkadatta become her husband in her future life.[24] Madirāvatī asks for mercy in the next birth.[25] There are many other references in the text which point at the belief in the next birth.[26]

There are various factors which are believed to determine one's future state of existence. It is held that a creature receives the form that he contemplates at the moment of death.[27] Lāvaṇyamañjarī abandons her life with thought intently fixed on her love. Therefore, she is born, in the next birth as a courtesan.[28] Dharmasena and Vidyullekhā die with their minds fixed on swans. So, they are born in the next birth as swans.[29] A dying Brāhmaṇa sees some fishermen eating fish, and his hunger causes desire for it in his heart. Therefore, in his next birth, he takes birth among the fisher-men.[30]

The transmigration of souls is chiefly based on the ethical grounds.[31]

It is believed that the impressions of previous births (Saṁskāras) are carried away with the soul when it takes another birth. These impressions are supposed to play an important part in the nature of every individual. Hatred and affection are commonly produced in living beings in this world owing to their impressions of previous births.[32] Wives and others are friendly or hostile to men in this world due to their impressions of the previous birth.[33]

An apparently causeless affection of the heart is a sign of friendship in a former birth.[34] Jīmūtavāhana is brought to the Śavara King Pulindaka to be sacrificed to the goddess. But the moment, the king beholds him, he feels pity for him. This confirms the belief that the both must have been friends in their previous birth.

Intimacy in a former birth results into affection.[35] The belief that the heart of creatures recognizes friendship formed in a previous birth[36] is found in the 'story of the king Vikramasiṁha and the two Brāhmaṇas' in which a Brāhmaṇa meets another Brāhmaṇa and though they have never met before, they feel intimacy at first sight.[37]

Love at first sight proves relations of the previous birth. The King Pālaka says that Suratamañjarī without doubt was the beloved of his son Avantivardhana in a former birth, and this is proved by his falling in love with her at first sight.

Success in achieving high goals also depends on the impressions of knowledge attained in the previous birth.[38] Sātavāhana easily acquires the knowledge of Sanskrit because he was a learned sage in his previous birth.

Moreover, one's desires in this life are also influenced by one's impressions of the previous birth. For instance, Hemaprabhā is fond of amusing herself by swinging, on account of the impressions of her roaming through the air in her former birth when she was a Vidyādharī.[39]

In the Hindu Faith, the doctrine of the transmigration of souls is inextricably linked up with the law of Karman according to which the everlasting soul takes birth again and again in high or low position in accordance with the acts performed in a previous existence.[40] It is supposed that every moment man is on his trial, and every honest effort will do him good in his eternal endeavour. The law of Karman opens up a vast vista where there will be an ample scope for self development.[41]

The Kathāsaritsāgara clearly states the belief in the role of Karman in determining one's future state of existence. It is believed that all the beings, bound by various works. good or evil, are ever revolving in the state of mundane existence in the three worlds, to receive the fruits blessed or miserable of their actions done in their previous births.[42] The people of the world are described as blind men, being led to the place of recompense by their own actions going before them.[43]

Whatever seed of works any man has sown in a former life, of that he, without doubt, would reap the fruit,[44] and none can escape its inevitable consequences.[45] It is believed that even gods are not able to alter the mighty influence of one's actions in a previous state of existence.[46] Vidhi himself cannot alter the effect of previous actions.[47]

The doctrine of Karman gives a most satisfactory explanation of present prosperous or miserable condition of an individual. In this world all the good and bad fortunes that befall all the beings at all times are earned by actions in a former life.[48] From their birth, all the beings enjoy the fruits of the tree of their former actions.[49] Infact, no man does anything for anyone or gives anything to anybody.[50] It is one's deeds in a former state of existence that give and do.[51]

It is believed that deformed and diseased creatures are born into the world on account of the evil actions done in a former life.[52]

There is an interesting belief that many sons are born to a person due to his evil actions of former life.[53] The children themselves are those persons who have committed sins in their previous life. They are born to poor persons in order to suffer as a result of their evil actions of the former existence.[54]

In the Kathāsaritsāgara, one continually comes across people undergoing hardships, suffering poverty or experiencing misery due to the effect of their evil acts of former life. It is held that for one whose merits in a former life are meagre, even a wish-yielding tree is ungenerous, even a Buddha is wanting in compassion, and even gold becomes a stone.[55] The 'story of the king Lakṣadatta and his dependent Lābhadatta' clearly shows how one's present is conditioned by one's actions of former life. It is maintained in this story that until a suitor's evil acts of the previous birth standing in his way, are removed, a king, even though disposed to give, cannot give. But when a man's guilt is effaced, a king gives, though strenuously dissuaded from doing so.[56] The story points at the belief that Lābdhadatta is merely working out his evil Karman of former life and his lot cannot be changed unless all his evil acts of previous birth are expiated in the present one.

Man's present is considered to be an offshoot of the past. It is deeply affected by the consequences of the actions of his previous life. The assertion of the inevitability of experiencing the results of one's own actions of previous life culminates in the concept of Fate[57] which shapes the very course of One's life. In Hindu way of life everything is predetermined according to one's actions of former life. The concept of Fate is only held as the sensible solution of life.

Bhavitavya, Bhavitavyatā, Bhāvi, Daiva, Deva, Dhātṛ, Vedhas, Vidhātṛ and Vidhi are the various words used in the Kathāsaritsāgara in the sense of Fate or destiny. As Fate depends on the actions of former life, it is described as unpredictable and mysterious.[58]

It is believed that man is merely a puppet in the hands of Fate. He is given no choice but to face the consequences of the actions of his previous life. Fate is all powerful. It's will is supreme.[59] None can change, modify or avert what is predestined to him.[60] Even Brahmā himself cannot overstep Fate.[61]

Not only human beings but heavenly beings are also influenced by Fate, and reap the fruits of the actions of their former existence. They descend from heaven to earth by appointment of Fate.[62]

What to talk of changing one's Fate, it is even held impossible to change the place and manner of the decreed event. A man is to undergo the experience which Fate has set for him, at the specific place and in the specific manner.[63]

In the Kathāsaritsāgara, sometimes, Fate is depicted as an inspiring force,[64] which directs human life and activity. It even bewilders a person.[65]

It is believed that Fate plays a very vital role in life. It can make or mar our lives. It can lead to prosperity or destruction.[66] No man can do anything in the world at any place or time unless Fate is favourable to him.[67] If Fate is adverse, it is even impossible to die.[68]

Fate favours one who is destined to be prosperous.[69] It produces unexpected results.[70] It brings about a thing that otherwise cannot be accomplished.[71]

Every misery of human life is attributed to the effect of Fate.[72] When Fate has turned against man, everything in this world also turns its face.[73] A wish-yielding tree, in the case of ill-fated persons, often becomes a Palāśa tree. It does not gratify their hopes.[74] Even great hardships bring no reward to them.[75]

Sometimes, importance of Puruṣārtha is also acknowledged in the text. It is believed that Fate produces fruit for every man according to his resolution.[76] Pleased with resolute men who undertake mighty enterprises, it makes all things subserve their ends.[77]

The World

The curiosity to know the origin of the world gives rise to the cosmological speculations,[78] The sectarian Faiths connect the task of the creation of the Universe with their gods. In the Kathāsaritsāgara, Śiva, Viṣṇu, Brahmā and Chaṇḍikā are separately called the ultimate cause of world.[79] The Cosmic Egg Theory explains the creation of the world from the cosmic egg which is associated with Śiva.[80]

An interesting allegory[81] in the text explains the mystery of the world. It shows the belief that Māyā revolves the wheel of mundane existence with all its creatures.[82] Impelled by her, creatures resort to righteousness or unrighteousness and perform good or evil actions accordingly. They acquire properties arising from their actions and become good or evil creatures. With their energy, they produce offsprings which get happiness or misery according to their actions. While attached to sons and other worldly connections, they are bitten by Death (Kāla) with its two mouths i.e. the good creatures with the white mouth symbolical of good fortune, the other with the black mouth symbolical of evil fortune. Then the Māyā plunges them into various wombs and they again emerge from them. They assume forms good or bad corresponding to what they had in their previous birth. They again become attached to the world. Tortured by the miseries of life, the evil creatures invoke the Supreme Lord for help. Beholding this the good creatures also become averse to their state and invoke the Supreme

Lord. Then the Lord consumes their webs of Karman with the fire of knowledge. All the creatures ascend into the orb of the Sun, and reach the 'Highest Home' (Parama Dhāma), which lies above it. And then Māyā vanishes with the revolving wheel of births and with her righteousness (Dharma) and unrighteousness (Adharma). The allegory clearly points at the belief that according to their actions, good and evil creatures revolve in the circle of existence.[83]

Besides the allegory which explains the functions of Māyā, there are other references in the text which assert the belief that the world is an illusion of the creator[84] and may be compared to the show of a juggler.[85]

It is believed that there are seven Pātālas[86] (nether regions) below the earth. Besides the names of Rasātala[87] and Pātāla,[88] there are references to the second,[89] third[90] and the fourth[91] Pātālas.

Mythological law about the food-taboos in the underworld is a matter of belief in the Kathāsaritsāgara. There is a 'story of the adventures of King Bhūnandana' in which an ascetic asks his pupil not to take fruit of Jambu tree in nether region. Inspite of this warning, a pupil eats a fruit of the tree. Immediately, he becomes rigid and motionless.[92]

Kalpānta (the day of doom) is held as sunless and moon-less.[93] The water of the ocean overflows its bank at this day. Wind raised at this time makes the three worlds tremble, and shakes the mountains.[94] The night of destruction at the end of the world carries off all living creatures.[95]

The doctrine of Yugas[96] shows progressive degeneration. The misery of the Kaliyuga has been eloquently described in the Kathāsaritsāgara. It is held that Kali allows those born under his sway to take pleasure in wickedness and break through the bound of rule. The evil effect of Kali is accepted in the 'story of Nala and Damayantī'. It is said that when Kali enters the body of the king Nala, the king abandons righteousness and acts as he pleases. He plays dice, loves females, utters untruth, sleeps in the day, keeps awake at night, becomes angry without cause, takes wealth unjustly, despises the good and honours the bad.[97]

Salvation

Emancipation from the bondage of births and deaths is believed to be the ultimate goal of human life. It consists in attaining to the state of universal spirit when the soul is lifted above the wheel of the world, the Saṁsārachakra, with its perpetual rhythm of growth and decay, birth and rebirth.[98]

The idea of salvation is present in the Kathāsaritsāgara. The perishable nature of the world is repeatedly asserted in the text. It is said that all the things of the world are frail as bubbles produced on the surface of water.[99] The body is perishable, loathsome and full of pain.[100] Men are ever miserable.[101] No one is born free from sorrow in this world.[102] As long as one retains one's body, how can one's woes come to an end.[103] Enjoyments of the world are unsubstantial and insipid.[104] All aggregation end in destruction, all progress end in fall, all union end in separation and all life end in death.[105] Prosperity is fickle.[106] None can retain it for ever.[107] Infact, there is no enjoyment in life of a man which involves separation from relations, friends and attendants very hard to bear, and the pain arising from loss of wealth, old age, disease, etc.[108] Passions are in the end distasteful[109] and the desire for pleasure tortures a person.[110] Life is really full of woe, but owing to delusion, people think that happiness is to be found in it.[111]

Even gods like Brahmā, Indra, Viṣṇu and Rudra are called perishable.[112] The perishable joys of heaven are described as far inferior to the everlasting bliss of liberation. Therefore, those men who desire liberation have no attraction for the joys of heaven.[113] Some means of attaining salvation are referred to in the text. The knowledge of the Reality is considered essential for its attainment.[114] It is held that without knowledge, liberation cannot be attained even by taking a hundred vows.[115] Pride is termed as an impediment of knowledge.[116] Lust and wrath[117] are described as two bolts on the door of salvation.

In some passages, asceticism is also cherished as a means to Eternal Bliss. The king Chirāyus,[118] Niśchayadatta, Somasvāmin,[119] and the hermit Śubhanaya[120] attain salvation by performing many austerities.

It is believed that human beings can also be liberated by propitiating the Supreme Lord.[121] The worship of the great god Śiva is called the bestower of emancipation.[122]

Pilgrimage is considered to be another means of attaining salvation.[123]

The word Sāṁkhya and yoga occur in the Kathāsaritsāgara.[124] There is a reference in the text, which, in accordance with the Sāṁkhya system of Philosophy, traces the creation of the universe to Prakṛti.[125] An indication to the theory of Satkāryavāda which establishes a relation between cause and effect,[126] is traced in another reference which shows that the quality of a cloth will be that of the thread from which it is made.[127]

There is a reference to an ascetic grove full of great sages, engaged in Yoga, sitting in the posture called Padmāsana.[128]

Yoga is described here as a supernatural power. It is the domination over matter that is characterised by lightness (Aṇimā) and the other mystic properties.[129] It is said that the Brāhmaṇa Kāla obtains independence and everlasting supernatural power by Yoga.[130] A hermit named Brahmasiddhi also possesses supernatural power by practising Yoga.[131]

It is believed that the art of entering another body (Parakāyapraveśa)[132] can be attained through Yoga.[133] The words Dehāntarāveśa or Anyadehapraveśa are used for this art in the Kathāsaritsāgara. By the Yoga, Chandraprabha enters the body of a hero[134] and Indradatta enters the body of the dead King Nanda.[135] An ascetic abandoning his own body, at once enters by Yoga a young Brāhmaṇa's body and the young Brāhmaṇa is returned to life.[136]

It is held that a man who does not die of his own free will and is born in another womb, does not remember anything, as his memory is destroyed by old age and other afflictions. But whoever of his own free will enters another body, through Yoga, without his mind and intellect being impaired, passes, as it were, from one house to another. Such prince among Yogins has supernatural knowledge and remembers all.[137]

In the Kathāsaritsāgara, the grace of God[138] is considered to be extremely effective. Everything can be accomplished through it.[139] Even a child can attain self-control by the favour of God.[140]

The philosophico-religious and the philosophico-mythical beliefs in the Kathāsaritsāgara depict that the sectarian Faiths consider gods like Śiva, Viṣṇu, Chaṇḍikā and Sūrya as the Ultimate Reality. The concept of Trimūrti helps in meditating on Brahmā, Viṣṇu and Śiva in the light of their unity. The belief in the transmigration of souls makes people think about the previous and next births. It is related with the law of Karman which is believed to determine one's fate. The sectarian Faiths connect the task of the creation of the universe with Śiva, Viṣṇu, Brahmā and Chaṇḍikā. The concept of Māyā is accepted by those people who think that Māyā revolves the universe.Mythological Law about the food-taboos in the Pātāla is a matter of belief. Salvation is held as the ultimate goal of one's life. Sāṁkhya, Yoga and the doctrine of grace are considered as important spiritual systems.

Footnotes Of Chapter VI

1. Vide pp.13-14,48-49,53-54,58 supra.

2. Monier Williams holds that it is probable that Veda is the real source of this triad of personification which was foreshadowed in the Vedic association of the three gods Agni, Indra and Sūrya (Hinduism, p.25) or in the triple form of fire (Indian Wisdom, p.324). The thirty-three gods (3 multiplied by 11) of the Ṛg Veda points to the same idea of triple manifestation. (Indian Wisdom, p.324, f.n.2).

According to A.A. Macdonell, threefold Agni is the earliest Indian trinity, and there may be a historical connection between this triad and the conception of the later Hindu trinity of Brahmā, Viṣṇu and Śiva (Article in the Encyclopaedia of Religion and Ethics, Vol. 12,p.605).

A. Barth opines that the dogma of the sectarian trinity found a point of support in this ancient triad. But it differs from it too much to be directly derived from it.Here, in fact, the point is not, as formerly, a cosmographic distribution of the deified forces of nature, but a threefold evolution of the divine unity (The Religions of India, p.180).

The Concept of Trimūrti is well established in the Purāṇas (Cf. Kūrma Purāṇa, I,6; I,91,26).

3. Goldstücker, Theodore, Sanskrit and Culture, pp.58-59.

4. यतो वा इमानि भूतानि जायन्ते
येन जातानि जीवन्ति
यत् प्रयान्त्यभिसंविशन्ति ।

Taittirīya Upaniṣad, 3.1.

5. Thomas, P., Epics, Myths and Legends of India, p.21.

6. यावच्च नाच्युतेशानविरिञ्चिष्वेकतामतिः ।
भेदोपासनजास्तावद्भङ्गुरा एव सिद्धयः ॥
तदभेदधिया ध्यायन्ब्रह्मविष्णुमहेश्वरान् ।
KSS. 12.6.170-71.

7. In the Ṛg Veda one cannot clearly trace the origin of the belief in the transmigration of the soul though some reference to future life is found in it (Cf. Ṛg Veda, X.58.16.3). However, it begins to appear in a more positive way, in the Brāhmaṇas (Cf. Śatapatha Brāhmaṇa, XI,6.1.1;X). In its fully developed form, we find it for the first time in the Upaniṣads (Bṛhadāraṇyaka Upaniṣad, III.2.13f; IV.4,2,5; Chhāndogya Upaniṣad, V.3; Kauṣitakī-Upaniṣad, I.1).

8. प्राक्तनं जन्म KSS. 6.1.101;
पूर्वजन्म KSS. 6.1.88;
पूर्वत्र जन्म KSS. 4.3.46;
प्राग्जन्म KSS. 3.2.20;
प्राग्जाति KSS. 4.3.42;
पूर्वजाति KSS. 4.3.46.

9. KSS. 1.7.15.

10. KSS. 3.2.120.

11. KSS. 1.5.127.

12. KSS. 1.7.29.

13. KSS. 4..2.53.

14. KSS. 5.1.232.

15. KSS. 7.9.154.

16. KSS. 6.3.7.

17. KSS. 6.1.129-30.

18. KSS. 12.2.164.

19. KSS. 7.2.14.

20. KSS. 6.1.84.

21. अन्य जन्म KSS. 17.5.170;
जन्मान्तर KSS. 16.2.99;
जननान्तर KSS. 7.9.163.

22. KSS. 9.3.159.

23. KSS. 4.2.164.

24. KSS. 12.36.51.   25. KSS. 13.1.137-38.

26. KSS. 8.2.42; 12.7.29-30; 12.11.84; 12.13.41; 12.28. 29-30.

27. यद्भावितात्मा म्रियते जन्तुस्तद्रूपमश्नुते ।

KSS. 12.2.159.

Cf. यं यं वापि स्मरन्भावं त्यजयन्ते कलेवरम् ।
तं तमेवैति कौन्तेय सदा तद्भावभावितः ॥

Śrimadbhagavadgītā, VIII,6.

28. KSS. 12.5.159,162.   29. KSS. 12.2.127-28.

30. KSS. 16.2.139-41.

31. For details on this point vide pp. 156-157 infra.

32. किं च देव विरोधो वा स्नेहो वापीह देहिनाम् ।
प्राग्जन्मवासनाभ्यासवशात्प्रायेण जायते ॥

KSS. 4.3.30.

33. इत्थं दारादयोऽपीह भवन्ति भुवने नृणाम् ।
प्राक्संस्कारवशायातवैरस्नेहा महीपते ॥

KSS.4.3.51.

34. वक्ति जन्मान्तरप्रीतिं मनः स्निह्यदकारणम् ।

KSS. 4.2.65.

35. आशु बध्नाति हि प्रेम प्राग्जन्मान्तरसंस्तवः ।

KSS. 6.2.117.

Cf. also प्राग्जन्मसंबन्धः प्रायः प्रीत्यै शरीरिणाम् ॥

KSS. 16.2.146.

36. चित्तं जानाति जन्तूनां प्रेम जन्मान्तरार्जितम् ।

KSS. 6.1.190.

37. KSS. 16.2.110.

38. अक्लेशलभ्या हि भवन्त्युत्तमार्था महात्मनाम् ।

जन्मान्तरार्जिताः स्फारसंस्काराक्षिप्तसिद्धयः ॥
KSS. 1.7.19.

39. KSS. 10.10.138.

40. The belief in the doctrine of the transmigration of souls rested in our country on ethical grounds right from the Vedic period (Cf.Śatapatha Brāhmaṇa, 11.2,7,33; Taittirīya Upaniṣad, I, 11; Bṛhadāraṇyaka Upaniṣad, 4.4; Chhāndogya Upaniṣad, III.14.1; IV, 14.3; V.3-10; Kausītakī Upaniṣad, 1,4; III,8; Kaṭha Upaniṣad, 2.2,6-7.

41. Radhakrishnan, S., The Heart of Hinduism, p.96.

42. विचित्रसदसत्कर्मनिबध्दाः सञ्चरन्ति हि ।
जन्तवस्त्रिजगत्यस्मिन् शुभाशुभफलाप्तये ॥
KSS. 6.1.77.

Cf. also - इत्यैहिकेन च पुराविहितेन चापि
स्वेनैव कर्मविभवेन शुभाशुभेन ।
शश्वद् भवेतदनुरूपविचित्रभोगः
सर्वो हि नाम ससुरासुर एष सर्गः ॥
KSS. 6.1.209.
and KSS. 1.3.19; 7.9.155, 181.

43. अन्धस्येवास्य लोकस्य फलभूमिं स्वकर्मभिः ।
पुरोगैर्नीयमानस्य – – – – – – – – – – ॥
KSS. 4.1.132.

44. सत्यं कर्मैव बलवद् भोगदायि शुभाशुभम् ॥
KSS. 6.1.78.
Cf. also - यत्कर्मबीजमुप्तं येन पुरा निश्चितं च तद्भुंक्ते ।
KSS. 12.19.45.

45. कस्य प्राक्कर्म केनेह शक्यते कर्तुमन्यथा ॥
KSS. 12.5.193.
Cf. also - कृतं दुःखेन हि शक्यं पूर्वकर्मातिवर्तितुम् ।
KSS. 12.34.296.

46. KSS. 12.34.199.

47. पूर्वकृतस्य हि शक्यो विधिनापि न कर्त्तुमन्यथाभावः ।

KSS. 12.19.79.

48. एवं भवति लोकेऽस्मिन् देव सर्वस्य सर्वदा ।
प्राक्कर्मोपार्जितं जन्तोः सर्वमेव शुभाशुभम् ॥

KSS. 7.6.113.

49. आगर्भाज्जन्तुरश्नाति पूवकर्मतरोः फलम् ।

KSS. 7.6.109.

50. विना हि प्राक्तनं कर्म न दाता कोऽपि कस्यचित् ।

KSS. 7.6.109.

51. प्राक्तनं कर्म हि करोति च ददाति च ॥

KSS. 7.6.78.

52. KSS. 7.6.30.

53. पूर्वदुंष्कृतभोगाय जातोऽतिबहुबालकः ॥

KSS. 6.4.93.

A tremendous change in the attitude of the society of the Kathāsaritsāgara has taken place in this respect. Whereas the Vedic Aryans always desired for many sons, the text attributes the birth of many sons to the evil actions of one's former life.

54. – – – – – – – दुखाय जायते ।
प्रजेयं पापभूयिष्ठा दरिद्रेष्वेव भूयसी ॥

KSS. 4.1.137.

55. कल्पद्रुमोऽप्यदातृत्वं सुगतोऽप्यदयालुताम् ।
आयाति मन्दपुण्यस्य सुवर्णमपि चाश्मताम् ॥

KSS.17.4.32.

56. क्षयो यावन्न वृत्तो हि पापस्य परिपन्थिनः ।
तावद्दानप्रवृत्तोऽपि दातुं शक्नोति न प्रभुः ॥
परिक्षीणे पुनः पापे वार्यमाणोऽपि यत्नतः ।
ईश्वरः प्रददात्येव कर्मायत्तमिदं किल ॥

KSS. 9.3.6-7.

57. Cf. Yājñavalkya Smṛti, I.348; Manu Smṛti, VII.205.

58. गतिः शक्या परिच्छेत्तुं न ह्यद्भुतविधेर्विधेः ।
KSS. 3.4.267.
कोऽत्र जानाति कीदृशी भवितव्यता ॥
KSS. 5.3.90.
विधेर्विलासानब्धेश्च तरङ्गान्को हि तर्कयेत् ॥
KSS. 5.3.18.
अचिन्त्यं दैवम् ।
KSS. 6.8.214.
अहो विधेरचिन्त्येव गतिरद्भुतकर्मणः ॥
KSS. 12.7.205.
किं वा भगवतो वेत्ति भवितव्यस्य को गतिम् ।
KSS. 12.19.60.
शक्या हि केन निश्चेतुं दुर्ज्ञाना नियतेर्गतिः ॥
KSS. 12.34.196.
को वेद देवस्य गतिम् ।
KSS. 18.4.341.

59. विधि प्रभुः --- KSS. 14.2.57.

60. ---- सततन्यस्तपदा सर्वस्य मूर्धनि ।
कामं भगवती केन भज्यते भवितव्यता ॥
KSS. 5.3.24.
कोऽन्यथाकर्त्तुं शक्तो हि भवितव्यताम् ॥
KSS. 6.1.86.
को देवलिखितं भोगं लङ्घयेत् ।
KSS. 7.6.31.
को हि स्वशिरसश्छायां विधेश्चोल्लङ्घयेद् गतिम् ॥
KSS. 9.2.211.
यद्यस्य लिखितं धात्रा ललाटाक्षरपङ्क्तिषु ।
तदवश्यमसम्भाव्यमपि तस्योपतिष्ठते ॥
KSS. 12.19. 155.

61. भवितव्यं हि धात्रापि न शक्यमतिवर्त्तितुम् ॥
KSS. 7.3.236.

62. इतीहावतरन्त्येव निरागस्त्वादयोनिजाः ।

भूतले कारणवशाद्दिव्या देवतनिर्मिताः ॥

KSS. 6.8.90.

63. तस्माद्यत्र तथा यद्भवितव्ये यस्य देवयोगेन ।
तत्र तथा तत्प्राप्त्यै विवशोऽसौ नीयतेऽत्र न भ्रान्तिः ॥

KSS. 12.19.80.

64. देवप्रबोधितः KSS.1.5.86.
देवचोदितः KSS. 3.4.206.
देवेनेव नियुक्ता KSS. 10.10.51.
विधिप्रेरितः KSS. 6.4.134.
विधिचोदितः KSS. 12.25.48.
विधिनियोगतः KSS.12.13.47.
विधिप्रेरणोत्पन्नबुद्धिः KSS. 12.13.28.

65. विधिविमोहितः

KSS. 9.4.109.

66. इत्थं चोपार्जितो यत्नाद्गुणोऽपि विधुरे विधौ ।
सम्पत्तये न न परं जायते तु विपत्तये ॥

KSS. 12.29.43.

67. ---- सर्वमाचेष्टते विधिः ।
न शक्यं पुरुषस्येह क्वचित्किञ्चित्कदाचन ॥

KSS. 12.29.13.

68. तदेवं नेच्छति विधो न मर्त्तुमपि लभ्यते ।

KSS. 12.29.22.

69. भव्यानां शुभसिद्धयुपायरचनाचिन्तां विधत्ते विधिः ॥

KSS. 7.9.256.

Cf. also - रक्षन्ति भाविकल्याणं भाग्यान्येव ।

KSS. 3.6.19

and - विधिरेव हि जागर्त्ति भव्यानामर्थसिद्धिषु ।
असञ्चेतयमानानां सद्भृत्यः स्वामिनामिव ॥

KSS. 6.4.91.

70. विधिर्हि घटयत्यर्थानचिन्त्यानपि सम्मुखः ।

KSS. 13.1.194.

71. असाध्यं साधयत्यर्थं हेलयाभिमुखो विधिः ॥

KSS. 6.4.124.

72. Cf. KSS. 4.1.118; 12.33.30; 17.6.8; 18.4.224.

73. अहो विधौ विपर्यस्ते न विपर्यस्यतीह किम् ।

KSS. 12.20.47.

74. कल्पवृक्षोऽप्यऽभव्यानां प्रायो याति पलाशताम् ।

KSS. 9.3.35.

Cf. also - कल्पवृक्षोऽप्यधन्यानां नाशां पूरयति ध्रुवम् ।

KSS. 18.2.102.

75. तत्सर्वथा ह्यभव्यानां कृतः क्लेशो महानपि ।
न फलाय विधिस्तेषु यथा वामो हि वर्त्तते ।

KSS.12.6.163.

76. फलति सर्वस्य विधिः सत्त्वानुसारतः ।

KSS. 10.10.109.

77. चित्रं धातैव धीराणामारब्धोद्दामकर्मणाम् ।
परितुष्यैव सामग्रीं घटयत्युपयोगिनीम् ॥

KSS. 3.4.359.

Cf also - दैवमेव हि साहाय्यं कुरुते सत्त्वशालिनाम् ।

KSS 3.4.311.

and - सत्यमेवं सुसत्त्वानां साहाय्यं भजते विधिः ।

KSS. 7.1.52.

78. The beginning of such speculations can be traced back to a very remote period. Even the Vedic thinkers were aware of the philosophical problems of the origin and nature of the world as they have given expression to their cosmological beliefs in the later portion of the Ṛg Veda. (10,72, 6, 121,3, 129, 190).

79. Vide pp. 14,48-49,52,53 supra.

80. Vide p.14 supra.

81. KSS. 12.3.89-97.

82. The Doctrine of Māyā (cosmic illusion) has its origin in the Upaniṣads. It is an important tenet in the Vedānta philosophy. Gauḍapāda, in his Kārikās, strongly supports it. Śaṁkara gives final form to it. Therefore, it is popularly known as his Māyāvāda.

For details vide the article 'Māyā' by J. Allan, Encyclopaedia of Religion and Ethics, Vol. viii, pp. 503-5.

83. या दृष्टा स्त्री त्वया सा माया भ्रामितं च यत् ।
तया संसारचक्रं तद्यो भृङ्गास्ते च जन्तवः ॥
वृषगदर्भरूपौ तौ धर्माधर्मौ पृथक् पृथक् ।
श्रितास्तद्वान्तदुग्धासृग्रूपे सुकृतदुष्कृते ॥
स्वस्वाश्रयोत्थ संसेव्य भूत्वा च श्वेतकल्मषाः ।
द्विविधा जालकाराभा विष्टब्धा निजवीर्यतः ॥
निर्माय द्विविधानेव जालपाशान् सुतादिकान् ।
सत्पुष्पविषपुष्पाभसुखदुःखानुषंगिणः ॥
यथास्वं तेषु संसक्ताः कालेनोरगरूपिणा ।
शुभाशुभाभ्यां वक्त्राभ्यां हताः पुत्र ! यथोचितम् ।
ततो घटकरूपासु नानायोनिषु मायया ।
स्त्रीरूपया तया क्षिप्तास्तथैवोत्थाय ते पुनः ॥
तुल्यासु वर्तिताः श्वेतकृष्णाकृतिषु द्विधा ।
पुत्रादिजालपाशेषु सुखदुःखानुबन्धिषु ॥
प्रवृत्ताः क्रन्दितुं विग्नाः शरणं परमेश्वरम् ॥
तद्दृष्ट्वा जातवैराग्यास्ते श्वेता अपि जन्तवः ।
प्रारब्धा निजजालस्थास्तमेवाक्रन्दितुं प्रभुम् ॥
ततः प्रबुध्य देवेन तेन तापसरूपिणा ।
ज्ञानाग्निज्वालयादग्धपाशाः सर्वेऽपि ते कृताः ॥
तेन विदुमसद्दण्डरूपमादित्यमण्डलम् ।
प्रविश्य तत्तादूर्ध्वस्थं परमं धाम ते श्रिताः ॥
नष्टा च चक्राकारेण संसारेणेव सहैव सा ।
माया वृषखराकारधर्माधर्मसमन्विताः ॥
एवं भ्रमन्ति संसारे शुक्लकृष्णाः स्वकर्मभिः ।

KSS. 12.3.107-19.

84. KSS. 1.5.103. 85. KSS. 16.1.87.

86. KSS. 8.2.161. The seven nether regions are named as Atala, Vitala, Sutala, Rasātala, Talātala, Mahātala and Pātāla. (Apte, V.S., The Students Sanskrit- English Dictionary, p . 330).

87. KSS. 4.2.253.
88. KSS. 2.2.53.

89. KSS. 8.2.151.
90. KSS. 8.2.134.

91. KSS. 12.33.16. For the description of Pātāla vide pp. 94-95 supra.

92. KSS. 12.6.127-28.
93. KSS. 15.1.83.

94. KSS. 15.1.117,119.
95. KSS. 12.7.286.

96. The doctrine of the four Yugas appears for the first time in the Aitareya Brāhmaṇa (VII.15). For the doctrine of the ages of the world or cosmic cycles (Yugas) in the mythologies of other countries vide Mackenzie, Donald A.,Indian Myth and Legend, Introduction, pp.XLIV, 108.

97. KSS. 12.35.75.

98. Radhakrishnan, S., Indian Philosophy, Vol.II.p.640.

99. - - - - - -- - एतस्मिन्भवाम्बुधौ ।
आशरीरमिदं सर्वं वीचिविभ्रमचञ्चलम् ॥
KSS. 12.30.18.
Cf. also - समुद्रलहरीलोलो विद्युत्स्फुरितभङ्गुरः ॥
जीवलोको ह्ययं याव्राद्युत्सवक्षणभङ्गुराः ।
KSS. 10.10.33.

100. KSS. 4.2.40; 5.3.16; 12.30.14-17.

101. मनुष्या नित्यदुःखिताः ।
KSS. 1.1.47.

102. निर्दुःखो नाम कश्चात्र संसारे भद्र जायते ॥
KSS. 1.1.47.

103. यावदयं देहस्तावद्दुःखक्षयः कुतः ।

KSS. 12.6.169.

104. किं तदस्ति हि संसारे पर्यन्तविरसं न यत् ॥

KSS. 9.1.25.

Cf. also– असारेऽस्मिन्भवे तावद्भावाः पर्यन्तनीरसाः ।

KSS. 16.1.67.

105. संयोगा विप्रयोगान्ता मरणान्तं हि जीवितम् ।
सर्वे क्षयान्ता निचयाः पतनान्ताः समुच्छ्रयाः ॥

KSS. 9.1.27.

106. प्रवातदीपचपलास्तथा कस्य कृते श्रियः ।

KSS. 4.2.40.

Cf. also - विशेषेणाचिरस्थायिप्रकाशप्रविलायिनी ।
सन्ध्या विद्युच्च लक्ष्मीश्च दृष्ट्वा कुत्र कदा स्थिरा ॥

KSS. 10.23.19.

and - अर्थानां शरदभ्रचला गतिः ।

KSS. 12.29.24.

107. KSS. 12.29.25.

108. - - - - भोगे मानुष्यके तु के ।
यत्र बन्धुसुहृद्भृत्यविप्रयोगाः सुदुःसहाः ॥
धननाशजरारोगाद्युद्भवा यत्र च व्यथा ।

KSS. 18.1.31-32.

109. KSS. 17.6.216.

110. KSS. 4.3.37.

111. KSS. 17.1.31.

112. ब्रह्मेन्द्रविष्णुरुद्राद्या यत्रावश्यं विनाशिनः ।

KSS. 12.27.135.

113. KSS. 1.5.138; 8.2.82.

114. KSS. 12.5.317.

115. ज्ञानं विना च नास्त्येव मोक्षो व्रतशतैरपि ।

KSS. 1.5.137.

116. ज्ञानमार्गे ह्यहङ्कारः परिघो दुरतिक्रमः।

KSS. 1.5.137.

117. KSS. 3.6.130. 118. KSS. 7.7.55.

119. KSS. 7.3.242. 120. KSS. 12.5.276.

121. ईश्वराराधनादेव विमुच्यन्ते च जन्तवः।

KSS. 10.3.119.

122. Vide pp.19-20 supra.

123. Vide p.119 supra.

124. इत्युक्त्वाख्याय सांख्यं च योगं च सरहस्यकम्।

KSS. 8.2.79.

125. KSS. 1.2.11-12.
Cf. - पङ्ग्वन्धवदुभयोरपि संयोगस्तत्कृतः सर्गः।

Sāṁkhyakārikā, 21.

126. Sāṁkhyakārikā, 9.

127. KSS. 8.2.80-82.

128. प्राप तपोवनं चास्य योगनिष्टैर्महर्षिभिः।
पद्मासनोपविष्टैश्च ब्रह्मलोकमिवावृतम्॥

KSS. 15.2.23.

129. अणिमा लघिमा प्राप्तिः प्राकाम्यं महिमा तथा।
ईशित्वं च वशित्वं च तथा कामाऽवसायिता॥

Quoted by M. Monier-Williams, A Sanskrit-English Dictionary, p.1216.

130. KSS. 8.2.112. 131. KSS. 12.1.16-17.

132. This art is variously known as Paraśarīra-āveśa, Parapurapraveśa and Parakāyapraveśa..

133. योगमन्यदेहप्रवेशदम्।

KSS. 8.2.78

134. KSS. 8.2.119. 135. KSS. 1.4.101.

136. KSS. 12.30.34-35.

137. अस्वतन्त्रो मृतोऽन्यत्र गर्भे यो जायते न सः ।
किञ्चित् स्मरत्यन्तरितः क्लेशैस्तैर्मरणादिभिः ॥
स्वातन्त्र्येण तु योऽन्यस्मिञ्छरीरे योगयुक्तितः ।
अन्तःकरणमाविश्य प्रविशेदिन्द्रियाणि च ॥
अविप्लुतमनोबुध्दिर्गृहादिव गृहान्तरम् ।
सहसा स स्मरत्येव ज्ञानी योगेश्वरोऽखिलम् ॥
KSS. 8.2.59-61.

138. The doctrine of grace can be traced back to the Upaniṣads which declare that God can be realised by that aspirant only whom He wishes to favour (Cf. Svetāśvatara Upaniṣad, 3.20; Kaṭha, Upaniṣad,. 1.2.23; Muṇḍaka Upaniṣad, 3.2.2. The Śrīmadbhagavadgītā affirms full faith in the divine grace (4.11;4.31; 18.66).

139. तत्क्षणं किं न कुर्याद्धिप्रसादः पारमेश्वरः ।
KSS. 1.6.164.
Cf. also - प्रसन्ने हि किमप्राप्यमस्तीह परमेश्वरे ।
KSS. 18.2.131.

140. ईश्वरानुगृहीतो हि कश्चिद् बालोऽपि शम्यति ।
KSS. 9.1.34.

Chapter VII

TĀNTRIKA PRACTICES

Religion concentrates on the relation of man with gods and lesser divine beings and aims to cultivate their goodwill by means of hymns as well as sacrifice, in order to induce them to bestow in return the benefits which man desires.[1] In contrast to it, Tantra endeavours to gain its ends by influencing the course of events, without the intervention of divine beings.[2] Tantra proceeds on mechanical rather than on emotional[3] lines and gives supreme importance to spells and ritual. Its purpose has always been either to produce or to avert evil. It is directed against demoniac and hostile agencies and aims at the acquisition of different Siddhis (supernatural powers). In ancient India, Tāntrika practices were generally undertaken by Śaivas and Śāktas.[4]

Tantra consists of Mantra and ritual. The Kathāsaritsāgara does not throw much light on the Mantra part of Tāntrika practices. Tāntrika rituals are described in an elaborate style. Detailed and vivid descriptions of many Tāntrika practices in the Kathāsaritsāgara show that such descriptions must have been incorporated on the basis of actual facts.

Tāntrika practices are generally undertaken by Kāpālikas,[5] Mahāvratins[6] or Pāśupatas[7] who live in cemeteries and possess supernatural powers.

Tāntrikas believe that every desired object can be attained from a Vetāla[8] by propitiating him with Tāntrika practices. It is said that the king Trivikramasena obtains the sovereignty of the Vidyādharas by the favour of a Vetāla.[9]

A Vetāla is invited and pleased[10] for the attainment of various desired objects. The mendicant Kṣāntiśīla wishes to please a Vetāla for obtaining overlordship of the Vidyādharas through him.[11] Vikramakesarī gets a Mantra and ritual for pleasing Vetāla to bring about reunion with his master.[12] Devadatta believes that propitiation of a Vetāla is the only recourse for taking revenge on wicked ascetic Jālapāda.[13] Vetāla is also pleased for curing diseases.[14]

The ceremony of Vetāla-Sādhanā is always described as Vīrasādhya –possible only with the help of a hero,[15] who is undaunted in performing rites like sitting on the corpse in a cemetery on a dark night and carrying on worship there with full concentration. Success (Siddhi) in the propitiation of a Vetāla can be gained when the obstacles to it are swept away by the aid of a hero.[16] A certain Tāntrika says that he can please a Vetāla with the help of a brave man.[17] It is believed that the raising of a Vetāla produces disagreeable results for a man of little courage.[18]

As far as the magical conditions and agencies are concerned, the ceremony of raising a Vetāla is undertaken in a cemetery. A Kāpālika sits on a corpse and mutter charms in a cemetery.[19] A hypocritical Kāpālika offers a burnt offering (Homa) in a cemetery.[20] An ascetic goes into a corner of a cemetery and performs worship by night.[21] Another Kāpālika comes near the pyre with the magic staff dancing on his shoulder and the booming drum in his hand. He quenches the flame of the pyre by throwing ashes on it. Then the dead body rises up uninjured and follows him drawn by his magic powers.[22] Vikramakesarin gets hold of a corpse in a cemetery. He washes it and performs all the necessary processes with regard to it. He summons a vetāla into it by means of a spell and duly worships him.[23] Devadatta also goes at night to a cemetery for pleasing a Vetāla.[24]

The night of the fourteenth day of the black half of a month (Kṛṣṇachaturdaśī) is considered to be very significant in Tāntrika practices. A mendicant tells a king, "On the fourteenth day of the black fortnight now approaching, I have to perform a certain incantation at nightfall, in a cemetery outside a town."[25] Later on, the king sees the ascetic pleasing Vetāla at the night of the black fortnight.[26] Another Tāntrika asks Śrīdarsana to come to the cemetery at nightfall on the fourteenth of the black fortnight.[27]

The Tāntrika practices are conducted in a cemetery because one can get dead bodies there and summon Vetāla in them. Moreover, the secluded environment of a cemetery helps the Tāntrikas to concentrate on their task. Strict secrecy is required in these rites and the cover of darkness provides a good opportunity to the Tāntrikas to perform their practices without others taking note of them.

There are charms for mastering a Vetāla.[28] A mighty Vetāla is summoned by the power of spells.[29]

The process of pleasing a Vetāla appears uniform in many stories of the Kathāsaritsāgara. The performer sits under a Banyan tree[30] in a cemetery with his body smeared with ashes from a funeral pyre using the hair of a corpse as his sacred thread, with a turban made from the cloth that is used for covering the dead and having put on a black garment.[31] He sends the hero to bring the corpse which is temporarily inhabited by the Vetāla or he himself goes to bring it if he has sufficient courage. Such a corpse is to be found hanging down a Śiṁśipa tree situated in the southern direction[32] of a cemetery. The Tāntrika honours the corpse with blood, garlands and unguents.

A circle is already prepared to receive the Vetāla, under the Banyan tree. The circle is a special and a spacious – one drawn by the yellow powder of human bones. The ground within the circle is smeared with blood. The jars full of blood are placed in the direction of the cardinal points. The ground is richly illuminated with candles of human fat, and near it is a fire fed with oblation. The circle is full of all the necessary preparations for a sacrifice, and in it the Tāntrika engages himself in his rite. He bathes the corpse, anoints it, throws a garland round it and places it within the circle. Then the mendicant summons that mighty Vetāla by the power of spells, and makes him enter the corpse and proceeds to worship him. He sits on the corpse, and holding in hand a ladle and spoon devised of a human bone, he begins to make an oblation of clarified butter in its mouth. He offers to him an Arghya of white human flesh in a skull by way of an Arghya vessel, and he presents to him flowers and fragrant unguents, and he gratifies him with the savoury smoke of human eyes, and makes an offering to him of human flesh.[33] For instance, Devadatta summons at the foot of a tree a Vetāla into the body of a man, and after worshipping him, he makes an oblation of human flesh to him. But Vetāla is not satisfied. Then, Devadatta prepares to cut off his own flesh to gratify him.[34] Vikramakesarin also satisfies a Vetāla with human flesh.[35] The 'Story of the king Trivikramasena and the mendicant' shows that the king is to be offered as a victim at the end of evil mendicant's worship.[36]

Maṇḍala or magic circle is drawn in the practices of black magic. It commands every point of compass and can be regarded as the inner circle of the horizon itself. There is a symbolism in the rites of centre (circle). In fact a Maṇḍala represents a whole series of circles, concentric or otherwise, inscribed within a square.[37] It indicates an 'ideal point' which belongs not to the profane geometrical space, but to the sacred space; a point in which communication with heaven or hell may be realised.[38] It is held up to be a potent centre of psychic energy.[39] It is a stronghold of the magician. The evil spirits cannot break through it. The magician can force the evil power, captured in the magic circle, to obey him. The magic circle helps the magician to concentrate on his task. It also serves as a protective barrier to the dead.

Another important constituent of the Tāntrika rites is the human body, dead or alive. All kinds of powers are attributed to the fat or the juices derived from the human body. Even ashes from the funeral pyre and the cloth used for covering the dead provide material to the Tāntrikas.

Black, red and yellow are the favourite colours of the Tāntrikas.

The use of fire in magic is wide-spread because fire is considered to be a purifying element. Garlands, flowers, fragrant unguents, clarified-butter, wine and blood are also used in Tāntrika practices. Animals, especially goats, are offered to please Vetālas.

The ceremony of the pleasing of a Vetāla is deemed successful if a flame rises from the widened mouth of a corpse. The ceremony is over when a handful of mustard seeds are found in the mouth of the dead body. These mustard seeds are believed to possess all possible magic powers that one can imagine.

There are rites for exorcising Bhūtas.[40] Bhūtas are worshipped for acquiring worldly gains.[41]

Piśāchas are pleased[42] for curing diseases,[43] attaining wealth and other desired objects. Yajñadatta gains the help of a Piśācha by a charm and obtains wealth through him.[44]

Yakṣas are adored for obtaining desired object.[45] There is a charm by which one can gain the help of a Yakṣa.[46] Piṅgadatta knows a charm to please the Yakṣa Sthūlaśiras.[47]

Brahma-Rākṣasa is worshipped in a magic-circle. The story of 'the Brāhmaṇa boy who offers himself to save the life of a king' shows the rite of worshipping a Brahma-Rākṣasa in the following manner.

The victim is adorned with garland and anointed with unguents. The priest draws a circle near the Aśvattha tree, and performs the required rite, and offers an oblation into fire.[48] The body is placed in front of the Brahma-Rākṣasa and his mother takes hold of his hands and his father of his feet.

The study of the Kathāsaritsāgara reveals that besides Vetālas, Bhūtas, Piśāchas, Yakṣas and Brahma-Rākṣasas, Bhairavas,[49] Yoginīs,[50] Yakṣiṇīs,[51] Vidyādharīs,[52] Śākinīs[53] and Ḍākinīs[54] are also the objects of worship in Tāntrika practices.

Some persons believe in performing certain magic rite (Kṛtyā) for the destruction of their enemies.[55] As a consequence of this rite, Yogananda is caught by a burning fever, and dies when the seventh day arrives.[56]

There is a reference to a peculiar practice of black magic in the text. The king Vikramāditya draws the figure of a man on the earth, and cuts off its hand with his sword. The hand of the Vetāla Yamaśikha is broken on account of this practice.[57] The king Vikramāditya proceeds to cut off the head of a figure of a man he has drawn, that makes Vetāla's neck stream with blood.[58]

This shows the belief that enemies can be destroyed or injured with the help of imitative magic. Perhaps the most familiar application of the principle of 'like produces like' is the attempt which has been made by many people in many ages to injure or destroy an enemy by injuring or destroying an image of him.[59] Piercing an image to make the enemy suffer or operating with a name as if it affected the owner of the name are not illogical acts when one believes that image and name are parts of a personality.[60]

The'story of the Kanakapura' contains reference to an act of foeticide. Kanakarekhā tells Śaktideva that in the eight month of the pregnancy of Bindurekhā, he must cut her open and take out the foetus.[61] An ascetic cooks an embryo with rice and eats it.[62] Supernatural powers are attributed to the extraordinary act of foeticide. It is believed that a magical sword (Khaḍagasiddhi) can be attained by performing this act.[63]

The act of foeticide does not seem merely the product of the story-teller's imagination. It must have formed part of the Tāntrika practices during the era of the Kathāsaritsāgara.

The Kathāsaritsāgara also refers to a belief that candles of human fat can be usefully employed in act of thieving. The candle of human fat possesses the property of searching hidden treasures.[64] A certain Pāśupata ascetic makes search of treasures with a candle of human fat. The candle falls from his hand which shows that the treasure is concealed on the spot.[65]

Magic in Medicine

It is generally held that the science of medicine grew out of black magic. The horned witch-doctor was the forerunner of our physicians and surgeons. His cauldron of crabs, scorpions, vipers, hyena's teeth and noxious weeds was the first laboratory in the world, and out of it grew the science of chemistry and medicine.[66]

In the Kathāsaritsāgara, magic has largely entered into medicine. It is believed that diseases can be cured by gaining the help of Vetālas and Piśāchas with various incantations and spells. A certain enchanter (Mantravādin) makes a promise that he can certainly put an end to the illness by getting a Vetāla into his power.[67] A Vetāla is propitiated for curing a disease like Yakṣmā (consumption).[68]

Services of Piśāchas are secured for curing a wound.[69] A friend of a Brāhmaṇa advises him to secure the services of a Piśācha to cure his wound which is about to become fatal. He gives him a Mantra with the instructions about the necessary accompanying ritual. The ritual is described in the following manner.

Rise up in the last watch of the night, and with dishevelled hair and naked, without rinsing your mouth, take two handful of rice as large as you can take with your two hands, muttering the Mantra go to a place where four roads meet, and there place the two handful of rice and return in silence without looking behind you. Do it until the Piśācha appears.[70]

By performing this rite, the wound of the Brāhmaṇa is healed by the Piśācha.[71]

In this Tāntrika ritual, special significance has been attached to the cross-road i.e. the place where roads cross one another. The chief factor, prompting crossroad as a special place for Tāntrika rites, must be due to the fact that it is a place which points out to all the four main directions i.e. east, west, north and south. People coming from different directions must meet here. Crossroad is considered particularly efficient in unburdening oneself of diseases which may pass to another person who comes from any of the four directions and puts his foot over the place. Due to its connection with disease transference, crossroad is considered to be a fit place to conjure up Piśāchas.[72]

The naked body is used as an instrument for gaining control over a Piśācha. This shows that nothing is considered vulgar in the sphere of innocence and religious sincerity. Complete nudity is regarded as most conducive to the effective operation of Tāntrika rites. There are various reasons behind the cult of nudity. It is believed that clothing contaminates and impairs the innate potencies of men and women. All the powers engendered during the ritual acts are diffused in a natural manner around the body without any impediment and serve to augment the efficacy of the rite and give force and direction to the sacrifice.[73] N.M. Penzer has enumerated a number of reasons for the use of nudity in Tāntrika practices. The nudity is preferred to dress, because the dress pollutes. In Tāntrika rites clothes become taboo and cannot be used again. In these rites the performer is required to be abnormal. Nudity is a great asset and complete nudity represents total submission to the power of spirit whose aid is needed in the particular rite to be carried out. Again, nudity is supposed to shock the spirits and so force them to grant the desired aid. Lastly, nudity is advocated due to the belief in the apotropaeic powers attributed to the sexual organs.[74]

There is a belief that fever is caused by a demon. People perform an incantation with all due rites for obtaining control over the fever-demon who has the power of removing fever. There is a ritual for curing fever (Jvarachetaka). It is held that the performance of this magic rite cures a person suffering from fever. The wicked Kanakamañjarī undertakes to perform this ritual which is told to her by some Yoginī.[75]

The ritual for curing fever begins at night in a holy temple of Śiva. There a goat is to be killed with sword and the image of Śiva to be bathed with its blood. All other items of worship of Śiva are also to be taken from the slaughtered goat – its flesh as cover, its heart as flowers, its eyes as incense and its head as Bali. Then the platform in front of the image of Śiva is to be sprinkled with red sandal. On it a lotus with eight petals is to be drawn with yellow pigment. In its centre the image of fever is to be prepared with blood and flour. The image should have three faces, three legs and has its fists filled with ashes by way of weapon. Having thus prepared fever demon with its concomitants, it is to be invited with a Mantra and worshipped with human blood, bones, flesh, etc. from the body of a person who is killed then and there.

A person is cured of his madness by striking him with charmed hand. There are ascetics who indulge in such a practice. An ascetic strikes the mad son of Upendraśakti by the charm-bearing hand. He, thus, makes him free from madness.[76]

Magical Incantations and Spells

Tāntrikas use incantations and spells to gain their desired ends.[77] Different Vidyās or Siddhis (supernatural powers) are attained by using Tāntrika spells. The Kathāsaritsāgara refers to the Prajñapti,[78] Māyāvatī,[79] Mohinī and Parivartinī,[80] Viparivartinī,[81] Kṛtyā,[82] Hemasiddhi,[83] Kālasaṁkarṣiṇī[84] and Iṣṭasaṁpādiṇī Vidyās.[85]

There are instances in the text which show the belief that a person can be excited, conciliated, attracted and bewildered by the power of charms. Somaprabhā is agitated with excitement inspired by charm. She is also conciliated by the magic power of a charm.[86] Kuvalayāvalī endeavours to attract a man by a spell, to offer him as a victim.[87] A hypocritical Kāpālika begins to draw Madanamañjarī to him by means of a spell.[88] Ghaṭa goes with the wandering mendicant, who is muttering spells and bewilders the guards.[89]

Some of the charms are described as having the inherent power of raising the dead to life.[90] It is also believed that one's life can be prolonged with the help of a charm known as Kālasaṁkarṣiṇī Vidyā. A powerful witch instructs Vāmadatta and his wife in the method of gaining the life-prolonging charm with the proper initiatory rites.[91]

The 18th story of the Vetāla gives some details of a charm called 'Iṣṭasaṁpādinī' i.e. that which fulfils the desires. The ritual is to be undertaken in water. While the aspirant is muttering spells under the water, the Vidyā creates delusion to bewilder him, so that he does not attain success. For there he sees himself born again as a boy. Later he grows into a young man, gets married and supposes that he has a son. And he is falsely deluded, supposing that one person is his friend and another his enemy, and does not remember his birth, nor that he is engaged in a magic rite for acquiring the Vidyā. But whosoever, when he seems to have reached twenty four years is recalled to consciousness by the knowledge of his instructor, and being firm in soul remembers his real life and knows that all, what he supposed himself to experience, is the effect of illusion, though he is under the influence of the illusion, he enters the fire, attains the Vidyā, and rising from the water, sees the real truth. But if the Vidyā is not attained by the pupil on whom it is bestowed, it is lost to the teacher also, on account of its having being communicated to an unworthy person.[92] This belief is shown in the story of the Brāhmaṇa's son who fails to acquire the magic power. The hermit of this story looses his mastery over the charm because he has bestowed it on an undeserving aspirant.[93]

Survey of the Tāntrika practices points at their great popularity in the society of the Kathāsaritsāgara. The Vetālas, Bhūtas, Piśāchas, Brahma-Rākṣasas, Bhairavas, Yoginīs, Yakṣiṇīs, Vidyādharīs, Śākinīs and Ḍākinīs are worshipped with the belief that they can bestow every desired object to their worshippers. People undertake practices of black magic, thinking that these can destroy or injure their enemies. Act of foeticide is considered to be the bestower of supernatural powers. It is held that hidden treasures can be searched by using the candles of human fat. Performance of various Tāntrika rites is held as extremely beneficial in curing diseases. Though the Tāntrika practices are widely popular in the society, these are generally looked down upon with contempt. A Brāhmaṇa, who leaves his own duties and indulges himself in the Tāntrika practices, does not command respect in the society.[94] The Brāhmaṇa Jīvadatta, who knows the Tāntrika rite of restoring dead person to life, is considered as degraded.[95] A hermit refuses to take food from the house of a Tāntrika Brāhmaṇa[96] and calls him sinner and Brahmarākṣasa.[97] The Tāntrika practices have drawn upon themselves the unfavourable criticism[98] because people perform all kinds of excesses under the cover of Tāntricism. Such practices have been unequivocally condemned by scholars. Sir Monier Williams hold that Tāntricism is the Hinduism arrived at its last and worst stage of medieval development.[99]

Footnotes Of Chapter VII

1. Macdonell, A.A., Article in the Encyclopaedia of Religion and Ethics, Vol.8, p.311.

2. Cf. "Tantra conveys the notion of power, by whatsoever means acquired, wielded by the Tāntrika as his own, and not as that of a higher being whose cooperation is only obtained by supplication and self-abasement." Hartland, E.S., Ritual and Belief, Vol.8, p.246.

3. Eliot, Hinduism and Buddhism, Vol.II, p.274.

4. Traces of some aspects of Tāntricism are suspected to be found in India as early as pre-historic period. Tāntrika practices are deeply rooted in the Ṛg Veda (V. 55; VI .52; VII. 50, 104; X.58, 60, 7-12; X.136.3; X.145; 162-63, 166, 185), Yajurveda (Vājasaneyī Saṁhitā, I.8) and Atharva Veda (IV.36).

5. KSS. 18.2.16
Cf. Buddhasvāmin, Bṛhatkathāślokasaṁgraha, canto XXII.

6. KSS. 7.3.54.

7. KSS. 12.30.21.

8. वेतालात्सर्वमाप्यते

KSS. 12.8.19.

Cf. also KSS. 12.32.14,44.

9. KSS. 12.8.20.

10. KSS. 2.3.48.

11. KSS. 7.5.36-37.

12. KSS. 7.5.10.

13. KSS. 5.3.237.

14. Vide p.183 infra.

15. KSS. 12.8.35.

16. KSS. 7.4.55.

17. KSS. 12.6.278.

18. KSS. 12.6.165.

19. KSS. 3.4.153.

20. KSS. 18.2.13-15.

21. KSS. 5.3.205.

22. KSS. 18.5.8.10.

23. KSS. 12.32.48.

24. KSS. 5.3.237.

25. KSS. 7.4.53-54. Cf. also - 12.8.35, 37-38.

26. KSS. 12.32.2.

27. KSS. 12.6.278.

28. वेतालसाधनं मन्त्रम्।

KSS. 12.8.16.

29. KSS. 12.34.14.

30. Aśvattha or Vaṭa tree (the Banyan tree) is always associated with Tāntrika practices which are generally performed under it.

31. KSS. 9.9.11; 12.6.283.

32. As the southern direction belongs to Yama, the dead body is described as hanging on a tree situated in it.

33. KSS. 12.32.4,12-13. Cf. also - KSS. 12.6.305-7.

34. KSS. 5.3.238.

35. KSS. 12.32.49-50.

36. KSS. 12.32.44.

37. Eliade, Mircea., Images and Symbols, Translated by Philip Mairet, p.52.

38. Ibid, p.75.

39. Walker, Benjamin., Hindu World, Vol.II, p.21.

40. भूततन्त्रविधिक्रमम्

KSS. 12.4.140.

41. KSS. 15.1.16.
42. KSS. 6.2.184.
43. Vide p.183 infra.
44. KSS. 6.2.162.
45. KSS. 3.6.32.
46. यक्षसाधनमन्त्र KSS. 18.2.10.
47. KSS. 9.6.94,101.
48. KSS. 12.27.71,114.
49. KSS. 3.6.110.
50. KSS. 8.5.122.
51. KSS. 8.6.163.
52. KSS. 9.1.9.
53. KSS. 10.5.294.
54. KSS. 3.4.150.
55. कृत्यामसाधयत्। KSS. 1.5.121.
56. KSS. 1.5.122.
57. KSS. 18.2.212-13.
58. KSS. 18.2.208.
59. Frazer, James.,Golden Bough, Vol.I, pp.10 ff.
60. Hopkins, E.W., Origin and Evolution of Religion, pp.9-10.
61. KSS. 5.3.166.
62. KSS. 14.4.76.
63. KSS. 5.3.268.
64. There seem to be two distinct ideas connected with the use of the dead man's hand and the candle of human fat. The first, and much older, idea is that of homoeopathic magic of the dead. The second idea is that of various magical properties attributed to the mandrake. (vide Ocean, Vol.III, p.151).
65. KSS. 6.8.70.
66. Thomas, P., Epics, Myths and Legends of India, Introduction, p.1. The use of magic in medicine goes back to the period of Atharva Veda which contains songs and spells for the healing of diseases (Bhaiṣajayāni). This Veda has many songs

(II,31; V,23) which serve the purpose of exorcism and driving away all kinds of worms. "These songs of magic, together with the magic rites attached to them form the oldest system of Indian medical science."

Winternitz, M., History of Indian Literature, Vol.I,p.129.

67. KSS. 12.6.261.

68. KSS. 7.5.261.

69. KSS. 6.2.163.

70. KSS. 6.2.164-68.

71. KSS. 6.2.169.

72. James Frazer gives customs connected with crossroad from Japan, Bali, Guatemala, China, Bohemia and England. (vide Golden Bough, Vol. iii, p.59; Vol.IX, p.10, 49, 68,144).

73. Walker, Benjamin; Hindu World, Vol. II, p.135.

74. Ocean, Vol.II, p.117.

75. KSS. 12.4.207.

76. KSS. 12.6.382.

77. KSS. 18.2.6-7. Vide also pp.179,181,183 supra.

78. KSS. 9.1.51.

79. KSS. 7.8.38.

80. KSS. 8.3.118.

81. KSS. 8.6.121.

82. KSS. 1.5.121. Vide also p.182 supra.

83. KSS. 14.4.81.

84. KSS. 12.6.69.

85. KSS. Vide p.186 infra.

86. KSS. 3.3.130, 132.

87. KSS. 3.6.189.

88. KSS. 18.2.13.

89. KSS. 10.8.81-82.

90. KSS. 12.9.21.

91. KSS. 12.1.65.

92. KSS. 12.25.35, 50-56.

93. KSS. 12.25.86.

94. KSS. 12.16.37.

95. KSS. 9.2.113. 96. KSS. 12.10.21-31.

97. KSS. 12.10.20.

98. Cf. Varāha Purāṇa, 70.41; 71.9, 53-55; Manu Smṛti, XI.63.

99. Hinduism p.123. Cf. also "The Tāntrika religion became the worst of all forms which the various aberrations of the Hindu mind assumed" Goldstücker, Theodore; Sanskrit and Culture, p.132.

Chapter VIII

THE BAUDDHA FAITH

Many stories of the text[1] confirm the impact of the Bauddha Faith in the society.[2] The inclusion of such stories in the work of a great Śaivite Hindu author evidently shows his broadmindedness and religious tolerance.

There are Bauddha mendicants in the society of the Kathāsaritsāgara. The words Śramaṇa,[3] Bhadanta,[4] Bhikṣu[5] and Kṣapaṇaka[6] are used in the sense of a Buddhist mendicant in the text. There are some female Bauddha mendicants (Pravrājikas) also. Some of them are depicted as of a very low character. Yogakaraṇḍikā and her disciple Siddhikarī, living in the monastery of Buddha, have nothing religious about them as they indulge in all sorts of immoral acts only for acquiring worldly gains.[7]

There are monasteries (Vihāras,[8] Chaityas[9]) where Buddhist monks live. The city of Takṣaśilā has lofty Buddhist monasteries. There is a Buddhist monastery outside the city of Mathurā.[10] Sometimes, kings show their interest in getting these monasteries constructed. For instance, the king Vinītamati gets a monastery constructed for Buddhist monks.[11] Buddhist preachers give religious instructions in monasteries.[12]

Besides, male and female Buddhist monks, some kings and their subjects are also described as followers of the Bauddha Faith. The king Kaliṅgadatta of Takṣaśilā is a distinguished Buddhist, all whose subjects are devoted to Buddha.[13] The king Vinītamati is also devoted to

Buddha.[14] The Buddhist merchant Vitastādatta is exclusively devoted to the honouring of Buddhist mendicants.[15]

Some people, being convinced with the teachings of Buddhism and desiring salvation, become Buddhists. A young and handsome prince becomes a Buddhist monk.[16] Being afraid of death, a merchant's son Ratnadatta becomes a Buddhist. Desiring salvation, he asks the king Kaliṅgadatta to teach him the Bauddha Faith.[17]

Conflicts between the followers of the Bauddha and the Hindu Faiths are clearly discernible in the society of the Kathāsaritsāgara. The merchant Vitastādatta is a Buddhist whereas his son Ratnadatta is an admirer of the Hindu Faith.

Ratnadatta calls his father as an impious man and talks to him with bitter scorn – 'You abandon the religion of the three Vedas and cultivate 'Adharma'. You neglect the Brāhmaṇas by always honouring Śramaṇas. What have you to do with that Buddhist discipline, which all kinds of low-caste men resort to, to gratify their desire to have a Vihāra to dwell in, released from bathing and other strict ordinances, loving to feed whenever it is convenient, rejecting the Brāhmaṇical lock and other prescribed methods of doing the hair, quite at ease with only a rag round their loins.'[18]

The Buddhist mendicant Ratnachandramati challenges the king Vinītamati to dispute on the following terms, 'if you are vanquished, O king you must adopt Buddhism. If I am vanquished, I will abandon the rags of a Buddhist mendicant and serve the Brāhmaṇas.'[19] The discussion continues for seven days. On the eight day, the Buddhist mendicant defeats the king in the dispute. Being subdued in spirit the king asks the mendicant to teach him the Bauddha Faith.[20]

The Buddhists hold their Faith in high esteem. A Buddhist merchant Vitastādatta says that religion is not confined to one form; a transcendent religion is a different thing from a religion that embraces the whole world.[21] He lays stress on the point that one should not blame the Bauddha Faith, which gives security to all the creatures, due to the fall of an individual.[22]

Preaching of Bauddha are told with devotion. The king Vinītamati tells Somaśūra the injunctions of the Bauddha Faith with all its secrets.[23]

The Buddhist do not believe in the existence of God.[24] Though Buddhism denies the existence of God as a creator or does not use the idea for the promotion of righteousness, and it practically denies the existence of the human soul as a substance, still it has the needful personal element in the shape of its founder.[25] The Kathāsaritsāgara refers to a monastery full of many images of Buddha.[26] Buddha is worshipped as God. Somaprabhā worships Buddha with a multitude of pearls, beautiful gems and golden lotuses.[27]

The Buddhist believe in the doctrine of Bodhisattva. The word 'Bodhisattva' literally means 'one whose essence is perfect knowledge'. Bodhisattva is a person who is on the way to the attainment of perfect knowledge. In other words, Bodhisattva is a person who will be a future Buddha. It is believed that the compassionate, generous and gifted persons spring from a portion of a Bodhisattva. In the Kathāsaritsāgara, Jīmūtavāhana, who is of great courage, compassionate to all creatures, attentive to the instruction of all spiritual advisers, has been considered as a portion of Bodhisattva.[28] Nāgārjuna, who springs from a portion of Bodhisattva, gives his head ninety nine times in his previous births and once in this birth.[29] There is a son of a rich merchant who is described as a partial incarnation of Bodhisattva.[30] He keeps his wife alive by giving her his own flesh and blood. Though exhausted with the long fast, the brave man enters a river rescues a mutilated person.[31] There is another man of noble soul who is held as an incarnation of portion of a Bodhisattva.[32]

Even some grateful animals are considered as the portions of Bodhisattva. Thus, Hemaprabha, the king of the parrots, is called an incarnation of a portion of Buddha. He is rich in chastity.[33] There is a wise boar who is an incarnation of the portion of Buddha. He is described as the benefactor of all creatures. He throws himself into a pit and sacrifices his life for a petitioner.[34]

Three truths[35] of the Bauddha Faith are referred to in the text. According to the Buddhists, one's heart is quieted by practising the four meditations (Chaturbhāvanā).[36] The word 'Chaturbhāvanā' of the text may refer to the four points of Buddhism – (i) Everything is momentary and momentary alone, (ii) Everything is pain and pain only, (iii) Everything is individual and individual only, (iv) Everything is baseless.

Many passages in the text which show that the world is misery, must have been influenced by the Bauddha Faith according to which everything is misery. The 'Story of the seven princesses', which resembles the Saptakumārikāvadāna, contains the belief that the world is unreal and so also the body and joys as the union with the loved ones are baseless fabric of a dream.[37] Another story of the dejected prince who takes out his own eye for the sake of a woman whose beauty she admires, shows that there is no beauty in this perishable body.[38]

The Buddhistic concept of Nirvāṇa also finds place in the Kathāsaritsāgara. Nirvāṇa is described as that state which allays the fire of desire.[39] The highest goal of life is considered to be the attainment of the state of Buddha which means freedom from the bondage of births and deaths.[40]

It is believed that one who knows the real truth about that which is to be rejected and which is to be chosen, attains the rank of an Arhat.[41] A man, who with the intent concentration of a person, averts his attention from all outward things, has intuition for truth. One who has seen the truth (Tattva) is not bound in the snare of Karman.[42]

Tapa and Yoga are considered to be means of attaining the highest perfection (Parama Siddhi). By the power of austerities, Malayamālin is said to have attained the rank of an Arhat.[43] Similarly, the generous Indraprabha attains the rank of Bodhisattva through austerities.[44] The king Vinītamati and his pupil Somaśūra gain the highest illumination through supernatural powers acquired by Yoga.[45]

Self mutilation and sacrificing one's life for others are considered to be other means of attaining perfection. There is a story of the prince who tears out his own eye, regardless of his lovely body, and passes on to perfection[46]. The 'story of the seven princesses'[47] shows that the princesses attain highest perfection through self-sacrifice.

In the Kathāsaritsāgara, the stories of faithless wives have Buddhistic influence which dissuades man from worldly life. Such stories especially occur in the tenth Lambaka of the text, where the heroes speak out the evil nature of ladies[48] and after the experience that there is no faithful woman in the world, become monks.

Bauddha Ethics

Ethics is an inseparable part of the Bauddha Faith which is a system of duty, morality and benevolence. The great discipline of a Bodhisattva is to be followed by those who are free from sins and by no other.[49]

The Bauddhas hold that those wise men who embark on the six perfections (Pāramitās), taught by Buddha, cross the ocean of temporal existence.[50] These six doctrines of perfection are illustrated by stories in the Kathāsaritsāgara. The doctrine of the perfection of charity[51] is elucidated by the 'story of the generous Induprabha',[52] the perfection of character[53] by the 'story of the parrot who is taught virtue by the king of the parrots',[54] the perfection of patience[55] by the 'story of the patient hermit Śubhanaya',[56] the perfection of perseverance[57] by the 'story of the preserving young Brāhmaṇa',[58] the perfection of meditation[59] by the 'story of the merchant who falls in love with a painting'[60] and the perfection of wisdom[61] by the 'story of robber who won over Chitragupta'.[62]

The Bauddha Faith is rich in the merit of giving benefit to all creatures.[63] The 'story of the seven princesses'[64] illustrates the belief that to give benefit to others is the only real thing in this revolving world. These princesses decide to do good to their fellow-creatures flinging their bodies, while they are alive, to the eaters of raw flesh in a cemetery.

Generosity, compassion and self-sacrifice are preached by the Bauddha Faith. It is stressed that a wise man should do what is beneficial to others. He should abstain from selfish aspirations. He should even sacrifice his own body in order that he might obtain perfection in insight (Samyakasambodha).[65]

As all creatures fear death, the Buddhists hold that there is no higher piety than giving the benefit of preserving creatures from the fear of death.[66] The main principles of the Bauddha Faith are giving security to all the creatures,[67] abstinence from injuring any creature[68] and bringing liberation.[69]

The study of the Hindu and the Bauddha Faiths reveals that though the former prevails in the Kathāsaritsāgara, some impact of the latter is also clearly visible. The Bauddha Faith serves as a missionary religion as some people, being fascinated by its teachings, have adopted it. But, it has not yet been able to capture the high position of the Hindu Faith. Mutual rivalries are also observed. Disputes and discussion between the followers of both the Faiths indicate the deep attachment of the followers to their respective Faiths. As far as Ethics is concerned, there is no great difference between the basic principles of both the Faiths which agree on the point that Upakāra is Dharma.[70]

Footnotes Of Chapter VIII

1. Cf. KSS. 5.6-7; 10.8-9; 12.5. For Buddhistic stories in the Kathāsaritsāgara vide Winternitz, M., History of Indian Literature, Vol.III, Part I, pp.355-56, 361; Weber, A., Story of Vararuchi, The Indian Antiquary, Vol.II, p.146.

2. There is no clear reference to the Jaina Faith in the text. The word 'Jina' (KSS. 9.1.205; 11.1.76) denotes Buddha only.

3. KSS. 9.1.118.

4. KSS. 9.3.40.

5. KSS.12.5.93.

6. KSS. 7.5.59.

7. Vide Story of Guhasena and Devasmitā (KSS. 2.5.88-90, 113-38, 144-45); Story of Siddhi (KSS. 2.5.93-112).

8. KSS. 10.9.132.

9. KSS. 6.1.13.

10. KSS.2.4.148-49.

11. KSS. 6.3.37.

12. KSS. 6.2.8.

13. तस्यां कलिङ्गदत्ताख्यो राजा परमसौगतः ।
अभूत्तारावरस्फीतजिनभक्ताखिलप्रजः ॥

KSS. 6.1.12.

The words "सौगत" and "जिनभक्त" are used in the sense of a Bauddha.

14. जिनपूजापरायणः

KSS. 12.5.99.

15. KSS. 6.1.15.

16. KSS. 6.2.18.

17. KSS. 6.1.42.

18. स च तं पितरं शश्वत्पाप इत्याजुगुप्सत ॥
तात त्यक्तत्रयी धर्मस्त्वमधर्मं निषेवसे ।
यद् ब्राह्मणान् परित्यज्य श्रमणाञ्शश्वदर्चसि ॥
स्नानादियन्त्रणाहीनाः स्वकालाशनलोलुपाः ।
अपास्तसशिखाकेशकौपीनसुस्थिताः ॥
विहारास्पदलोभाय सर्वेप्यधमजातयः ।
यमाश्रयन्ति किं तेन सौगतेन नयेन ते ॥

KSS. 6.1.16,18-20.

19. त्वया जितेन राजेन्द्र ग्राह्यं सुगतशासनम् ।
मया जितेन शुश्रूष्या विप्राः सन्त्यज्य चीवरम् ॥

KSS. 12.5.95.

20. KSS. 12.5.98-100.

21. - - - - न धर्मस्यैकरूपता ।
अन्यो लोकोत्तरः पुत्र धर्मोऽन्यः सार्वलौकिकः ॥

KSS. 6.1.21.

22. किं च दर्शनमेतत्त्वं सर्वसत्त्वाभयप्रदम् ।
प्रायः पुरुषदोषेण न दूषयितुमर्हसि ॥

KSS. 6.1.23.

23. अन्येद्युश्च क्रमात् तस्मै सोमशूराय शासनम् ।
स विनीतमतिबौद्धं सरहस्यमुपादिशत् ॥

KSS. 12.5.366.

24. अनीश्वरः

KSS. 18.1.50.

25. Bhandarkar, R.G., Vaiṣṇavism, Śaivism and Minor Religious Systems, pp.2-3.

26. नानाजिनाकारं विहारम् ।

KSS. 6.2.7.

27. KSS. 6.3.38-40.

28. KSS. 12.23.8-9, 106.

29. KSS. 7.7.10, 47-48, 51, 53, 188-89.

30. KSS. 10.9.2.
31. KSS. 10.9.6,10.
32. KSS. 10.9.45-46.
33. KSS. 12.5.237
34. KSS. 12.5.380.
35. त्रिःसत्य

KSS.5.1.100.

36. KSS. 10.8.161.
37. असारं विश्वामेवैतत्तत्रापीदं शरीरकम्।
तत्राप्यभीष्टसंयोगसुखादिस्वप्नविभ्रमः ॥

KSS. 6.2.15.

38. KSS. 6.2.18-23.
39. तृष्णासंतापशमनं निर्वाणम्।

KSS. 18.1.116.

40. KSS. 7.7.53.
41. सहेतुहेयोपादेयतत्त्वज्ञोऽर्हत्वमाप्तपवान् ॥

KSS. 12.5.316.

42. एकाग्रो हि बहिर्वृत्तिर्निर्वृत्तस्तत्वमीक्षते।
दृष्टतत्त्वश्च न पुनः कर्मजालेन बध्यते ॥

KSS. 6.1.52,53.

43. KSS. 12.5.316.
44. KSS. 12.5.235.
45. KSS. 12.5.368.
46. KSS. 6.2.21.
47. KSS. 6.2.13-17, 42-43.
48. न स्नेहोऽस्ति न दाक्षिण्यं स्त्रीष्वहो चापलादृते ॥

KSS. 10.8.93.

गृहे नार्यो निबन्धनम्।

KSS. 10.8.108.

सन्निकृष्टे निकृष्टेऽपि कष्टं रज्यन्ति कुस्त्रियः

KSS. 10.8.124.

हा धिक् निम्नाभिपातिन्यो लोला दूरान्मनोरमाः ।
सुक्षोभ्या न स्त्रियः शक्याः पातुं ह श्वाभ्रापगा इव ॥

KSS. 10.8.149-50.

49. - - - -विगतकल्मषैः ।
बोधिसत्त्वमहाचर्या चरितव्यैह नेतरैः ॥

KSS. 12.5.101.

50. एवं चारु नौतुल्यां तरन्त्यैव भावाम्बुधिम् ।
वत्स बुद्धोक्तदानादिषट्कपारमितां बुधाः ॥

KSS.12.5.362.

51. दानपारमिता ।

KSS. 12.5.236.

52. KSS. 12.5.219-36.

53. शीलपारमिता ।

KSS. 12.5.236.

54. KSS. 12.5.237-59.

55. क्षमापारमिता ।

KSS. 12.5.259.

56. KSS. 12.5.260-77.

57. धैर्यपारमिता ।

KSS. 12.5.277.

58. KSS. 12.5.278-83.

59. ध्यानपारमिता ।

KSS. 12.5.283.

60. KSS. 12.5.284-318.

61. प्रज्ञापारमिता।

KSS. 12.5.318.

62. KSS. 12.5.319-61.

63. - - - सौगतं मतम्।
सत्त्वोपकारपुण्याढ्यं – – – – – – ॥

KSS. 12.5.98.

64. KSS. 6.2.13-17, 42-43.

65. आ शरीरमतः सर्वेष्विष्टेष्वाशानिवर्तनात्।
प्राज्ञः सत्त्वहितं कुर्यात्सम्यक्सम्बोधलब्धये ॥

KSS. 6.2.12.

66. ईदृगेव हि सर्वस्य जन्तोर्मृत्युभयं भवेत्।
तद्रक्षणोपकाराच्च धर्मः कोऽभ्यधिको वद ॥

KSS. 6.1.39.

Cf. also
भूतेष्वऽभयदानेन नान्या चोपकृतिर्मम ।

KSS.6.1.24.

67. सर्वसत्त्वाभयप्रदम्।

KSS. 6.1.23.

68. अहिंसाप्रधाने

KSS. 6.1.25.

69. मोक्षप्रदायिनि ।

KSS. 6.1.25.

70. उपकारस्य धर्मत्वे विवादो नास्ति कस्यचित्।

KSS. 6.1.24.

Part II

BELIEFS

Beliefs regarding omens, dreams and evil spirits are fairly universal among mankind. From the cradle to the grave, man is their slave. Sincere persons give expression to the fact that while rational in intention, they are unable to resist the temptation to react in some special way to those situations where superstition is traditionally sanctioned.[1] A superstitious mind, quite independent of education and training holds many superstitions which are not founded on reasonable conceptions of the world and of human life, its necessities and obligations. Such superstitions flourish in the atmosphere of ingnorance. Fear is another element contributing towards their formation. It is the irrational fear which forms the base of the bogey of superstitions.[2]

The following chapters are based on beliefs in popular superstitions.

---

1. Goldenweiser, A.A., Early Civilisation, p.196.

2. Knowlson, T. Sharper; The Origin of Popular Superstitions and Customs, p.3.

Chapter IX

OMENS

An omen is a casual event of occurrence, phenomenon or incident which is supposed to be a portent of either the good or the evil destiny.[1] It is a sign believed to prognosticate a future event between which and the event foretold there appears no relation of cause and effect but which is usually received as an intimation of things to come from a superior power.[2] According to Varāhamihira, it indicates the future result of the action performed in the previous birth.[3]

Belief in omens is almost universal. Both educated as well as uneducated people believe in them. The belief is common among primitive people. The tendency to believe in omens seems to be inherent in human race. Curiosity, the desire for knowledge, the craving to penetrate mysteries and to know what the future holds in store, are feelings natural to mankind. Added to them an animistic attitude of mind and a vague sentiment of awe towards uncomprehended things are at the root of belief in omens.[4] Omens are generally based on superstitions and like all other superstitions, their origin is found in the atmosphere of ignorance and fear. Application of false inductive logic has contributed to their growth. The principle of direct symbolism still accounts for a fair proportion of them.[5]

Belief in omens is as old as mankind. In the Sanskrit literature, it can be traced back to the Vedic period.[6]

In the Kathāsaritsāgara, omens of both good and evil nature are accepted as of unquestionable validity. Belief in both types of omens is prevalent among the people in all walks of life. Good omens portend joy and evil omens misery to the characters of the text. The king of Vatsa is cheered up with omens which portend victory.[7] Beholding an auspicious omen, Śrīdatta goes in search of his wife.[8] People are quite afraid of evil omens. Viṣṇudatta believes in the evil effect of inauspicious omens. As he sets forth and sees an evil omen, he tells his friends that it is advisable to turn back and set out again with good hope of success only when they have an auspicious omen.[9] Somaprabhā sees an unfavourable omen and asks Kaliṅgasenā not to meet Udayana.[10]

Many stories of the Kathāsaritsāgara confirm the belief that good or evil omen always shows its effect. A king first, has happiness announced by omens[11] and then he beholds Anaṅgaprabhā. Śrīdatta beholds unlucky omens and afterwards he sees all his friends, together with Bhāvanikā, wounded in the road.[12]

It is widely held that any work which is undertaken without first counteracting the evil omen will end in calamity.[13] Visnudatta sets forth and sees an evil omen. He asks his friends not to set out in wake of an inauspicious omen. But his friends do not listen to him. On account of the effect of the evil omen, they are charged with the murder of a Śavara.[14] The two chiefs of bandits named Piṅgeśvara and Guheśvara, though they see an evil omen, do not turn back, and reach and plunder the whole city and even temple of god. Śiva in his wrath then punishes the bandits by making them blind.[15]

It is believed that one who proceeds to fight one's enemy after an inauspicious omen cannot win. The king of the Asuras, though warned by omens to desist from proceeding against his enemy goes to fight and meets destruction in his fight with Muktāphaladhvaja.[16]

Any work done after an evil omen is sure to bring distress. Though previously forbidden by her friend Somaprabhā, Kaliṅgasenā sends her chamberlain, giving him her message for the king of Vatsa. In consequence of the inauspicious omen, her marriage is put off by six months.[17] Later on, she realises her mistake. She thinks that this is due to her own folly in sending a messenger to the king after an evil omen.[18]

Many good and evil omens are referred to in the Kathāsaritsāgara. Prosperous events happening at the very beginning of an undertaking are good omens and portend its final success.[19] The king of Vatsas finds a jewelled throne. The ministers rejoice exceedingly making certain of the king's victory.

Good luck befalling one also indicates success in an undertaking.[20] Śaktideva going in search of Kanakapura, meets his relation Viṣṇudatta in the way. He considers that the accomplishment of his object is near at hand for this is an auspicious omen.

It is one of the most common and most widely spread beliefs that birds and animals have the faculty of seeing things which escape the notice of men. They act under supernatural impulses. Therefore, many omens are connected with birds and animals. It is an evil omen to see a crow at the time of one's journey.[21] Crow on one's left hand, a dog running form one's left to right, a snake appearing on one's right and left arms are considered to be inauspicious omens.[22] Terrific howl of a female jackal is ominous.[23] The merchant Samudrasena, Kīrtisenā and others reach an entrance of a forest. A female jackal, like a messenger of Yama, utters a terrific howl. Thereupon, the merchant who understands what that means becomes apprehensive of an attack by bandits.[24] The unfavourable omen immediately shows its effect. In the dread of night a large force of bandits suddenly falls upon the caravan with uplifted weapons, and surrounds it on all sides. Bandits kill the merchant prince Samudrasena and his followers, and run away with all his wealth.[25]

A partridge appearing on one's right hand and a jackal howling on one's left hand are sure prophets of evil. Brāhmaṇa Agniśarman sees such evil omens.[26] As a result, he is handed over to the executioners by the orders of a king.

Appearance of an owl is considered to be inauspicious.[27] Encircling of one's head by vultures too is an evil omen.[28]

Natural phenomena indicate good and evil omens to the characters of the Kathāsaritsāgara. The red sky portends that the earth will soon be dyed crimson with blood.[29] The 'story of Sūryaprabha' shows the evil effect of this omen. The sky becomes red and after sometimes there ensues a fierce battle in which many persons are killed.

Peaks reddened with the evening light foreshadow the bloodshed of the approaching battle.[30] Blowing of the terrible wind, earthquake, breaking of mountains and rumbling of sky though cloudless are alarming omens because these omens announce the approach of evil. A detailed description of these omens connected with natural phenomena is observed in the 'story of Naravāhanadatta'.[31] The story shows that suddenly great portents manifest themselves in the grove of ascetics. A very terrible wind blows, uprooting gigantic trees, the hills break, and the sky rumbles awfully, though cloudless. As a result of these portents, there arises a battle between the party of Naravāhanadatta and that of his enemy Mānasavega.

Lightning too has ominous import.[32]

No unexpected or unusual occurrence is too trivial to be the subject of an omen. The 'story of Somaprabhā' shows that the girl born to Chandraprabha speaks distinctly and gets up and sits down. The women in the lying-in-chamber are astonished and terrified to see this evil omen. So much so that her father Dharmagupta himself goes in a state of alarm.[33] Due to these evii omens, the girl is regarded as inauspicious. Later it is said, as the result of evil omens manifested at the time of her birth, Guhasena, whose son Guhachandra is married to this girl, dies soon after the marriage.

It is considered to be an evil omen if a horse of a bridegroom is stolen. A horse of a bridegroom is stolen by the Brāhmaṇa Hariśarman from the house of Sthūladatta. The friends of the bridegroom are unable to find the horse. Sthūladatta is distressed at this evil omen.[34]

Enmity between religious sects has caused the sight of a person belonging to one sect as inauspicious omen for the person of the other sect. This is the reason why the sight of a Buddhist monk is considered to be an evil omen.[35]

Belief in omens from bodily signs is also mentioned in the Kathāsaritsāgara. Involuntary twitching or itching are looked upon with great apprehension. Movements of the right limbs of men signify good luck but of the left, bad luck. With women, these omens are reversed. Throbbing of right eye in men indicate good fortune.[36] The throbbing of right eye and fluttering of a woman's heart predict evil fortune.[37] The throbbing of the left arm and shoulder of men are held as inauspicious omens.[38]

In magnanimous men, the spirits, by being elevated or depressed, indicate before hand the approach of good or evil fortune.[39] For instance, listening to the 'story of the devoted couple Śūrasena and Suṣeṇā', Naravāhanadatta thinking over it, suddenly becomes dejected. This is an evil omen. Later on, he comes to know that his father-in-law and mother-in-law have died and his father, Yaugandharāyaṇa and others have hurled themselves from a mountain cliff.

Birth marks on the body of a person are interpreted as auspicious or inauspicious. Many characters of the Kathāsaritsāgara are described as possessed of auspicious marks. For instance, sons of the minister of Udayana, Kīrtisenā,[40] daughters of the hermit Parvata,[41] son of the Brāhmaṇa Chandrasvāmin,[42] and Tārāvaloka[43] have auspicious marks on their bodies.

Some of the auspicious marks are mentioned in the Kathāsaritsāgara. Signs of umbrella, chowries, line, banner and such other marks on feet and of line, umbrella, banner etc. on hands indicate future sovereignty.

Future emperors are described in the text as possessing such auspicious marks on their bodies. Naravāhanadatta bears the marks of umbrella and chowries on his feet.[44] Tārāvaloka is distinctly marked with the signs of a great emperor.[45] The foot of the Vidyādhara king Madanavega is marked with umbrella and banner.[46] A person is distinguished from the auspicious marks on his body.[47]

Auspicious marks on one's body indicate approaching good fortune.[48] Auspicious marks on the sons of the ministers of Udayana portend good fortune.[49] Future glory of Sūryaprabha is indicated by his exceedingly auspicious marks.[50] Auspicious marks on the son of Dhanavatī foreshadow his lofty destiny.[51] There is a belief that no ill fortune can befall a lady with auspicious marks.[52]

In marriage, auspicious marks on the body of a girl are taken into account.[53] The king Devasena sends some Brāhmaṇas to find out whether Unmādinī possesses auspicious marks or not. On the false report of the Brāhmaṇas, the king declines to take her as his wife.[54]

The 'story of the woman who has eleven husbands' shows that the children with inauspicious marks are always the destroyers of their families. According to this story, as soon as a daughter is born to a certain householder, her mother dies, and a few days later, one of the man's sons dies. Then his brother dies also. The householder believes that owing to the birth of this ill-omened girl, three have met their death.[55] The story further tells the destructive character of the ill-omened girl. When the ill-omened girl gets married, she loses eleven husbands.

The story of the 'Dhūrtamaṭhādhīśa' also confirms the belief that children with inauspicious marks indicate misfortune in the form of the destruction of their families. The story shows that people are afraid of such children and want to get rid of them. In this story, a certain ascetic cleverly tells a man that his daughter has inauspicious marks and when she marries, his wife, sons and other relatives will undoubtedly perish. The father casts her in the Ganges out of fear.[56]

There is a belief that moles on one's body too portend one's future. People give due consideration to such moles. Guṇaśarman knows the meaning of moles, and tells Agnidatta what these portend when appearing on every single limb, both in men and women.[57] Moles on the nose and breasts of a girl portend that she will have rival wives.[58]

This chapter shows that the superstitious people of the society of the Kathāsaritsāgara believe in the unquestionable validity of both good and evil omens which portend joy and misery to them and which are often connected with birds and animals, natural phenomena, usual occurrences and the sight of a particular person. Omens are generally based on the principle that whatever is agreeable to human life and whatever is pleasing to the human mind is considered to be auspicious. On the contrary, whatever creates trouble in human activities and whatever causes fear to human beings is inauspicious. Involuntary twitching or itching is looked upon as ominous. Birth-marks on one's body are interpreted as auspicious or inauspicious. Moles too are believed to indicate one's future.

Footnotes Of Chapter IX

1. Cf. शक्नोति शुभाशुभं विज्ञातुमनेनेति शकुनम्।

Śabdakalpadruma, Kāṇḍa V, p.2.

2. Mc Donnald, A.H., The Encyclopaedia Americana, Vol. XX, p.682.

3. -- अन्यजन्मान्तरकृतं कर्म पुंसां शुभाशुभम्।
यत् तस्य शकुनः पाकं निवेदयति गच्छताम् ॥

Varāhamihira, Bṛhatsaṁhitā, Adhyāya 86/5,p.500.

4. Burne, C.S., The Handbook of Folklore, p.124.

5. Tylor, E.B., Primitive Culture, Vol.I, p.120.

6. Cf. Ṛg Veda, 2/42/2,3; 10/165/1-5; Atharva Veda 10/164/5; 19/8/4,5,6,8. Ṣaḍviṁśa Brāhmaṇa, Prapāṭhaka 5, Khaṇḍa 3,6,8,9-11,12; Aitareya Āraṇyaka, Āraṇyaka 3, Adhyāya 2, Khaṇḍa 4(10).

7. प्रीते निमित्तैर्जयशंसिभिः।

KSS. 3.5.62.

8. KSS. 2.2.152.

9. प्रस्थितश्चाग्रतोऽकस्मादनिमित्तमुपस्थितम्।
दृष्ट्वा सोऽत्र वयस्यांस्तान् सहप्रस्थायिनोऽभ्यधात्।
अनिमित्तमिदं हन्त युक्तमद्य निवतितुर्म्।
पुनरेव प्रयास्यामः सिद्ध्ये शकुनान्वितः ॥

KSS. 6.6.46-47.

10. अद्याशुभं मया किञ्चिन्निमित्तमुपलक्षितम् ॥
तदिदं दिवसं तूष्णीमुद्यानेऽस्मिन्नलक्षिता।
अधितिष्ठस्व मा कार्षीः सखि दूरं गतागतम् ॥
KSS. 6.5.48-49.

11. शकुनैः पूर्वमाख्यातशुभः।
KSS. 9.2.198.

12. KSS. 2.2.116.

13. अव्यपोह्यानिमित्तं हि कार्यं यत्क्रियते सखि।
तदनिष्टाय कल्पेत – – – – – – – ॥
KSS. 6.6.41.

14. KSS. 6.6.46 ff.

15. KSS. 17.1.119.

16. KSS. 17.5.72,90.

17. KSS. 6.5.52-53, 93.

18. दृष्टाशकुनया सख्या निषिद्धापि व्यसर्जयम्।
त्वत्पार्श्वं यदहं दूतं तस्य चेदं फलं मम ॥
KSS. 6.8.8.

19. आमुखपातिकल्याणं कार्यसिद्धिं हि शंसति।
KSS. 3.4.49.

20. अन्तरापाति हि श्रेयः कार्यसम्पत्तिसूचकम्।
KSS. 5.2.71.

21. KSS. 6.6.52.

22. आगान्मार्गे च सुबहुन्यनिमित्तान्यवैक्षत।
वामस्तस्याभवत्काकः श्वा वामाद्दक्षिणं ययौ।
दक्षिणोऽहिरभूद्वामः संस्कन्धश्चास्फुरद् भुजः।
अशुभं सूचयन्त्येतान्यनिमित्तानि मे ध्रुवम् ॥
KSS. 8.6.128-30.

23. अशिवं चारुवञ्शिवाः।
KSS. 17.3.3.

24. चक्रे कृतान्तदूतीव शब्दं भयकरं शिवा ॥
तदभिज्ञो वणिग्लोके चौराद्यापातशङ्किनी ।
KSS. 6.3.106-7.

25. KSS. 6.3.119.

26. निर्गतस्य गृहात्तस्य दक्षिणोऽभूत्कपिञ्जलः ।
दक्षिणा च विरौति स्म शिवा वाष्पैकशंसिनी ॥
KSS. 18.5.108-10.

27. उलूकममङ्गलम् । KSS. 10.6.27.

28. प्रावर्तन्तानिमित्तानि तस्य निर्गच्छतस्तदा ॥
– – – – – – भ्रेमुर्गृध्रास्तथोपरि ।
KSS. 17.3.2-3.

29. तावच्चाशङ्कितं तत्र नभः पिञ्जरतां ययौ ।
रक्तारुणत्वमभ्यर्णभाविशंसदिवात्मनः ॥
KSS. 8.1.134.

30. संध्यारुणा बभूवुश्च कैलासोत्तरसानवः ।
सूचयन्त इवासन्नसङ्ग्रामरुधिरोक्षणम् ॥
KSS. 15.1.94.

31. तत्राकस्मान्महोत्पाताः प्रादुरासंतपोवने ॥
एवं शूराः पतिष्यन्ति रणेऽत्रेति वदन्निव ॥
किमत्र स्यादिति भयादिव भूमिरकम्पत् ।
भीतावकाशदानार्थमिवादीर्यन्त सानवः
विद्याधराः प्रभुं यत्नादमुं रक्षत रक्षत ।
इत्यब्रवीदिवानभ्रं घोरशब्दं नभस्तलम् ॥
नरवाहनदत्तश्च सोऽस्मिन्नुत्पातसंभ्रमे ।
ध्यायन्निष्कम्प एवासीद्भगवन्तं त्रिलोचनम् ॥
अनिष्टाशङ्किनो वीरास्तं रक्षन्तोऽवतस्थिरे ॥
मुमुचुः सिंहनादांश्च व्याधूतासिलतावनाः ।
भर्त्सयन्त इवोत्पातानहितागमशंसिनः ॥
KSS. 14.3.88-94.

32. प्रावर्तन्तानिमित्तानि तस्य निर्गच्छतस्तदा ॥
ध्वजेषु विद्युतः पेतुः – – – – – –॥
KSS. 17.3.2-3.

33. सा कन्या जातमात्रैव कान्तिद्योतितवासका
चक्रे सव्यक्तमालापमुत्थायोपविवेश च ॥
ततो विस्मितवित्रस्तं स्त्रीजनं जातवेश्मनि ।
दृष्ट्वा स धर्मगुप्तोऽत्र समयः स्वयमाययौ ॥
KSS. 3.3.66-67.

34. KSS. 6.4.103.

35. स दृष्ट्वा मातुलुङ्गं तद्वक्त्रे कार्पटिका ततः ।
आददे शकुनापेक्षी दत्वास्मै वस्त्रयोर्युगम् ॥
KSS. 9.3.50.

36. KSS. 4.2.106; 9.1.4; 11.1.68.

37. पद्मावत्याश्च तत्कालमदक्षिण्यं प्रदर्शयत् ।
पस्पन्दे दक्षिणं चक्षुरकम्पत च मानसम् ॥
KSS. 17.4.141.

38. आगान्मार्गे च सुबहुन्यनिमित्तान्यवैक्षत ।
– – – – वामः सस्कन्धश्चास्फुरद् भुजः ॥
KSS. 8.6.128-29.

39. महात्मनां विना हेतोर्दुस्थितः सुस्थितोऽपि वा ।
सूचयत्यन्तरात्मा हि पुरो भावि शुभाशुभम् ॥
KSS. 16.1.49.

40. KSS. 6.3.161.

41. KSS. 8.2.348.

42. KSS. 9.6.6.

43. KSS. 16.3.21.

44. KSS. 4.3.70; 7.9.212; 14.2.6.

45. KSS. 16.3.26.

46. KSS. 6.7.178.

47. सापि तं वीक्ष्य राजानं शुभशरीरलक्षणम् ।
पुरुषातिशयो पूर्वः कोऽयं स्यादित्यचिन्तयत् ॥
KSS. 12.14.78.

48. भाविकल्याणसूचकाः शुभलक्षणाः ॥
KSS. 4.3.54.
Cf. also - KSS. 12.6.178.

49. KSS. 4.3.54.

50. KSS. 12.19.99.

51. लक्षणानुमितायतिम् ।
रेखाच्छत्रध्वजाद्यङ्कपाणिपादशुभाकृतिम् ॥
KSS. 12.26.47.

52. सुलक्षणया ईदृश्या ह्याकृतेरशुभं कुतः ॥
KSS. 8.6.209.

53. KSS. 12.31.26.

54. KSS. 3.1.68, 71,72; 6.7.63; 12.24.13,17.

55. त्रयोऽनया लक्षणया जातया मारिता ।
KSS. 10.10.81.

56. KSS. 3.1.36,38-39.

57. KSS. 8.6.210.

58. सपत्न्योऽस्या भविष्यन्तीत्यग्निदत्तमुवाच तम् ॥
नासायां तिलकोऽस्त्यस्यास्तत्सम्बन्धाच्च वच्म्यहम् ।
उरस्यस्ति द्वितीयोऽपि तयोश्चैतत्फलं विदुः ॥
KSS. 8.6.205.

Chapter X

DREAMS

From the point of view of psycho-physiology, dreaming is only a part of the more general phenomenon of sleep. But, the superstitious mind attaches emotional and religious values to dreams. It always gives specific and conventional interpretations of them thinking that during sleep the superior soul leaves the body and goes about its own affairs which become the substance of dreams.[1] Another idea behind dream is that the liberated spirit visits the spirit world and there secures information.[2] According to the Kathāsaritsāgara, a man under the influence of sleep, with mind bewildered by the quality of passion and withdrawn from outward objects, sees in dream on account of various reasons.[3] False analogy and symbolism have influenced the origin and growth of superstitions connected with dreams.

The belief that in dreams an insight is given into the future event is universally prevalent.[4]

In the Kathāsaritsāgara, dreams are divided into three categories: (i) Anyārtha, (ii) Yathārtha and (iii) Apārtha. A dream which quickly reveals its meaning is called Anyārtha. A dream in which a propitious god gives a command is called Yathārtha and one which is brought about by deep thinking and anxiety is called Apārtha (meaningless).[5]

The fulfilment of a dream depends upon the time when it is seen. It is believed that a dream which is seen at the end of a night is qui kly fulfilled.[6]

Many characters of the Kathāsaritsāgara believe in the ominous nature of dreams. They are afraid of inauspicious dreams which predict evil to them. Anichchhasena's fears are aroused by a threatening dream.[7]

Whenever a superstitious person sees a dream, he becomes apprehensive of its result. In the Kathāsaritsāgara, it is very common with the characters to think over the implications of their dreams. Sometimes, a character tells the ominous nature of a dream to another character. Sūryaprabha dreams towards the end of a night, that he and his friends are all carried away by a great stream of water. While they are swept away, they keep dancing and do not sink at all. The stream is turned back by a contrary breeze. Then a certain man of fiery brightness draws them out and throws them into the fire and they are not burnt by the fire. Then a cloud rains a stream of blood, and this blood fills the whole sky.[8] Suvāsakumāra tells to Sūryaprabha that this dream indicates success preceded by a struggle. The stream of water signifies battle. It is due to valour that they do not sink but dance and are carried along by the water. The wind that turns back the water for Sūryaprabha is some saviour to whom men resort for protection. The men of fiery brightness who draws him out of it, is Śiva in bodily form. And that he throws him into the fire means that he is cast into a great war. The rising of the cloud means the return of fear. The rain of a stream of blood means the destruction of fear and filling of all the quarters with blood means great success for him.[9]

Some people ask others about the meanings of their dreams. The king Kanakavarṣa beholds a dream[10] and asks a mendicant about its meaning. The latter tells him that the fact that the king has seen his necklace and crest jewel taken away means that he will be separated from his wife and his son. And the fact that he has escaped from the sea and finds them again means that he will be reunited with them, when the calamity comes to an end.[11]

The minister Vimalabuddhi tells Mṛgāṅkadatta the implications of the latter's dream[12] which indicates that Śiva has shown him favour.

He tells that as Mṛgāṅkadatta obtains the necklace and drinks up the sea, he shall, without fail, obtain Śaśāṇkavatī and will rule the earth. But the rest of the dream indicates some trivial misfortune.[13]

Another dream[14] portends the end of a curse.[15] Guṇāḍhya believes that the woman who visibly entered the king's mouth in dream was Sarasvatī.[16]

Implications of various other dreams are given in the Kathāsaritsāgara. It is held that if a person beholds in a dream, a lady taking away from him a black blanket, his disease will be cured.[17] If a person is seen, in a dream, dragged away by a black female towards the southern quarter which is assigned to Yama, it proclaims his death.[18]

A dream seen by a pregnant woman indicates the future of the child. In her dream, Vāsavadattā rises high in the sky, while Vidyādhara ladies, singing melodious songs, wait on her.[19] This dream indicates that her son will be the lord of the Vidyādharas. Tārādattā beholds in a dream a flame descending from heaven and entering her womb. The king thinks that some divine being has entered her embryo.[20]

Dreams are accepted as legitimate source of divine communication. In a dream, the deity is believed to reveal himself in a special way to the individual declaring the will of heaven and predicting the future. This is the chief principle underlying superstitions about Yathārtha dreams in which propitious gods who watch over their devotees, reveal the future to them in a distinct and superior manner.

There are many references to Yathārtha dreams in the Kathāsaritsāgara. Such references show the revelation, in a dream, by Śiva,[21] Viṣṇu,[22] Gaṇeśa,[23] Indra,[24] Agni,[25] Kārttikeya,[26] Sūrya,[27] Devī,[28] Gaurī,[29] Sarasvatī[30] and Gaṅgā.[31]

The characters of the Kathāsaritsāgara believe in these Yathārtha dreams. It is said that words of Śiva, uttered in a dream, cannot be falsified.[32] Many characters are rejoiced and consoled by such dreams and they act according to the instructions of their dreams. The king Dīpakarṇi, who is instructed by Śiva in his dream, rejoices remembering his dream.[33] The king Udayana delights his minister, two queens and the subjects by telling them his dream[34] in which Śiva has told him that he will soon have a son who will become the king of all the Vidyādharas. The king Karpūraka is delighted[35] to know in a dream from Śiva that a daughter shall be born to him who will be superior to a son, and whose husband shall obtain the sovereignty of the Vidyādharas. The king Hemaprabha becomes pleased[36] to know from Śiva that he will beget a son and a daughter. The minister Vichitrakathā says to Mṛgāṅkadatta that he will succeed in all undertakings by the grace of Śiva which is promised to him in a dream.[37] Haṁsāvalī thinks that as directed by Viṣṇu in a dream, she will obtain Kamalākara as her husband. So she decides to go somewhere and wait a little so that the dream may come to be true.[38] Vararuchi is encouraged by his dream[39] in which Sarasvatī tells him that Upakośā was his wife in a former birth also. The queen of the king Pratāpamukuṭa consoles her daughter on the strength of a dream in which some heavenly woman tells her that she must not give her daughter Madanalekhā to anyone but Aśokadatta for she is his wife, acquired by him in a former birth.[40]

Believing in the Yathārtha dreams, many characters of the Kathāsaritsāgara act according to the instructions of the divine beings which are given to them in their dreams. For instance, in a dream, Śiva asks Hiraṇyavatī and her daughter Dhanavatī to leave a boy alongwith a thousand gold pieces, early in the morning, at the door of king Sūryaprabha. And relying upon the dream, they take the boy and the gold, and lay together at the gate of the king's palace.[41] The king Prasenajit, having been urged by the god in a dream gives Kuraṅgī to a young Chaṇḍāla.[42] The god Śiva commands Brāhmaṇas in a dream to take food from the house of Mātaṅga Utpalahasta. They accordingly agree to do so.[43] Śaktideva, remembering his dream gladly accepts the proposal of Bindumati. He marries her as his wish is fulfilled by her brothers who receive the command to do so from Durgā in a dream.[44] Umā announces to the king Alaṅkāraśila in a dream that his son should be devoted to Dharma. Therefore, the king names him Dharmaśila.[45]

In the Yathārtha dream, sometimes, a divine being is seen giving fruit or something else to a person. The superstitious mind interprets such happenings of a dream and considers the dream as indicating some future event. For instance, a certain man with matted locks gives the queen Vāsavadattā a fruit in her dream. The king Udayana interprets it as indicative of Śiva blessing her with a son.[46] Vāsavadattā also believes in the validity of her dream and thinks that she will soon beget a son.[47] In a dream, Śiva gives a fruit to the queen of the king Vikramāditya. The king rejoices in the hope that Śiva has blessed him with a son.[48] Padmāvatī tells to her friend Manohārikā that she has seen a dream in which Pārvatī was about to throw a garland of lotuses round her neck but desisted from her intention and said that she would give it to her on some other occasion. She believes that the goddess wishes in this way to tell her that her union with her husband will be hindered.[49]

Many stories of the Kathāsaritsāgara are framed in such a way that they confirm the superstitions about the Yathārtha dreams. For instance, Śiva commands the king Sūryaprabha, in a dream, to lift a child from the gate of his palace. Accordingly, in the morning, the king finds the child[50] at the palace gate. Śiva in a dream informs Gomukha of his success, and some heavenly nymph seizes him and brings him to Naravāhanadatta.[51] Viṣṇu tells the father of Haṁsāvalī that his fever will be allayed by her touch and prince Kamalākara is destined to be her husband. When the father wakes up, his fever is cured by her touch. Later on, the marriage of Kamalākara and Haṁsāvalī takes place.[52] Indra tells Chaṇḍamahāsena in a dream that he will be blessed with a daughter. Later on, the prophecy comes out to be true.[53] Pārvatī tells Hiraṇyākṣa, in a dream, that he will be delivered from his curse by the touch of the hand of a female ascetic and then he will quickly marry Mṛgāṅkalekhā. Similarly, she says to Mṛgāṅkalekhā, in a dream, that she will have Hiraṇyākṣa as her husband. This dream also comes out true.[54] There are many other references in the text which confirm belief in the validity of such dreams in which a deity reveals himself to his devotee.[55]

Thus, the superstitious people of the Kathāsaritsāgara attach emotional and religious values to their dreams. They are afraid of inauspicious dreams as these predict some evil to them. Some of the dreams are given specific implications while others, in which a propitious god gives a command are always considered to be true. Dreams brought about by deep thinking and anxiety signify nothing to a superstitious mind. The fulfilment of a dream is connected with the time of its vision. Superstitions about the Yathārtha dreams are based on religious feelings. Revelation of a god in a dream is attributed to the merits (Puṇya) of a person.[56]

Footnotes Of Chapter X

1. The Standard Dictionary of Folklore, Mythology and Legend,Vol.I, p.224.

2. Encyclopaedia of Religion and Ethics, Vol.V, p.33. Cf. "Dreams and other psychio phenomena confirm man's belief in an after-life and in invisible world where spirits move and hold communion with the sub-conscious mind." – Thomas,P., Epics, Myths and Legends of India, p.93.

3. रजोमूढेन मनसा बाह्यार्थविमुखेन हि ।
जन्तुर्निद्रावशः स्वप्नं तैस्तैः पश्यति कारणैः ॥
KSS. 8.3.150.

4. The New Popular Encyclopaedia, Vol.X, p.164. Belief in superstitions about dreams is found even in the Vedic literature (Cf. Ṛg Veda Saṁhitā, 8/47/14; Atharva Veda, 19/53/3; Aitareya Āraṇyaka, Āraṇyaka 3, Adhyāya 2, Khaṇḍa 4(10).

5. स्वप्नश्चानेकधान्यार्थो यथार्थोऽपार्थ एव च ।
यः सद्यः सूचयत्यर्थमन्यार्थः सोऽभिधीयते ॥
प्रसन्नदेवतादेशरूपः स्वप्नो यथार्थकः ।
गाढानुभवचिन्तादिकृतमाहुरपार्थकम् ॥
KSS. 8.3.147-48.

6. चिरशीघ्रफलत्वं च तस्य कालविशेषतः ।
एष रात्र्यन्तदृष्टस्तु स्वप्नः शीघ्रफलप्रदः ॥
KSS. 8.3.150.

7. KSS. 7.8.153.

8. KSS. 8.3.137-41.

9. आयासपूर्वोऽभ्युदयः स्वप्नेनानेन सूचितः ॥
यो जलौधः स संग्रामो धैर्यं तद्यदमज्जनम् ।

नृत्यतां ह्रियमाणानां जलैस्तत्परिवर्त्तकः ॥
यो युष्माकं मरुत् सोऽपि शरणः कोऽपि रक्षिता ।
यश्चोद्धर्ता ज्वलत्तेजाः पुमान् साक्षात् स शङ्करः ॥
क्षिप्ता स्थाग्नौ च यत्तेन तन्नयस्ताः स्थ महामृधे ।
मेघोदयस्ततो यच्च स भूयोऽपि भयागमः ।
रक्तौधवर्षणं यच्च तद् भयस्य विनाशनम् ॥
दिशां यद्रक्तपूर्वत्वमृद्धि सा महती च वः ॥

KSS. 8.3.142-46.

10. KSS. 9.5.133-36.

11. या त्वयैकावली दृष्टा हृता चूडामणिस्तथा ।
सैष देव्या वियोगस्ते पुत्रेण च भविष्यति ॥
प्राप्ते चैकावलीरत्ने यदुत्तीर्णाब्धिना त्वया ।
दुःखान्ते सोऽपि भावी ते देवपुत्रसमागमः ॥

KSS. 9.5.139-40.

12. KSS. 12.2.34-39.

13. मन्त्री विमलबुद्धिस्तं नन्दत्स्वन्येष्वभाषत ।
त्वं देव धन्यो यस्यैवं विहितानुग्रहो हरः ॥
स्वप्ने मुक्तावलीं लब्ध्वा यत्पीतश्च त्वयाम्बुधिः ।
तच्छशाङ्कवतीं प्राप्य भोक्तासि पृथिवीं ध्रुवम् ॥

KSS. 12.2.40-43.

14. KSS. 10.10.160,164.

15. प्रत्यासन्नं च शापान्तं तव स्वप्नो वदत्यसौ ।

KSS. 10.10.165.

16. ----मन्ये सा च सरस्वती ।
देवस्य वदने साक्षात् सम्प्रविष्टा न संशयः ॥

KSS. 1.6.140.

17. जाने जहार पृष्ठान्मे स्वप्ने स्त्री कृष्णकम्बलम् ।
तन्निश्चितमिमं रोगं हरिष्यति भवान्मम ॥

KSS. 6.3.165.

18. KSS. 16.1.51-53.

19. KSS. 4.2.10.

20. KSS. 6.1.74 ff.

21. KSS. 1.3.21; 1.6.91; 2.5.78; 3.5.6-7; 4.1.143; 4.2.122; 7.9.145; 7.1.103-6; 9.2.389; 10.3.168; 12.26. 48-50, 52-53; 14.4.60; 16.2.181-82; 18.1.36-43.

22. KSS.12.4.120.

23. KSS. 12.33.53.

24. KSS.2.3.76.

25. KSS. 12.6.59.

26. KSS. 1.2.45; 7.9.50,52.

27. KSS. 9.6.48.

28. KSS. 1.2.3; 1.7.25; 4.3.38-47; 5.3.62; 5.3.148-54; 7.4.48; 7.8.118-19; 10.10.103; 12.36.37,57; 14.4.85.

29. KSS. 7.1.135; 9.1.17; 10.9.231.

30. KSS. 1.4.9.

31. KSS. 12.7.119.

32. न मृषा स्यान्मुनिवचः स्वप्नादेशश्च शांभवः ॥

KSS. 17.6.149.

33. अथ प्रबुद्धस्तं स्वप्नं स्मरन्राजा जहर्ष सः ।

KSS. 1.6.93.

34. अनन्दयच्च सचिवान् प्रातः स्वप्नेन तेन सः ।
व्रतोपवासक्लान्ते च देव्यौ द्वे पुष्पकोमले ॥

KSS. 3.5.9.

Cf. also - तत्स्वप्नकीर्तनसुधारसतर्पितास्ताः ।

KSS. 4.1.146.

35. निवेद्य बुद्धिकार्ये च देव्यै स्वप्नं तदोत्थितः ।
प्रहृष्टः – – – – – – – – – – – – – – – ॥

KSS. 7.9.147.

36. आनन्दयदलङ्कारप्रभां स्वप्नं निवेद्य सः ।

KSS. 7.1.107.

37. सर्वं सेत्स्यति ते हरात्स्वप्नदृष्टानुग्रहात् ।

KSS. 12.2.76.

Cf. also -

तत्स्वप्नदृष्टगिरिजादयितप्रसादात्सेत्स्यभीष्टमचिरेण तवापि देव ॥

KSS. 12.2.184.

38. KSS. 12.4.188-90.

39. प्रबुद्धो जातास्थः

KSS. 1.4.9.

40. KSS. 5.2.166-68.

41. KSS. 12.26.50-56.

42. KSS. 16.2.108.

43. KSS. 16.2.181-82.

44. KSS.5.3.155.

45. KSS. 9.1.17.

46. KSS. 4.1.148.

47. स्वप्नसत्यत्वसञ्जातपुत्रप्राप्तिनिश्चया।

KSS. 4.3.15.

48. KSS. 18.1.36-43.

49. KSS. 17.4.166-68.

50. KSS. 12.26.55-56.

51. KSS.14.4.60.

52. KSS. 12.4.120 ff.

53. KSS. 2.3.76-77.

54. KSS. 10.9.231.

55. KSS. 10.10.103 ff; 17.5.135,138; 17.6.71-76, 80-90, 95.

56. KSS. 7.9.53.

Chapter XI

EVIL SPIRITS

The realm of the unknown is inhabited by many monstrous spirits of prevailing evil nature. Rākṣasas, Piśāchas, Bhūtas, Pretas, Vetālas and water-spirits are the mythical beings which are generally held as evil spirits. Besides them, some women are charged with being witches. The chief function of these evil spirits is to cause damage and destruction in the sphere of human life.

There is no rational explanation for superstitions about these evil spirits. Such superstitions are the creation of a primitive mind which requires no earthly model for the creatures of his fancy and symbolizes everything – his ideals, his desires, his hopes and his fears. Just as a highly imaginative child symbolizes his fears with terrifying monsters, so, it may be inferred, does primitive man conceive with childlike mind of evil spirits thirsting for his blood.[1]

The Kathāsaritsāgara shows belief in the existence of the following evil spirits.

The Rākṣasas[2]

The word 'Rākṣasa' may be derived from the root 'Rakṣ'–to injure. It is, however, possibly connected with the ordinary root 'Rakṣ' 'to protect'. Thus, the word 'Rākṣasa' means both 'the injurer' and 'the protector'. Rākṣasa was, at first, one of the many harmful spirits, a nocturnal power, a demon of darkness, and therefore, evil. But as 'the injurer' of those opposing it, the Rākṣasa is also 'the protector' of what it values.[3] In fact, according to our ethical conceptions there is neither perfect good nor absolute evil. The conception of good and evil arises out of the inherent incapacity of the mortal mind to perceive realities.[4] The derivation of the word Rākṣasa also shows that the conceptions of both good and evil are included in it.[5]

In the Kathāsaritsāgara, the Rākṣasas are held as the enemies of human beings. They kill human beings[6] or swallow them.[7] A Rākṣasa devours the king Vīrabhuja along with his relatives and attendants.[8] A Rākṣasī devours, with utmost delight, the flesh of Nisthuraka after killing him.[9] When children ask their terrible Rākṣasī mother to give them food, she says that she will give them the flesh of a Brāhmana.[10] The arms of Rākṣasa has been described as a swift wand of death to hundreds of men.[11]

It is believed that the Rākṣasas haunt cemeteries.[12] The Rākṣasī Vidyuchchhikhā tells Aśokadatta that she always comes to the cemetery on the fourteenth night of the black fortnight.[13]

Some of the Rākṣasas are supposed to reside in certain trees, particularly the Vaṭa tree. It is held that they drink the blood and tear out and devour the hearts of those persons who go near such trees. Even the gods cannot trespass their places.[14]

In appearance, the Rākṣasas are held as terrifying and monstrous.[15] They have upstanding tawny hair,[16] terrible mouths with projecting tusks,[17] gigantic bodies which are as black as a cloud or smoke[18] and have pendulous breasts and bellies.[19] Their eyes shine like lightning.[20] They have cavernous mouths which are as black as darkness and which remain gaped wide making loud roar.[21]

Many supernatural powers are attributed to the Rākṣasas. They can fly through the air. The Rākṣasī Vidyuchchhikhā, by the power of her magic, carries Aśokadatta through the air to a cemetery.[22] The Rākṣasas can change their from at their will[23] and can also disappear.[24] A Rākṣasa named Agniśikha assumes the form of a crane.[25]

There is a belief that the Rākṣasas have a magical power which makes their life hard to destroy. They can be killed like any ordinary person if their secret is discovered and their magical power disincanted. Indīvarasena frequently cuts off a Rākṣasa's head but it grows again. Seeing this magic power of his having a sign made to him by the lady at the Rākṣasa's side, the prince, after cutting off the head of the Rākṣasa, again cuts it in two with a stroke of his sword. Then the magic of the Rākṣasa is baffled by contrary magic and his head does not grow again, and the Rākṣasa dies of the wound.[26]

The Rākṣasas are generally held as beings of horrible appearance and malicious nature who haunt cemeteries, harass people, devour human beings and afflict them. But, sometimes, they become friendly to human beings and protect them. A Rākṣasa becomes a friend of Vidūṣaka and appears before him as soon as the latter calls him to his mind.[27] Vararuchi also has a Rākṣasa as his friend.[28] He tells Śakaṭāla that he cannot be slain since he has a Rākṣasa friend, who will come to his aid immediately on being thought of, and at his request will devour the whole world.[29]

The Rākṣasas possess remarkable riches. The city of the Rākṣasa Agniśikha is described as the abode of all riches.[30] The city of the Rākṣasī Vidyuchchhikhā is built of gold on a peak of the Himālayas.[31] The great hall of the Rākṣasas is paved with gold and jewels and is adorned with jewelled pillars and is full of jewelled vessels.[32]

The Piśāchas

The etymological sense of the word 'Piśācha' is the 'eater of raw flesh'. In the Kathāsaritsāgara, the Piśāchas appear both as evil spirits and as human beings living in Vindhya forests.[33]

Piśāchas are the evil spirits who lead people out of their way, haunt cemeteries, eat human flesh and practise every kind of wickedness. The Brāhmaṇa Govindaswāmin tells his son Vijayadatta, ' There is a cemetery, so how can you go to the place made terrible with the presence of Piśāchas and other evil spirits'.[34] The 'story of Brāhmaṇa and Piśācha' has been narrated to show the evil importunity of Piśāchas.[35]

People believe in the healing power of the Piśāchas. A Piśācha being conciliated by a Brāhmaṇa, brings heavenly herbs from a lofty peak of the Himālayas and heals a wound.[36]

It is maintained that the Rākṣasas and Piśāchas have no power in the day being dazed with the brightness of the Sun and it is at night alone that their power is at its height[37] and it is then that they roam about the cremation grounds in search of human bodies.

The Rākṣasas and Piśāchas grow in those places only where gods and Brāhmaṇas are not worshipped and where men eat contrary to the holy law.[38] But they do not go to those places where there is a man who abstains from flesh or a virtuous woman. They never attack chaste men, heroes and men awake.[39] As they are the evil spirits, they cannot set foot on the mountain of the rising sun (Udayādri) inhabited by the pure spirits Siddhas.[40]

The Bhūtas and the Pretas

Fear of Bhūtas and Pretas is universal. Bhūtas are malignant spirits and Pretas are the spirits of the newly dead persons.[41] They are designated as beings of a rather vicious disposition, small and great, and can be very likely included at first in subdivisions of the particular groups known by special names as cannibalistic night – wanderers. But as ghosts are also by predilection malicious, the term Bhūta had a tendency to interchange with Preta, till the modern equivalence, Bhūta Preta, becomes thoroughly established.[42]

The Kathāsaritsāgara presents Bhūtas as the malicious spirits who haunt cemeteries[43] and lurk in trees.[44] They can assume any form. They can assume form of a fish even. They insinuate any person and laugh at the exceeding want of discernment in kings.[45]

Bhūtas are held as flesh relishing and blood-drinking creatures.[46] They take delight in battles. The battle which takes place between Sūryaprabha and Śrutaśarman gives delight to them.[47]

People are afraid of these ghosts. They think that they seize a person, delude him[48] and even devour him. A merchant is terrified to see that his servant has been seized by a ghost.[49] A Brāhmaṇa says, surely some Bhūta has smitten his sight and bewildered him.[50] Mṛgāṅkadatta thinks that his friends are devoured by Bhūtas on a tree.[51] A person possessed by a Bhūta eats his own flesh with his teeth.[52]

Charms, fire, light and iron are said to scare away evil spirits. A place can be secured from hostile beings by using innumerable charms, spells and other incantations. The birth chamber of Vāsavadattā is rendered secure by conjurers who go through these incantations.[53] It contains various weapons which are rendered auspicious by being mixed with the gleam of jewel lamps, shedding a light up which is able to protect the child from the evil spirits.[54]

The period of child-birth is the most critical one in which evil spirits are believed to take advantage. The custom of keeping lights in the birth-chamber to scare away evil spirits is almost universal. This is a trait surviving from what is perhaps the oldest phase of the cult of fire as warding off the attack of evil spirits.[55]

The original cause of the dread of iron by evil spirits appears to be simply that the spirits themselves date back to the Stone Age. The discovery of iron had enormous advantages over stone. Miraculous powers are attached to it and the evil spirits, in their ignorance, came to dread it.

The sacred plants of Arka and Śamī also act as a protection against the evil spirits. The description of the birth-chamber of Vāsavadattā shows that the windows of the room are covered with the leaves of these plants.[56]

The Vetālas

The spirits which animate dead bodies are known as Vetālas. A Vetāla is a vitalised corpse that the visitor from the other world comes to human appetites, constantly endowed with more than human strength and malignity.[57] It is the spirit who haunts cemeteries and lives in dead bodies.

In the Kaṭhāsaritsāgara, the burning ground of Mahākāla in Ujjayinī is described as densely tenanted by Vetālas.[58] Aśokadatta enters the cemetery in which Vetālas make terrible music with the clapping of their hands.[59] The Brāhmaṇa Vidūṣaka sees three impaled thieves tenanted by Vetālas.[60] Another Vetāla enters the corpse that is in the circle of adoration.[61]

The twenty-five stories of Vetāla (Vetālapañchaviṁśati) contain beliefs about the appearance and the nature of the Vetālas.[62] A Vetāla is described as tall and black.[63] He has neck of a camel, head of an elephant, legs of a bull, eyes of an owl and the ears of an ass.[64]

The Vetālas are held as very mischievous. The Vetālas in the bodies of three impaled thieves strike the Brāhmaṇa Vidūṣaka with their fists.[65] Another Vetāla cuts the nose of a lady with its teeth.[66] Sometimes, Vetālas swallow a person. A Vetāla pursues a sorcerer and swallows him whole.[67]

The Vetālas take delight in wars.[68] The corpse that is animated by a Vetāla, utters a terrible shriek.[69] The king Trivikramasena flings the dead body to the ground and the moment it is flung down it cries out, as if in pain. Then the corpse makes a loud demonaic laugh and the king understands that the dead is tenanted by a Vetāla.[70] Another reference shows that the king sees the corpse lying on the ground groaning.[71]

The superstitious people believe that the Vetālas are expert in magic.[72] According to them, the Vetāla can fly through the air,[73] and can go by their supernatural deluding power (Yogamāyā) to the place they desire.[74] They are able to change their forms. A Vetāla transforms himself in many possible ways.[75] The minister Bhīmaparākrama follows a lion who becomes a deformed giant and tells him that he is a Vetāla.[76]

Vetālas are attributed with the power of deluding people. The king Trivikramasena sees as many corpses of similar appearance hanging on a tree and they are seem to be possessed by Vetālas. Later on, the Vetāla withdraws the delusion. Then the king beholds only one Vetāla on the tree in the corpse of a man.[77]

There is a belief that the Vetālas are endowed with the healing power also. Śrīdarśana cuts off some of his own flesh and gives it to a Vetāla. Then pleased with him, the Vetāla restores his body as before.[78]

Many references in the text show the belief that the Vetālas become pleased with one's courage, wisdom, bravery, patience and such other virtues.[79] A Vetāla is pleased with Śrīdarśana's courage.[80] Another Vetāla tells the king Trivikramasena that he loves the king because he is wise and brave.[81]

Water-Spirits

There is a belief that some of the spirits live under water and seize them who go near the water place. The story of Mṛgāṅkadatta shows the belief in the dread of water-spirits. When the king of the Śavaras named Māyāvaṭu has bathed, three water spirits rise simultaneously and seize him.[82]

The Witches

In the Kathāsaritsāgara some of the women are held as witches who have been classified into Śākinī, Yoginī, Ḍākinī and Yakṣiṇī. All these four classes of witches are different from each other with regard to their activities and Siddhis. The dreadful deeds of all of them are described as follows.

Śākinī

A Śākinī employs the method of the charmed grains and can turn a human being into a goat.[83] The Mantras used by a Śākinī require only barley seeds or some other corn which she sows at mid-night in a secluded chamber of her own house. The seeds which grow immediately, are plucked, sifted, fried, pounded and placed in a pot of white copper.[84]

Sometimes, Śākinī throws a charmed dust on a person and transforms him into an animal. The Śākinī Śaśiprabhā throws some dust on the face of Vāmadatta and changes him into a buffalo.[85]

Yoginī

The term 'Yoga' has many shades of meaning from that of a saint to that of sorcerer or charlatan.[86] In the Kathāsaritsāgara, the word 'Yoginī' has been used in the sense of a witch. Somadā,[87] Bandamochanikā,[88] and Sukhaśayā[89] are called Yoginīs.

Just as Śākinī is known for her charmed grains, Yoginī is held to be expert in her string method. She can transform man into a monkey, a bull, a peacock or even a mare or a cow by fastening charmed string into his neck. The Yoginī Sukhaśayā knows two spells. By reciting one of them, one can be made in a moment a monkey, if a string is fastened round one's neck, and by the second if the string is loosened, one will immediately become a man again.[90] She fastens a thread on the neck of Somaṣwāmin and makes him a monkey.[91] The Yoginī Mokṣadā employing a spell, looses the string and makes him a man as before.[92] The Yoginī Somadā ties a string around the neck of Bhavaśarman and he is immediately turned into an ox.[93] The Yoginī Bandhamochanikā looses a string and again makes him a man.[94] A wicked Yoginī ties a thread on Bhīmaparākrama's neck and transforms him into a peacock.[95] The moment this thread is loosened from its neck, the peacock becomes the minister Bhīmaparākrama.[96]

Charmed water is also used by Yoginīs. A witch sprinkling Vāmadatta with some charmed water, releases him from his buffalo condition.[97]

It is believed that Yoginīs come at night longing for men's flesh and blood.[98]

Ḍākinī

In the Kathāsaritsāgara, some women are called Ḍākinīs. A king thinks that a barber's wife is a Ḍākinī.[99] The king Karṇotpala believes that beautiful Padmāvatī is a Ḍākinī and has really destroyed his child.[100]

The following is a description from Kathāsaritsāgara of the Ḍākinī Kālarātri.

Her eye-brows meet, she has dull eyes, large cheeks, widely parted lips, projecting teeth, a long neck, pendulous breasts, a large belly and broad expanded feet. She appears as if the creator has made her a specimen of skill in producing ugliness.[101]

Ḍākinī is considered to be a witch of more terrible aspect.[102] She can fly through the air.[103] She is a cannibal. Kuvalayāvalī and the other witches devour men.[104] Magic power of Ḍākinī's spells are attributed to her eating of human flesh.[105]

Yakṣiṇī

The following description of the activities of the Yakṣiṇī Śriṅgotpādinī throws some light on the beliefs about Yakṣiṇīs.

At night there comes dancing the Yakṣiṇī Śriṅgotpādinī, playing from afar on her lute of bones, and when she comes near, she fixes her eyes on one of the four Pāśupata ascetics and recites a charm, as she dances outside the circle. That charm produces horns on him and bewilders him. She rises up, and dances till he falls into the blazing fire. And when he has fallen, the Yakṣiṇī drags him half burnt out of the fire, and devours him with delight. Then she fixes up her eyes on the second

Pāśupata ascetic and in the same way recites the horn-producing charm and dances. The second one also has horns produced by that charm, and is made to dance and falling into the fire is dragged out and devoured before the eyes of the others. In this way the Yakṣiṇī charms one after another at night all the four ascetics, and after horns have been produced on them, devours them.[106]

The above account shows the beliefs that Yakṣiṇīs come at night. They play on the flute of bones, fix up their eyes on human beings and reciting a charm produce horns on them and devour them. The power of a Yakṣiṇī is contained in her flute of horns and in the charm which she recites on it. When the Yakṣiṇī Śriṅgotpādinī lays her flute on the ground and Niśchayadatta seizes the flute and begins to play on it the horn-producing charm, she is confused and horns are about to sprout on her own forehead.[107]

Evil Eye and Fatal Look

The basic concept of the very earliest ages which is still held every where by superstitious people, is that certain individuals have the power of casting a spell. This power is demoniac and is either voluntary or involuntary. The spell can produce some malignant effect upon every object animate or inanimate on which the evil eye of the individual rests. The superstitious belief about the disastrous influence of the malignant look is so deep rooted that every human mischance is attributed to the evil eye which brings pain, sickness and whatever is undesirable in life. Sometimes, it is believed to cause even death.

The belief in the evil influence of fatal look is also found in the Kathāsaritsāgara. It is said that a Kāpālika looks at the wife of the Brāhmaṇa Chandrasvāmin. She catches a fever from the moment he looks at her and in the evening she dies.[108]

The account of the superstitions regarding evil spirits amply proves that superstitious persons have a baseless terror in their mind which induces them to believe that there exist evil spirits like the

Rākṣasas, Piśāchas, Bhūtas, Pretas, Vetālas and water-spirits who are bent on doing much harm to human beings. Even some women are held as witches which are classified into Śākinī, Yoginī, Ḍākinī and Yakṣiṇī. People believe in the evil influence of the fatal look too.

Footnotes Of Chapter XI

1. Mackenzie, Donald.A., Indian Myth and Legend, p.71.

2. The belief in the existence of Rākṣasas goes back to the Vedic period (Cf. Atharva Veda, 8.6).

3. Hopkins, E.W., Epic Mythology,p.38.

4. Thomas. P., Epics, Myths and Legends of India, p.81.

5. The Rāmāyaṇa (7,4,4 &12) and the Viṣṇu Purāṇa (1, 5,41) give another derivation of the word 'Rākṣasa'. The Brahman himself created creatures to guard the waters. Some of them cried 'Rakṣāmah' while others cried 'Yakṣāmah'. So they became Rākṣasas and the Yakṣas respectively.

6. KSS. 2.4.132.

7. KSS. 12.19.122.

8. KSS. 7.8.138-39.

9. KSS. 2.2.72.

10. KSS. 1.5.21.

11. KSS. 3.4.281.

12. KSS. 5.2.181.

13. KSS. 5.2.215.

14. KSS. 12.27.71-73.

15. KSS. 2.2.73; 3.4.280,330; 7.8.124; 8.3.208.

16. KSS. 12.27.68; 17.1.107; 17.3.29.

17. KSS. 7.8.129; 17.1.107; 17.3.29.

18. KSS. 12.11.37; 12.27.68; 17.3.29.

19. KSS. 17.3.29.

20. KSS. 12.11.37.

21. KSS. 12.19.121.
22. KSS. 5.2.214.
23. KSS. 5.2.203.
24. KSS.12.11.113.
25. KSS. 7.5.60.
26. KSS. 7.9.131-34.
27. KSS. 3.4.341,347.
28. KSS. 1.5.53.
29. KSS. 1.5.45, 47.
30. KSS. 7.5.84.
31. KSS. 5.2.207.
32. KSS. 8.2.227-28.
33. Here we are concerned with Piśāchas as evil spirits only.
34. KSS. 5.2.96.
35. पिशाचदुराग्रहकथा –

    "SS. 6.2.156-84.
36. KSS. 6.2.169.
37. दिवा नैषां प्रभावोऽस्ति ध्वस्तानामर्कतेजसा।
    यक्षरक्षःपिशाचानां तेन हृष्यन्त्यमी निशि ॥

    KSS. 1.7.35.
38. न पूज्यन्ते सुरा यत्र न च विप्रा यथोचितम्।
    भुज्यतेऽविधिना वापि तत्रैते प्रभवन्ति च ॥

    KSS. 1.7.36.
39. अमांसभक्षः साध्वी वा यत्र तत्र न यान्त्यमी।
    शुचीन्छूरान्प्रबुद्धांश्च नाक्रमन्ति कदाचन ॥

    KSS. 1.7.37.
40. KSS. 3.4.
41. Cf.Atharva Veda, VIII.6
42. Hopkins, E.W., Epic Mythology, pp.37-38.
43. KSS. 12.6.43; 12.16.3.
44. KSS. 12.33.34.
45. KSS. 1.5.25.
46. KSS. 17.3.66.

47. KSS. 8.4.53, 92.
48. KSS. 13.1.65.
49. KSS. 2.5.110.
50. KSS. 10.6.67.
51. KSS. 12.33.34.
52. KSS. 10.7.118.
53. KSS. 4.3.63.
54. KSS. 4.3.62.
55. Ocean. Vol.II, p.167.
56. KSS. 4.3.61.
57. Ralston.,Russian Folk-Tales, p.306.
58. KSS. 2.4.47-48.
59. KSS. 5.2.136.
60. KSS. 3.4.149.
61. KSS. 18.2.26.
62. KSS. 12.35.19; 18.2.24.
63. KSS. 2.4.48; 12.35.19.
64. KSS. 12.35.19.
65. KSS. 3.4.149.
66. KSS. 12.10.68.
67. KSS. 12.6.309.
68. KSS. 14.4.107.
69. KSS. 12.6.290.
70. KSS. 12.8.51-54.
71. KSS. 12.9.2-3.
72. KSS. 12.10,93; 12.25.84.
73. KSS. 12.32.54.
74. KSS. 12.32.30; 12.11.138.
75. KSS. 12.30.2.
76. KSS. 12.2.26-27.
77. KSS. 12.25.3,6-7.
78. KSS. 12.6.302.
79. KSS. 12.19.3; 12.31.61.
80. KSS. 12.6.311.
81. KSS. 12.13.3.
82. KSS. 12.4.6.
83. KSS. 12.4.273.
84. KSS. 12.4.266-68.
85. KSS. 12.1.44-45.
86. Barth, A., The Religions of India, p.213.
87. KSS. 7.3.150.
88. KSS. 7.3.155.

89. KSS. 7.3.109.
90. KSS. 7.3.110-11.
91. KSS. 7.3.116.
92. KSS. 7.3.241.
93. KSS. 7.3.153.
94. KSS. 7.3.156-57.
95. KSS. 12.4.276-77.
96. KSS. 12.4.56.
97. KSS. 12.1.51.
98. KSS. 14.4.32.
99. KSS. 6.6.169.
100. ग्रस्तः सुतो मे डाकिन्या तयेत्युत्पन्ननिश्चयः ।

KSS. 12.8.180.

101. मिलद्भ्रुवं कातराक्षीं न्यञ्चच्चिपिटनासिकाम् ।
स्थूलगण्डीं करालोष्ठीं दन्तुरां दीर्घकन्दराम् ॥
लम्बस्तनीमुदरिणीं विदीर्णोत्फुल्लपादुकाम् ।
धात्रा वैरूप्यनिर्माणवैदग्धीं दर्शितामिव ॥

KSS. 3.6.108-9.

Meeting of eye-brows is considered to be a sign of being a witch.

102. KSS. 5.2.149.
103. KSS. 5.2.151.
104. KSS. 3.6.114.
105. इमा नृमांसाशनजा डाकिनीमन्त्रसिद्धयः ।

KSS. 3.6.104.

106. KSS. 7.3.64-70.
107. KSS. 7.3.72-74.
108. KSS. 18.5.5-6.

CONCLUSION

An exhaustive and comprehensive survey of the Kathāsaritsāgara from the point of view of faiths and beliefs has been presented in the foregoing chapters. We now sketch a consolidated picture of the faiths and beliefs depicted in the text.

In ancient times, when science was not so advanced, faiths and beliefs exercised powerful hold over the thoughts and actions of the people. It was but natural to find human society as a whole to be credulous. Presumably, without much reasoning, people in that age entertained various faiths and beliefs. The fact appears to be corroborated by the study of the faiths and beliefs in the Kathāsaritsāgara.

As the Kathāsaritsāgara contains remotely connected floating stories from heterogeneous sources, it represents the faiths and beliefs of the Indian Society spread over several centuries, starting from the pre-Vedic age and continuing in some modified form upto the eleventh century A.D.

The prevailing faiths in the society of the Kathāsaritsāgara were the curious medley of the Higher Hindu Faiths, of the Tāntrika practices and of the Bauddha Faith. The synthesis of the philosophical tenets of Hinduism and Buddhism and the animistic rites and practices of the forest tribes, had produced a mixture which was not calculated to impart either social or political stability to Hindu India in the coming struggle with Islam.[1]

The Hindus were divided into various sects. The Śaiva, the Gāṇapatya, the Vaisnava, the Brāhma, the Śākta and the Saura were the principal sectarian Faiths prevalent in the society. The Śaiva was the most prominent Faith. It was influenced by Tāntricism. The Gāṇapatya had also emerged as a powerful Faith. The Śākta was another popular Faith. Influence of Tāntricism was quite evident in the case of the Śāktas also. The Vaiṣṇava, Brāhma and the Saura Faiths were comparatively less important. Mutual sectarian rivalries are quite clearly discernible in the Kathāsaritsāgara. Sectarian tendencies are obvious in those portions of the text where each one of the sectarian god is looked upon as superior to the other gods.

The divine family had become very large in that period. It consisted of gods, goddesses, associates of gods, divine seers, divine races, enemies of gods, animal divinities, divine trees and groves, rivers and ocean. The group of gods had been much enlarged as both Vedic and the non-Vedic gods were included in that. Mythology was fairly consistent. There was not much discrepancy between the character of any one god in the period of the Kathāsaritsāgara and that of the same god in the earlier period. Sectarian tendencies inverted the position of the gods. Significant changes had occurred in the position of gods. The Vedic gods like Indra and others had been reduced in estate and the post-Vedic gods throned above them.

The ritual aspect of the Hindu Faith consisted in the performance of various religious practices belonging both to the Vedic and the non-Vedic traditions. Though the practice of the sacred prostitution was in vogue, it was not held in high esteem.

The belief in the concept of final judgment in the after-world helped in the uplift of the society as it laid stress on avoiding sins and leading a virtuous life. The belief in the concepts of curse and boon also helped in maintaining moral standards.

Certain days and moments were considered to be more auspicious than others. Great care was taken to perform every important work on the days and moments which were declared auspicious or favourable by astrologers. Influence of planets on human beings was duly regarded.

The practical aspect of the Hindu Faith consisted in morally high standards of behaviour. Various ethical virtues were recommended for spiritual development.

Philosophy formed an inseparable part of the Hindu Faith. Many philosophico-religious and philosophico-mythical views contained beliefs about God, soul, world and salvation. Sectarian Faiths held their respective deities as the Ultimate Reality. The concept of Trimūrti inspired people to meditate on Brahmā, Viṣṇu and Śiva in the light of their unity. Belief in the continuity of the soul was found in the theory of the transmigration of souls. People had strong faith in the law of Karman which was believed to determine one's Fate. The Sectarian Faiths connected the task of creation of the universe with their gods. The Cosmic Egg Theory which explains the creation of the universe from the Cosmic Egg, was associated with Śiva. People believed in the doctrine of Māyā which shows that Māyā revolves the wheel of the mundane existence. Mythological law about the food taboos in the under-world was a matter of belief. Salvation was considered to be the ultimate goal of human life. Sāṁkhya, Yoga and the doctrine of grace were held as the important spiritual systems.

The Tāntrika practices had become very popular in the society of the Kathāsaritsāgara. Performance of these practices was considered to be a certain way of attaining every desired object. Vetālas, Bhūtas, Piśāchas, Brahma Rākṣasas, Bhairavas, Yoginīs, Yakṣiṇīs, Vidyādharīs, Śākinīs and Ḍākinīs were worshipped. Black magic was performed for the destruction of enemies. Some Tāntrikas even did not object to perform the heinous act of foeticide for acquiring supernatural powers. Candles of human fat were attributed with the property of searching hidden treasures. Magic largely entered into the medicine of the days. People believed in the power of various magical incantations and spells. Inspite of their great popularity, the Tāntrika practices had attracted unfavourable criticism from the society of the Kathāsaritsāgara.

Though the Hindu Faith prevailed in the society, some influence of the Bauddha Faith is also observed in the Kathāsaritsāgara. The Bauddha Faith had become a missionary religion. The period of the Kathāsaritsāgara was marked by regular disputes and discussions between the followers of the Hindu and the Bauddha Faiths. The followers of the Hindu Faith regarded the Bauddhas as impious. But the Bauddhas held their Faith in great veneration and worshipped Buddha as God. Ethics formed an integral part of the Bauddha Faith. Six Pāramitās were cherished as the means of crossing the ocean of temporal existence. The text does not clearly refer to the Jaina Faith.

The people believed in many superstitions. Omens of both good and evil nature were of unquestionable validity. Good omens predicted joy and evil omens misery to the people who attached omens to birds and animals, natural phenomena, unusual occurrences and sight of a particular person. Involuntary twitching or itching and such other bodily signs predicted good or evil fortune to them. Birth-marks on one's body were interpreted as auspicious and inauspicious. Moles on one's body too were means to portend one's future.

Emotional and religious values were attached to dreams. The dreams were considered to be Anyārtha, Yathārtha and Apārtha. The fulfilment of a dream was associated with the time when it was seen. People believed in the efficacy of dreams which predicted future to them. They were afraid of inauspicious dreams. Various dreams had different implications for them. The belief in the Yathārtha dreams had its roots in religious feelings.

The superstitious people believed that the realm of the unknown was inhabited by many monstrous beings of evil nature. Rākṣasas, Piśāchas, Bhūtas Pretas, Vetālas, and the water-spirits were held as evil spirits. Some of the women were believed to be witches who were classified into Śākinī, Yoginī, Ḍākinī and Yakṣinī according to their activities and Siddhis. Believing in the malignant effect of the evil eye, the superstitious persons held that it could even become fatal.

The study of faiths and beliefs in the Kathāsaritsāgara is interesting and revealing as much as it covers man in the past as well as present. The detailed and vivid descriptions of some of the faiths and beliefs prevalent among Indians even today, are found in the text. The study amply shows that the faiths and beliefs have altered only a little since the days of the Kathāsaritsāgara. It points at the continuity of the Indian thought. Donald A Mackenzie[2] has rightly remarked.

People may change their weapons or language with the passage of time, but retain their ancient modes of thought.

---

1. Prasad, S.N., Studies in Guṇāḍhya, p.139.

2. Indian Myth and Legend, Introduction, p.XI.

BIBLIOGRAPHY

A. ORIGINAL TEXTS AND TRANSLATIONS

Aitereya Brāhamaṇa : Ed. B.R. Ghanekar, Nirṇaya Sāgara Press, Bombay, 1910.

Aitereya Upaniṣad : Trans.(H) with Śaṁkara's Comm. Gītā Press, Gorakhpur, 1961.

Arthaśāstra : Kauṭilya, Ed. Shama Shastry, Oriental Library Publications, Sanskrti Series No. 37/54, Mysore, 1919.

Āryāsaptaśatī : Govardhanāchārya, Ed. Pandit Durgaprasad and Kashinath Pandurang Parab and Vasudeva Laxman Shastri Panishikar, Nirṇaya Sāgara Press, Bombay,1934.

Aṣṭādaśasmṛtayaḥ : Ed. Bhimasena Sharma, Brahma Press, Etawa.

Atharvaveda : Ed. S.D. Satvalekar, Svādhyāya Maṇḍala, Aundh, 1939.

Bṛhadāraṇyaka Upaniṣad : Ed. Mādhavānanda, Advaita Āśrama, Mayavati, Almora, 1950.

Bṛhatkathāmañjarī : Kṣemendra, Nirṇaya Sāgara Press, Bombay, 1931.

Bṛhatkathāślokasaṁgraha : Buddhasvāmin, Ed. Felix Facôte, Paris, i-ix, 1908-9.

Buddhacharita : Aśvaghoṣa, Sanskrit Bhavan, Kathotia, Bihar, 1955.

Chāndogya Brāhmaṇa : Ed. D. Bhattacharya, Sanskrit College, Calcutta, 1958.

Chāndogya Upaniṣad : Nirṇaya Sāgara, Bombay,1918.

Dharma Sūtra : Āpastamba, Ed. George Bühler, Bombay Sanskrit Series Nos. XLIV and L, 1932.

Dharma Sūtra : Gautama, Ānandāśrama Saṁskṛta Granthāvali, No.60, 1966, Ed. Vedamitra, National Publications, New Delhi, 1969.

Harṣacharita : Bāṇabhaṭṭa, Ed. P.V. Kane, Motilal Banarsidass, Delhi, 1965.

Hitopadeśa : Nirṇaya Sāgara Press, Bombay, 1955.

Īśādi Nau Upaniṣad : Ed. Hari Krishnadas Goyanḍaka, Gītā Press, Gorakhpur, Saṁvat 2010.

Kathāsaritsāgara : Somadeva, Ed. Durgaprasad and Kashi Nath Panduranga Parab, Nirṇaya Sāgara Press, Bombay, 1930, Ed. Jagdish Lal, Motilal Banarsidass, Delhi,1970.

Eng. Trans. - C.H. Tawney, Jaico Publishing House, 1956; Ocean of Story, Ed. N.M. Penzer, 10 Vols, Motilal Banarsidass, 1968. H. Trans, Pandit Kedarnath Sharma Sarasvata, Bihar Rāṣṭra Bhāsa Parishad, Patna, Part I, 1960,1974; Part II, 1961; Jatashankara Jha and Praphulla Chandra Ojha, Part III, 1973.Ab. H. Trans. Gopal Krishan Kaul, Satsāhitya Prakāśana, Delhi.

Kauṣītaki Brāhmaṇa : Ed. H.N. Apte, Ānandāśrama Mudraṇālaya, Poona, 1911.

Mahābhārata : Gītā Press, Gorakhpur, 1966.

Manu Smṛti : Ed. Haragovinda Shastri, Chowkhamba Sanskrit Series, Vārāṇasī, 1970.

Meghadūta : Kālidasā, Ed. R.R. Deshpande & T.K. Tope, Bombay, 1942.

Muṇḍaka Upaniṣad : Nirṇaya Sāgara Press, Bombay, 1914.

Pañchatantra : Ed. Pandit Ramtejapandeya, Paṇḍita Pustakālaya, Kāśī, 1964.

Rājataraṅgiṇī : Kalhaṇa, Paṇḍita Pustkālaya, Vārāṇasī, 1960, Eng. Trans, M.A. Stein, Westminister, 1960. Eng. Trans. R.S. Pandit, Allahabad, 1935.

Rāmāyaṇa : Ed. Ramateja Shastri, Paṇḍita Pustakālaya, Kāśī, 1959.

Ṛg-Bhāṣya-Saṁgraha : Ed. Deva Raj Chanana, Munshi Ram Manohar Lal, Delhi, 1961.

Ṛgveda Saṁhitā : Svādhyāya Maṇḍala, Pāradī, Surata, 1957.

Sāṁkhyakārikā : Ed. Kantanath Shastri Telanga, Chowkhamba Sanskrit Series, Vārāṇasī, Saṁvat 2010.

Śatapatha Brāhmaṇa (Mādhandinīya School) : Vol.2, The Reasearch Institute of Ancient Scientific Studies, 1969.

Śrībhāṣya : 2 Vols. with Śrutaprakāśikā, Ubhayavedāntagranthamālā, Madras, 1967.

Śrīmadbhagavadgītā (Rāmānujabhāṣya) : Ānandāśrama Saṁskṛta Granthāvali No.92, 1923.

Śrīmadbhagavadgītā (Śāṁkarabhāṣya) : Gītā Press, Gorakhpur, Saṁvat 2024.

Stories from the Kathāsaritsāgara : P.V. Ramanujaswamy (Trans.), Part I, The Sanskrit Academy, Osmania University, 1959.

Stories from the Kathāsaritsāgara : S.V. Shastri (Trans.), Part II, The Sanskrit Academy, Osmania University, 1965.

Taittirīya Āraṇyaka : Prathama Bhāga, Dvitīya Bhāga, Ānandāśrama Saṁskṛta

Granthāvali, Poona, 1926, 1927.

Taittirīya Brāhamaṇa : Ānandāśrama Saṁskṛta Granthāvali, Poona, No.37, 1938.

Taittirīya Saṁhitā : Saṣṭha Bhāga 1948, Saptama Bhāga 1949, Aṣṭama Bhāga 1951, Ānandāśrama Saṁskṛta Granthāvali, Poona.

Taittirīya Upaniṣad : Gītā Press, Gorakhpur, 1920.

Vājasaneyī Saṁhitā : With Uvaṭ & Mahidhara's Comm.; Ed. P.J. Sreskthi, Bombay, 1929.

Vedārthasaṅgraha : Ed. J.A.B. Van Buitenen, Deccan College Monograph Series, 16, Poona, 1956.

Vetālapañchaviṁśati : Retold by S.N. Shastri and Pt. H.V. Kochar, Bhārtī Prakāśana Mandira, Delhi.

Vājñavalkya Smṛti : Nirṇaya Sāgara Press, Bombay, 1926.

Yajurveda : Vedic Yantrālaya, Ajmer, 1940.

Yoga System : Patañjali, Ed, Charles Rockwell Lanman, Harvard Oriental Series, vol. 17.

B. REFERENCE BOOKS

Advanced History of India : K.A. Nilakanth Shastri; G. Shrinivasachari, Allied Publishers, 1970.

An Advanced History of India : R.C. Majumdar, Macmillan Co., London, 1953.

Ancient India : H. Oldenberg, Chicago, 1898.

Ancient India : R.C. Majumdar, Motilal Banarsidass, Delhi, 1977.

Aspects of Early Viṣṇuism : J. Gonda, Motilal Banarsidass, Delhi, 1969.

The Bhagavadgītā : S. Radhakrishnan, George Allen & Unwin, London, 1963.

Chips from a German Workshop : Max Müller, 2 vols, London,1868.

The Classical Age : R.C. Majumdar, Bhārtīya Vidyā Bhavan, Bombay, 1962.

The Complete works of Swāmī Vivekānanda : Vol. III, Advaita Āśrama, Calcutta, 1960.

The Cultural Heritage of India : Vol.I (1958), Vol.II (1962), Vol.III (1953),Vol.IV (1956), The Ramakrishana Mission Institute of Culture, Calcutta.

Cultural Heritage of Kashmir : Suresh Chandra Banerji, Sanskrit Pustak Bhandar, Calcutta.

The Discovery of India : J.L. Nehru, Meridian Books, London, 1956.

The Early Hindu Civilization : R.C. Dutt, Punthi Pustak, Calcutta,1963.

Elements of Hindu Econography : T.A. Gopinatha Rao, Vol.I, Parts I-II, Motilal Banarsidass, Delhi, 1968.

Epic India : C.V. Vaidya, Bombay Book Depot, Bombay, 1933.

Epic Mythology : E. Washburn Hopkins, Indological Book House, 1958; Motilal Banarsidass, Delhi, 1974.

Epics, Myths and Legends of India : P. Thomas, D.B. Taraporevala Sons and Co., 1961.

Epic Sources of Sanskrit Literature : Juthika Ghosh, Sanskrit College, Calcutta,1963.

Ethics of India : E. Washburn Hopkins, Yale University Press, New Haven, 1924.

Evolution of Religion : Farnell, London, 1905.

Evolution of the Thoughts in Bhagvadgītā : Kumudranjan Ray, K. Ray, Calcutta, 1933.

Faith and Knowledge : John Hiçk, Cornell University Press, New York, 1957.

Faith and the Philosophers : John Hick, Macmillan & Co., New York, 1964.

Fundamentals of Hindu Faith and Culture : C.P. Ramaswami Aiyar, Ganesh & Co., Madras, 1959.

Golden Bough : J.G. Frazer, Macmillan, London, 1925.

The Handbook of Folklore : C.S. Burne, 1914.

Harṣacharita – Eka Sāṁskṛtika Adhyayana : V.S. Agrawala, Bihar Rāṣṭra Bhāṣā Parishad, Patna, 1953.

The Heart of Hinduism : S. Radhakrishnan, G.A. Natesan & Co., Madras.

Hindu Civilization : Radhakumud Mookerji, Longmans, Green & Co., London, 1936.

Hinduism : M. Monier-Willams, Rare Books, Delhi, 1971.

Hinduism at a Glance : Swāmī Nirvedānanda, Ramakrishna Mission, Calcutta, 1969.

Hindu Manners, Customs and Ceremonies : Abbe Dubois, Clarandon Press, Oxford, 1906.

The Hindu View of Life : S. Radhakrishnan, George Allen & Unwin, London, 1954.

History of Classical Sanskrit Literature : M. Krishnamachariar, Motilal Banarsidass, Delhi, 1974.

History of Dharmaśāstra : P.V. Kane, vol, I, Part I (1968), Vol.II, Parts I-II (1941)Vol.III (1946), Vol.IV (1953), Vol.V, Parts I-II (1958,1962), Bhandarkar Oriental Research Institute, Poona.

The History of Indian Literature : A. Weber, Chowkhamba Sanskrit Studies, Vol, VIII, Vārāṇasī, 1961.

History of Indian Literature : M. Winternits, Vol.III, Part I, Motilal Banarsidass, Delhi, 1963.

A History of Indian Philosophy : S.N. Dasgupta, Vols. I-II, The Cambridge University Press, 1963

History of Religions : E. Washburn Hopkins, Ginn & Company,1896.

A History of Sanskrit Literature : A.A. Macdonell, London, 1905.

A History of Sanskrit Literature : A.B. Keith, Oxford University Press, Bombay.

A History of Sanskrit Literature : S.N. Dasgupta; S.K. De; Classical Period, University of Calcutta, Calcutta, 1962.

Images and Symbols : Mircea Eliade, Trans. by Philip Mairet, Harvill Press, London, 1961.

India as Known to Pāṇini : V.S. Agrawala, Pṛthvī Prakāśana, Vārāṇasī, 1963.

Indian Culture Through the Ages : V.Venkateshwar, Vols, I&II, Longmans, London, Bombay, 1928.

Indian Myth and Legend : Donald A. Mackenzie, Sona Publication, 1971.

Indian Philosophy : S. Radhakrishnan, vols. I-II, George Allen and Unwin, London, 1966.

Indian Wisdom : M. Monier-Williams, Luzac & Co., London, 1836.

India of Dharma Sūtras : Veda Mitra, Veda Mitra & Sons, 1969.

India's Past : A.A.Macdonell, Motilal Banarsidas, Vārāṇasī, Delhi, Paṭna, 1958.

Indological Studies in India : V. Raghwan, Motilal Banarsidass, Delhi, 1964.

An Introduction to Indian Philosophy : D.M. Datta; S.C. Chatterjee, University of Calcutta, Calcutta, 1954.

Kādambarī - Eka Sāṁskṛtika Adhyayana : V.S. Agrawala, Chawkhamba Vidyā Bhavan, Vārāṇasī, 1958.

Kashmir (Retrospect and Prospect) : P.B. Gajendragadkar, University of Bombay, 1967.

Kathāsaritsāgara – Eka Sāṁskṛtika Adhyayana : Vachaspati Dwivedi, Susheel Kumar Dwivedi, Patna, 1977.

Kathāsaritsāgara Tathā Bhāratīya Saṁskṛti : S.N. Prasad, Chaukhamba Orientalia, Vārāṇasī, 1978.

Lectures on Ṛgveda : Ghate, Ed. V.S. Sukthankar, Oriental Book Agency, Poona, 1959.

Made in India : Cornella Spencer, Alfred.A.Knope, New York,1953.

Mohenjo Daro and Indus Civilization : John Marshall, Vol.I, London, 1931.

Monograph on Religious Sects in India among Hindus : D.A. Pai, Municipal Corporation, Bombay, 1928.

Myths of the Hindus and Buddhists : K. Coomaraswamy; Sister Nivedita, Dover Publications, New York, 1967.

New History of Sanskrit Literature : Krishna Chaitanya, Asia Publishing House, 1962.

The Nīlamata Purāṇa – A Cultural and Literary Study : Veda Kumari, J.K. Academy of Art, Culture and Languages, Srinagar, 1968.

Obscure Religious Cults : S.B. Dasgupta, Firma K.L. Mukhopadhyay, Calcutta, 1962.

Original Sanskrit Texts : J. Muir, Vols, I, IV. Trubner & Co.. London, 1890.

The Origin and Development of Religion in Vedic Literature : P.S. Deshmukh, Oxford University Press, London, 1933.

An Outline of the Religious Literature of India : J.N. Farquhar, Motilal Banarsidass, Delhi, 1967.

Paurāṇica and Tāntric Religion : J.N. Banerjea, University of Calcutta, Calcutta, 1966.

The People of India : H.H. Risley, Tacker and Co., Calcutta, 1915.

The Philosophy of Rāmānuja : K.D. Bhardwaj, Sir Shankar Lall Charitable Trust Society, New Delhi,1958.

The Philosophy of the Śrīmad-Bhāgavata : S. Bhattacharya, Vol.I (1960), Vol.II (1962), Viśva Bhāratī, Calcutta.

Position of Women in Hindu Civilization : A.S. Altekar, Motilal Banarsidass, Delhi, 1978.

Primitive Culture : E.B. Tylor, 1903.

Rāmāyaṇa Kālīna Saṁskṛti : S.N. Vyas, Sastā Sāhitya Maṇḍala, New Delhi, 1958.

Religion and Mythology of the Brāhmaṇas : G.V. Devasthali, Poona, 1965.

The Religion and Philosophy of the Veda and Upaniṣads : A.B. Keith, Motilal Banarsidass, Delhi, 1970.

The Religion of the Veda : M. Bloomfield, Nicker Bocker Press, 1908.

Religions of Ancient India : L. Renou, London, 1953

Religions of India : A. Barth, Trans, by Rev, J. Wood, The Chowkhamba Sanskrit Series, 1963.

The Religions of India : A.P. Karmarkar, Vol.I, Mira Publishing House, Lonavla (India), 1950.

The Religions of India : E. Washburn Hopkins, Boston,1895.

The Religions of Mankind : E.D. Soper, 1921.

The Religions of the Hindus : K.W. Morgan, New York, 1953.

Religious Life in India : J.N. Farquhar, Oxford University Press, London, 1916.

Religious Sects of the Hindus : H.H. Wilson, Susheel Gupta, Calcutta, 1958.

Ṛgvedādibhāṣyabhūmikā : Śrīmaddayānanda, Saraswatī, Vedic Yantrālaya, Saṁvat 2004.

Ṛgvedic and Vedic Religion : A.C. Clayton, London & Madras, 1913.

Ṛgvedic Culture : A.C. Das, R. Cambray & Co., Calcutta, 1925.

Ṛgvedic India : A.C. Das, Vol.I, Calcutta, 1921.

Saṁskṛta Sāhitya Kā Itihāsa : Baladeva Upadhayaya, Prathama Bhāga, Sārdā Saṁsthāna, Vārāṇasī 1973.

Sanskrit and Culture : Theodore Goldstücker, Indological Book House, 1971.

Social and Religious Life in the Gṛhayasūtras : V.M. Apte, The Popular Book Depot, Bombay, 1954.

A Socio-Political Study of the Vālmīki Rāmāyaṇa : R. Sharma, Motilal Banarsidass, Delhi, 1971.

Stories from the Indian Classics : V.S. Naravane, Asia Publishing House, 1962.

Studies in Guṇāḍhya : S.N. Prasad, Chaukhambha Orientalia, Vārāṇasī, 1977.

Studies in Indian History and Culture : U.N. Ghoshal, Orient Longmans, 1957.

Studies in Indology : Vasudev Vishnu Mirashi, Vol.I, The Vidarbha Saṁśodhana Maṇḍala, 1960.

Studies in the Epics and Purāṇas : A.D. Pusalker, Bhāratīya Vidyā Bhavan, Bombay, 1963.

Studies in the Purāṇic Records of Hindu Rites and Customs : R.C. Hazra, University of Dacca, Dacca, 1940.

Survey of Sanskrit Literature : Kunhan Raja, Bhāratīya Vidyā

Bhavan, 1962.

Tales of Ancient India : J.A.B. Van Buitenen (Trans.), The University of Chicago Press, 1959.

Tantras – Studies in their Religion and Literature : Chintaharan Chakravarty, Punthi Pustak, Calcutta, 1963.

Tree and Serpent Worship : James Ferguseon, Indological Book House, Delhi, Vārāṇasī, 1971.

Vaidika Sāhitya aura Saṁskṛti : Baladeva Upadhyaya, Śārdā Saṁsthāna, Vārāṇasī,1976.

Vaiṣṇavism, Śaivism and Minor Religious Systems : R.C. Bhandarkar, Indological Book House, Vārāṇasī, 1965.

The Vedic Age : R.C. Majumdar, George Allen and Unwin, London, 1951.

Vedic India : L. Renou, (Eng. Trans.), Calcutta, 1957.

Vedic India : Z.A. Ragozin, T. Fisher Union, London, 1899.

Vedic Mythology : A.A. Macdonell, Indological Book House, 1963; Motilal Banarsidass, Delhi, 1974.

Vedic Religion : A.Bergaigne, (Eng. Trans.) 2 Vols, Poona, 1971.

Wonder that was India : A.L. Basham, London, 1954.

C. ENCYCLOPAEDIAS AND DICTIONARIES

American English Usage :	Margaret Nicholson, Oxford University Press, New York, 1957
Cassell's Encyclopaedia of Literature :	Cassell & Company, London, 1953.
Catalogus Catalagorum :	Theodor Aufrecht, Parts I, II, III, Frenz Steiner Verlag, Gmbh Wiesbaden, 1962.
Chamber's Encyclopaedia :	International Learning System Corporation, London, 1969.
A Classical Dictionary of Hindu Mythology and Religion, Geography, History and Literature :	John Dowson, Routledge and Kegan Paul, 1968.
A Comparative Dictionary of Psychological and Psychoanalytical Terms :	Horace B. English; Ava Champney English, Longman, Gram, & Co., 1958.
A Dictionary English and Sanskrit :	M. Monier Williams, Motilal Banarsidass. 1956, 1975.
Dictionary of Comparative Religion :	S.G.F. Brandon, New York, 1970.
A Dictionary Sanskrit and English :	M.Monier-Williams, Motilal Banarsidass, Delhi, 1976.
The Encyclopaedia Americana :	A.H. Mac Donnald, Chicago, Washington, New York, 1958.

The Encyclopaedia of Philosophy : Paul Edwards, The Macmillan Company & the Free Press, New York, 1967.

An Encyclopaedia of Religion : V.Form, New York, 1945.

Encyclopaedia of Religion and Ethics : James Hastings, Ed. Vols.I-XII; Charles Scribner's Sons, New York, 1955.

The Funk and Wagnall's Standard Dictionary of Folklore, Mythology and Legend : Maria Leach, Ed, Funk and Wagnalls Company, New York, 1949.

Great Treasury of Western Thought : Moilimer J. Adler; Charles Van Doren (Ed.); R.R. Bowler & Company, New York, 1977.

Hindu World : Benjamin Walker, Vols.I & II, George Allen & Unwin, London, 1968.

The International Thesaurus of Quotations : Khoda Thomas Tripp (comp.), Penguin Books, 1976.

Modern English Usage : H.W. Fowler, Oxford University Press, New York and Oxford, 1965.

Nāmaliṅgānuśāsana or Amarakoṣa : Amarasiṁha, Ed. Pt. Haragovinda Shastri, Chowkhamba Sanskrit Series, 1970.

New Catalogus Catalogorum : V. Raghavan, Vol..III, Ed, University of Madras, 1967.

The New Century Dictionary of the English Language : The Century Co., 1929.

New Encyclopaedia of Philosophy : J.Grooten; G.J. Steenbergen, New York, 1972.

The New Funk and Wagnall's Encyclopaedia : Joseph Laffan Morse, Vol,13, Ed, Unicorn Publishers, New York, 1955.

New Practical Standard Dictionary of the English Language : Charles Earles Funk, Ed. Vol.I, Funk and Wagnall Company, New York, 1955.

Origins : Routledge & Kegan Paul, London, 1966.

The Oxford English Dictionary : The Clarendon Press, Oxford, 1961.

The Random House Dictionary of English Language : Jess Stein, (the Unabridged), Random House, New York, 1967, 1968.

The Reader's Digest Great Encyclopaedic Dictionary : Oxford University Press, London, 1964.

Śabdakalpadruma : 5 Volumes, Chowkhamba Sanskrit Series Office, Vārāṇasī, 1961.

Sanskrit-English Dictionary : V.S. Apte (3 vols.), Prasad Prakashan, Poona, 1957-59.

Standard French and English Dictionary : J.E. Mansion, Ed. Part II, George G., Harrap and Company, 1955.

The Students English Sanskrit Dictionary : V.S. Apte, Motilal Banarsidass, Delhi, 1963.

Usage and Abusage : Eric Partridge, Penguin Books, 1977.

Vāchaspatyam : Taranath Tarkavachaspati (Comp.), 6 Vols., Chowkhamba Sanskrit Series NO.94, Vārāṇasī, 1962.

Webster's Dictionary of Synonyms : G & C Merriam Co., 1961.

World University Encyclopaedia : (unabridged) Vol.II, New York, 1968.

D. ARTICLES

The Devadāsīs of India : T.V. Seshagiri Iyer, The Quarterly Journal of the Mythic Society, Vol. XIII, No.3, pp.689-91.

Essai Sur Gunadhya Et La Brhatkatha : Felix Lacote, Trans. by Rev. Father A.M. Tabard, The Quarterly Journal of the Mythic Society, Banglore, Vol.IV, pp.26-32, 64-73, 85-103, 141-56, 164-205; Vol.V, No,4; Vol,VI, No.3; Vol.XIII, No.4, pp.93-148.

History of Sanskrit Literature of Kashmir : Sunil Chandra Ray, The Indian Historical Quarterly, Calcutta, Vol. XXXI-3, 1955, 232-256.

The Home of the Sātavāhanas : T.N. Subrahmanyam, The Quarterly Journal of the Mythic Society, Bangalore, Vol.13, No.2, pp.591-594.

An Interpolation of Some Mss. of the Bṛhatkathāmañjarī : M.B. Emenesu, The Journal of the Royal Asiatic Society of Great Britan and Iraland, 1933, pp.821-30.

King Sātavāhana of the Coins : Sant Lal Katare, Indian Historical Quarterly, Calcutta, 1951, pp.210-14.

A Note on Folk Literature : Brij Bhushan Sharma, Folklore, Nov. 1967.

Note on the Original Home of Guṇādhya : S. Nath, The Journal of the Ganganath Jha Research Institute, Allahabad, Vol.23 (1967), pp. 147-50.

An Old Sanskrit version of the Bṛhatkathā : R. Narasimhachar, The Journal of the Royal Asiatic Society of Great Britain and Ireland, 1913, pp.389-90.

On the Immediate Source of the Kathāsaritsāgara : S. Rangacharya, The Indian Historical Quarterly, Calcutta, Vol.XIV, No.1, March, 1938, pp.57-73.

On the Vrihatkatha of Kshemendra : J.G. Bühler, The Indian Antiquary, Bombay, Vol.I, 1872, pp.302-9.

Paiśāchī Language and Literature : A.N.Upadhye, Annals of the Bhandarkar Oriental Research Institute, Poona,vol.21, 1939-40, pp.1-32.

The Phallus Worship in the Veda : Vidhushekhara Bhattacharya, Indian Historical Quarterly, Calcutta, Vol. IX.

Scepticism or Faith and Mysticism : Esther Soloman, journal of the Oriental Institute, Baroda, Vol. VIII, 1958-59, pp.219-33.

Story of Devasmitā : B. Hale Wortham, Journal of the Royal Asiatic Society of Bengal, Calcutta, Vol. XVI, New Series, 1884, pp.1-12.

The story of Jīmūtavāhana and Hariśarman : B. Hale Wortham, Journal of the Royal Asiatic Society of Bengal, Calcutta, Vol.XVIII, 1886, pp. 157-76.

Studies of the Kathāsaritsāgara : J.S. Speyer, Book Review by C.H. Tawney, Journal of the Royal Asiatic Society of Bengal, Calcutta, 1908, pp. 907-15.

Tradition about Vanaras and Rākṣasas : Chintaharana Chakravarti, Indian Historical Quarterly, Calcutta, Vol.I, No.1.

INDEX